AMERICA'S ARAB REFUGEES

AMERICA'S ARAB REFUGEES

Vulnerability and Health on the Margins

Marcia C. Inhorn

Stanford University Press
Stanford, California

Stanford University Press
Stanford, California

Printed in the United States of America on acid-free, archival-quality paper

Library of Congress Cataloging-in-Publication Data

Names: Inhorn, Marcia C., 1957– author.
Title: America's Arab refugees : vulnerability and health on the margins / Marcia C. Inhorn.
Description: Stanford, California : Stanford University Press, 2018. | Includes bibliographical references and index.
Identifiers: LCCN 2017017086 (print) | LCCN 2017019970 (ebook) | ISBN 9781503604384 (e-book) | ISBN 9780804786393 (cloth : alk. paper) | ISBN 9781503603875 (pbk. : alk. paper)
Subjects: LCSH: Refugees, Arab—Medical care—Michigan—Detroit. | Refugees, Arab—Health and hygiene—Michigan—Detroit. | Refugees, Arab—Michigan—Detroit—Social conditions.
Classification: LCC RA448.5.A73 (ebook) | LCC RA448.5.A73 I54 2018 (print) | DDC 362.108992/753077434—dc23
LC record available athttps://lccn.loc.gov/2017017086

Typeset by Thompson Type in 10/14 Minion

For Arab refugees everywhere

Contents

List of Acronyms

AAA (American Anthropological Association)
ACC (Arab American and Chaldean Council)
ACCESS (Arab Community Center for Economic and Social Services)
ALICE (asset limited, income constrained, employed)
ASRM (American Society for Reproductive Medicine)
CDC (Centers for Disease Control and Prevention)
CFR (Council on Foreign Relations)
CMES (Council on Middle East Studies)
DAAS (Detroit Arab American Survey)
DU (depleted uranium)
ESHRE (European Society for Human Reproduction and Embryology)
ESL (English as a Second Language)
EU (European Union)
FCSRCA (Fertility Clinic Success Rate and Certification Act)
FLCIVF (Friends of Low-cost IVF)
GCC (Gulf Cooperation Council)
GM (General Motors)
GWS (Gulf War syndrome)
HOMP (High-order multiple pregnancy)
IBC (Iraq Body Count)

ICSI (intracytoplasmic sperm injection)
IDP (internally displaced person)
IED (improvised explosive device)
IFHS (Iraq Family Health Survey)
IMHS (Iraq Mental Health Survey)
IOM (Institute of Medicine)
IRAP (Iraqi Refugee Assistance Project, renamed International Refugee Assistance Project)
IRIS (Integrated Refugee and Immigrant Services)
ISIL (Islamic State of Iraq and the Levant)
ISIS (Islamic State of Iraq and Syria)
IT (information technology)
IVF (in vitro fertilization)
KS (Klinefelter syndrome)
LCIVF (low-cost in vitro fertilization)
MAIC (Medical Aid for Iraqi Children)
MSF (Médecins Sans Frontières, or Doctors Without Borders)
NATO (North Atlantic Treaty Organization)
NGO (nongovernmental organization)
NIH (National Institutes of Health)
OCHA (Office for the Coordination of Humanitarian Affairs)
OEF (Operation Enduring Freedom, Afghanistan)
OIF (Operation Iraqi Freedom)
OHSS (ovarian hyperstimulation syndrome)
PCOS (polycystic ovary syndrome)
PLO (Palestine Liberation Organization)
PTSD (posttraumatic stress disorder)
RMA (Refugee Medical Assistance)
SLA (South Lebanon Army)
SMA (Society for Medical Anthropology)
SOHR (Syrian Observatory for Human Rights)
SSI (Supplemental Security Income)
TANF (Temporary Assistance to Needy Families)

TESA (testicular epididymal sperm aspiration)
UAE (United Arab Emirates)
UN (United Nations)
UNFIL (United Nations Interim Force in Lebanon)
UNHCR (United Nations High Commissioner for Refugees)
UNICEF (United Nations Children's Fund)
UNRWA (United Nations Relief and Works Agency)
USCIS (United States Citizenship and Immigration Services)
USCRI (United States Committee for Refugees and Immigrants)
USRAP (United States Refugee Admissions Program)
UXO (unexploded ordnance)
VolAg (voluntary agency)
WHO (World Health Organization)
WMD (weapon of mass destruction)
WMH (World Mental Health)

War in Lebanon: A Timeline

1970: Palestine Liberation Organization (PLO) arrives in Lebanon following "Black September" massacre of Palestinians in Jordan

1975: War officially begins in April between Christian Phalangists and PLO

1976: Arab League approves 40,000 Syrian troops as peacekeepers in Lebanon

1978: Israel invades southern Lebanon with aid of South Lebanon Army (SLA), a primarily Christian militia

1982: Israel launches full-scale invasion of Lebanon, occupying West Beirut, where it supports massacres by Phalangist militia in Sabra and Shatila Palestinian refugee camps

1983: Attack on the US embassy kills 63 people, followed by attacks on US and French military garrisons, leading to deaths of 241 US marines and 58 French soldiers

1984: Assassination of American University of Beirut President Malcolm Kerr by unknown assailants; US troops withdraw from the country

1985–1989: Most Israeli troops withdraw during period of intense fighting between shifting Muslim, Christian, and Druze factions

1989: Taif Agreement signed in Saudi Arabia to end war

1990: Civil war officially ends in October, although violence continues in early 1990s

1990–2000: Ongoing Israeli occupation of southern Lebanon, including April 1996 "Operation Grapes of Wrath," in which Israel bombs Hezbollah bases, killing more than 100 displaced civilians in the UN base in Qana

2000: Withdrawal of Israeli troops in May, after rapid advance of Hezbollah forces and collapse of SLA; political prisoners, including from the infamous Khiam Detention Center, are released

2003: US and British invasion of Iraq prompts anti-Western violence in Lebanon

2005: Assassination of Lebanese Prime Minister Rafik Hariri in February draws international scrutiny and leads Syria to withdraw its troops from Lebanon in April under international pressure

2006: Six-week summer war between Hezbollah and Israel inflicts heavy casualties

2007: Siege of Palestinian refugee camp Nahr al-Bared, following clashes between Islamist militants and Lebanese military

2011: Arab spring protests begin as Lebanese government collapses

2012: Syrian conflict, beginning in March 2011, spills over into Lebanon with deadly clashes between Sunni Muslims (opponents of Bashar al-Assad) versus Alawi and Shia militias (al-Assad's supporters)

2013: Sectarian tensions and border clashes flare between opponents and supporters of Syrian regime in Lebanon; dozens killed in deadly bomb attacks

2014: UN announces that over 1 million Syrians have registered in Lebanon; thus, one in every five people living in Lebanon is now Syrian

2015: January brings new restrictions on Syrians entering the country, intended to staunch the flow of people trying to escape the Syrian war

War in Iraq: A Timeline

1963: Arab Socialist Baath Party rises to power

1979: Saddam Hussein becomes president

1980–1988: Saddam Hussein initiates Iran–Iraq War, which kills more than 1 million and is the longest conventional war between two countries in the twentieth century

1988: Iraqi military attacks northern Kurdish town of Halabjah with poison gas, killing thousands

1990: Saddam Hussein invades Kuwait on August 2

1990–2003: Iraq is economically sanctioned over thirteen years by the UN Security Council for its aggression on its neighbors; all imports are restricted, except for vital medicines

1991: US and coalition of thirty nations invade Iraq in January, in the First Gulf War that leads to Saddam's surrender after six weeks

1991: Following Saddam's defeat, southern Iraqi Shia and northern Iraqi Kurds stage an intifada (uprising) against Saddam, supported by the US military; however, Saddam retaliates with a brutal crackdown, in which Shia and Kurdish populations are forced to flee

1991–1997: Southern Iraqis spend time in Saudi Arabian desert refugee camps, before being granted refugee admission to the United States; many end up in Arab Detroit

1995: Oil-for-Food Programme initiated by the United Nations to alleviate major sanction-induced food and medicine shortages; United Nations allows partial resumption of Iraq's oil exports

2003: United States declares war on Iraq on March 19, based on intelligence reports that Saddam Hussein possesses "weapons of mass destruction" (WMDs)

2003–2011: The Second Gulf War, also known as "Operation Iraqi Freedom" (OIF), is initiated, lasting nearly nine years and setting off years of violent conflict between sectarian and jihadist groups competing for power

2006: Saddam Hussein is executed for crimes against humanity

2007: President George W. Bush announces deployment of 30,000 more US troops, in Iraq "surge" to provide better security and to reduce casualties; Britain hands over its control of southern Iraq to Iraqi forces after five years

2007–2015: Second major wave of Iraqi refugee resettlement in the United States; 125,000 of 200,000 Iraqi refugees enter the United States

2009: Al-Quaeda–linked Islamic State of Iraq emerges, claiming responsibility for suicide bombings in Baghdad

2011: United States completes troop withdrawal on December 18, marking official end to US-led war in Iraq

2013: Islamic State of Iraq and Syria (ISIS) emerges as an independent Sunni jihadist group, declaring itself an "Islamic state"; reports being to emerge of a full-blown sectarian war in Iraq

2014: ISIS seizes Mosul, Iraq's second largest city

2015: Iraqi Army launches offensive against ISIS to take back key Sunni-dominant cities such as Tikrit, Ramadi, and Fallujah

2016: Iraqi government forces wage war against ISIS in city of Mosul, with US military support

Preface

THIS BOOK IS ABOUT A POPULATION OF POOR ARAB IMMIgrants and refugees, mostly from the countries of Iraq and Lebanon, who have fled from Middle Eastern war zones and who have subsequently struggled to make a life for themselves in America. I extend my deepest sense of gratitude to those individuals and couples whose stories of exile and hope are captured in the chapters that follow. Without their willingness to share their lives with me, I would not have been able to write this book.

As a scholar and a feminist, I have been deeply moved and inspired by two strands of theory and activism, which have helped me to frame the discussion of Arab refugee lives in America. The first is the Black Lives Matter movement, a movement that was started online by young black activists in the wake of multiple incidents of racial profiling and police brutality, particularly toward young black men. However, since its beginning in the summer of 2015, the Black Lives Matter movement has diversified, raising awareness about perceived injustices in a variety of social systems and among a variety of people of color and genders in this country. I am both impressed by, and grateful for, the Black Lives Matter movement and its agenda to achieve greater social justice in America. My gratitude is both personal and professional. On the personal level, my husband Kirk Hooks is black, and my children Carl and Justine Hooks are biracial. Thus, I hope that my children grow up in a fairer, less racist America. As a scholar, the Black Lives Matter movement has also motivated me to think about the profound struggles of another very oppressed minority group in America, namely, Arab Muslims, many of whom have come to this country as war refugees.

This book highlights the profiling of both black and Arab populations in this country and the widespread vilification of both black and Arab men as inherently violent and untrustworthy. Furthermore, the location of this ethnographic study in Detroit, Michigan—a predominantly black city, incorporating a substantial Arab ethnic enclave, and manifesting poverty so deep and pernicious that the collapsing urban infrastructure is reminiscent of a Middle Eastern war zone—facilitates this comparison of black and Arab lives.

America's Arab Refugees also draws conceptual inspiration from intersectionality theory, as defined by black feminist scholars,[1] and taken up by both black medical anthropologists and public health scholars.[2] Intersectionality theory elucidates the relationships among multiple forms of oppression based on gender, race, and class but also sexual orientation, age, ability, religion, and national origin. Rather than acting independently, systematic forms of oppression are interrelated and multiplicative in their effects, leading in many cases to poor health outcomes and premature mortality. Intersectionality theory has been applied primarily to the lives of black women and less so to those of Latinas in the United States. However, this framework has great utility in understanding intersecting oppressions facing other minority populations. In the case of Arab Muslim refugees, intersecting oppressions include, but are not limited to, discrimination based on ethnicity, religion, social class, race, gender, and appearance (for example, veiling). This book thus applies intersectionality theory to the study of Arab Muslims' lives in the United States, showing the utility of this theoretical approach in interrogating axes of oppression beyond the theoretical triumvirate of gender, race, and class.

For many years now, at both the University of Michigan and Yale, I have taught a feminist anthropology course on "Intersectionality and Women's Health: Ethnographic Approaches to Race, Class, Gender and 'Difference.'" I see myself as a committed feminist scholar, and I teach this course to make my generally privileged college students much more aware of the intersection of race, class, and gender oppression in the lives of poor urban and rural women in America.

Beyond all this, I have worked as a scholar for more than thirty years in the Arab world. This is a world about which I feel great passion—but also at this moment great heartache. The Arab world is currently imploding, causing massive human suffering in its wake. As I write this book in the midst of the worst refugee crisis since World War II, I hope to convince readers that the lives of Arab refugees matter and that America must care. That is the main message of this book.

Marcia C. Inhorn
Yale University

AMERICA'S ARAB REFUGEES

Prologue: Fatima and Sadiq

From Iraq to Michigan

On a sweltering Friday afternoon in August, I drove my minivan from Ann Arbor, Michigan, to Dearborn, the Arab ethnic enclave located about forty minutes to the east on the outskirts of Detroit. I made this trip to Dearborn on most Friday afternoons, passing the polluting smokestacks of the massive Ford Rouge auto factory. My destination in Dearborn was a nondescript two-story brick medical office building, located on a treeless cement-gray commercial boulevard.

Once inside the building's front door, however, I was transported into another world—the Arab world. Iraqi women dressed in black *abaya*s (traditional long cloaks) and Yemeni women wearing black *niqab*s (facial veils) pushed their sick children in strollers into the first-floor pediatrics clinic. Across the open foyer, older Arab gentlemen with white skullcaps visited the Lebanese-run pharmacy, usually after visits to Arab doctors' offices on the second floor. I would make my way upstairs to one of those offices, the satellite clinic of southeastern Michigan's largest infertility and in vitro fertilization (IVF) treatment center.

It was there on that late Friday afternoon in August that I met Fatima and Sadiq, an Iraqi-born couple who were struggling to overcome their infertility problem and many additional hardships. Fatima wore a *hijab* (Islamic headscarf), which framed her pretty face. Her husband Sadiq was also good looking, his full head of hair evenly shaved almost to the scalp. In excellent

English, Fatima and Sadiq poured out their story to me. I spent the rest of the afternoon listening to them, the three of us leaving the office as it was closing for the weekend.

I learned that both Fatima and Sadiq had grown up in Basra, a Shia Muslim–dominated city in southern Iraq. When Saddam Hussein invaded Kuwait in 1990, and President George H. W. Bush responded with Operation Desert Storm in early 1991, the population of southern Iraq was caught in the middle. Shia men had been encouraged by the US-led coalition to take up arms against Saddam Hussein after US forces withdrew in February 1991. However, this intifada (uprising) failed, leaving many Shia male fighters in the grips of Saddam's revenge. Those who were not disappeared or killed—often after periods of brutal imprisonment and torture—fled to neighboring countries. Families fled, too, given that Iraq's southern Shia Muslims were viewed as potential "enemies of Saddam."

Although Sunni Muslim–dominated Saudi Arabia was reluctant to take in nearly 40,000 fleeing Iraqi Shia refugees, the United States and United Nations put pressure on Saudi Arabia to open its borders. A desolate refugee tent camp was set up near Rafha, a Saudi town in the remote northern desert region. Conditions were harsh. Food was scarce and the water salty. Scorching heat and gusts of sand made skin and eyes burn, and high desert winds made the flimsy tents collapse. The Saudi camp guards were also reluctant "hosts," sometimes committing acts of violence against this vulnerable refugee population.[1]

Among these refugees were Fatima, age eight, and Sadiq, age eleven. Fatima's father had stayed behind to fight while his wife and their six young children fled to Saudi Arabia with his younger brother. Sadiq's father was not a fighter, but he feared for the lives of his wife and ten children, fleeing with them to Saudi Arabia.

It was in these unfortunate circumstances that Fatima and Sadiq spent their formative preteen years. They never knew each other in the Saudi refugee camp, nor did their families meet when both eventually were granted asylum in the unlikely American city of Lincoln, Nebraska. When I asked Fatima and Sadiq why they were resettled in America's heartland, Sadiq replied, "I don't know why. Why there? They just picked Lincoln, Nebraska, I guess." Fatima added, "Now Nebraska is supposed to be a good place for Iraqis. But when we were there, back in the early '90s, there were very little, not too many Arabs." For that reason, Fatima's family left Lincoln for Philadelphia within a year but decided to move permanently to Dearborn, with its growing Iraqi refugee population.

Sadiq's family stayed in Lincoln for several years, and Sadiq was somewhat nostalgic about his early days in Nebraska. Although he had neither been able to go to high school nor to learn English fluently, Sadiq was nonetheless able to obtain meaningful employment in Lincoln's Kawasaki factory, which manufactured all-terrain vehicles. Sadiq exclaimed, "I never looked for a job. The job looked for me!" But he then added, quietly, "Now I look for it, but I can't find it."

As I soon discovered, Sadiq was currently unemployed. When he had moved with his family to Dearborn seven years earlier, he had begun working as a busboy in a Lebanese restaurant, before landing a factory job in a company making plastic parts for the local automotive industry. As good factory jobs with accompanying benefits were hard to find in Michigan's depressed economy, Sadiq had been lucky to secure this kind of stable employment. He used his job to save money for his marriage. He also took a second night job in a Lebanese-owned Mobil gas station.

Through connections in the local Iraqi community, Sadiq met Fatima and married her on a cold winter day in January, shortly before he turned thirty. Sadiq was attracted to Fatima not only for her beauty but also because she was smart and was one of the few Iraqi refugee women attending the local branch of the University of Michigan. Fatima applied herself to her studies and was well on her way to obtaining a bachelor's degree in information technology (IT) management. In addition, Fatima had obtained a coveted government position at the state's unemployment agency. Being fully bilingual, Fatima was able to help local Arab refugees and immigrants fill out their unemployment forms. Fatima's position provided her with health insurance benefits and also allowed her to pay her own way through college, as her father could ill afford the tuition bills.

Fatima and Sadiq began their marriage with the highest hopes and aspirations. They both had good jobs with benefits. Fatima was on track to graduate from college. And in a depressed housing market with low interest rates, the couple was able to buy a small home on a tree-lined street in a mostly Lebanese Shia neighborhood. Living apart from their large families for the first time in their lives, Fatima and Sadiq also had some measure of marital privacy. Like most Arab newlyweds, they started trying to make a family from the first night of marriage.

But a year and a half later, the couple's plans had gone terribly awry. Metro Detroit was in an economic free fall. Sadiq's factory job, reliant on the local General Motors (GM) and Ford factories, swiftly disappeared due to downsizing. But Sadiq was most disturbed by the fact that he had not been able to impregnate Fatima, who was coming under community scrutiny for her inability to "prove" her fertility. Although Sadiq's wages as a gas station attendant were meager, he encouraged Fatima to make an appointment for both of them at the local infertility clinic.

When I asked Sadiq and Fatima how they had come to find this clinic, Fatima explained, "I heard about it from the community. It is 'known' in the Arab community as the only clinic for these kinds of things. So we came here, and they couldn't find anything [wrong]. When they started doing X-rays and check-ups, everything was perfect, except that I have an enlarged [fallopian] tube. That is the only problem. There were no sperm problems."

Fatima was suffering from tubal-factor infertility, the very condition for which IVF was initially developed. Although the Lebanese-American IVF physician explained to Fatima and Sadiq that they might eventually become pregnant without the help of IVF, the couple was quite eager to start a family. Throwing caution to the wind, they decided to put all of their remaining savings—$10,000, to be exact—into the purchase of a single IVF cycle, an elective procedure that was not covered by Fatima's health insurance plan. Furthermore, Fatima lost that plan when she decided to cut back to half-time employment. With the daily blood tests, ultrasound scans, and hormone injections, fitting her medical appointments into a full-time work schedule was too difficult. To add insult to injury, Sadiq lost his gas station job soon after Fatima began the IVF cycle. But because they were already committed—and had paid fully for the IVF cycle—they decided to press forward.

The IVF cycle itself seemed to be going well. Because Fatima was still young, in her late twenties, she produced twenty-six healthy eggs, a considerable number, which were retrieved from her ovaries in an outpatient procedure that was performed under general anesthesia. However, two days later, when Fatima was scheduled for the transfer of the embryos back into her uterus, she began to feel unwell. Her abdomen became extremely bloated, and she found herself gasping for breath. In addition, severe pain and cramping in her lower abdomen and legs meant that she could not walk or even stand on her own. Realizing that something was terribly wrong, Sadiq rushed Fatima to the emergency room of the local hospital, where she was admitted for ovarian hyperstimulation syndrome (OHSS). OHSS is a rare but potentially fatal complication resulting from some forms of fertility medication. Although most cases of OHSS are mild, involving abdominal bloating, nausea, and slight weight gain, Fatima's case was severe. She experienced marked abdominal bloating above the waist and shortness of breath due to pleural effusion, or the buildup of excess fluid in her lungs. The couple described the medical emergency—and the unpaid hospital bill totaling thousands—to me in this way:

FATIMA: I got sick, with fluid in the lungs. It was hyperstimulation. It was bad, and I was in the hospital for a whole week. I had pleural effusion.

SADIQ: Yeah, they had to put a tube in her. It drained all the fluid from her lungs. It was bad hyperstimulation, and she had to stay in the hospital until she got better.

FATIMA: I still have a lot of pain in my lower belly and back. My ovaries are big. They said they will get better after I have a period. But now, it's going to take three to four weeks before they will decrease in size.

SADIQ: But at least now she's feeling good. She can walk on her own and can breathe better.

FATIMA: This is the worst time *ever* in both of our lives. I *never* got that much sick before. This was the most toughest time I've ever had. And I had spent a lot of time coming for ultrasounds and blood work. It was costly, painful, and also time consuming. Every other day, I was doing treatment. But no one knew, not even the family. It was too personal, and I wanted to keep this to ourselves. Also, I had been working full-time for the state. But because we wanted to start a family, I cut to part-time and lost my state benefits. We started treatment from our own pockets. But when we left the hospital, the hospital bill was still unpaid. We're going to have to ask a charity to help pay for our hospital bills. It's a charity in the hospital. They will pay for the stay, but you have to prove that you're low income or not working. I wasn't expecting that I'm going to get sick when I saved just enough money for the in vitro. The IVF was maybe $10,000, all totaled with the medicine. At least that is paid for. But now we're so broke that I can't go back to school in the fall. I would register as a senior in the fall, but I don't think I can go back to school. The tuition is going up. Right now, to register for four classes, three to four months ago would have been $4,000. But there was a 7 percent [tuition] increase. So now it's $5,200 for one semester, for four classes, just for the tuition. I was planning to graduate on time, but this is never going to happen.

Because Fatima had revealed their financial woes to me, I asked the couple if their families could help provide them with any form of financial support. Sadiq was the first to respond, explaining how the Michigan economy was sinking:

> SADIQ: Businesses around here keep laying people off. So there are not that many people who can help us in our families. If we have no choice, then I've got to go to my family. But first, I must try my best. We just bought a house, but now she's sick, and I never thought this would happen.
>
> FATIMA: My dad worked for the largest oil company in Iraq as a supervisor for twenty years. They say in the news that things are getting better in Iraq with the government's help. But my dad and mom were in Iraq this year, trying to get his retirement. He hired an attorney, and for three months he stayed there, but nothing's happened. He owns a little business here, but he doesn't make much money. He needs his retirement [from Iraq], and he can't get it.
>
> SADIQ: We have not been back since we left in 1991. We've not been back there. If you want to go back home, and you see your country and feel bad all of the time, then you go there and get depressed. People say it got worse and worse. I don't think it's a good time to go to see the country. You'll look and see where your country is, and you'll just want to stay away until it gets better.
>
> FATIMA: I would like to go and visit someday. I would love to go to the Middle East. But definitely not now.

I told Fatima and Sadiq that few Americans probably realized that Iraq had once been a country known for its higher education, including an excellent health care system and many talented Iraqi physicians.[2] This caused Fatima to reflect on American attitudes toward Iraqis and Arabs more generally:

> FATIMA: From my experience, when I was at school and at work—and I went to school here, not back home [in Iraq]—I noticed people always look at you. They don't look at you as an Iraqi or Yemeni. You're all mixed up in their minds. You're an "Arab." They don't know the differences between the Lebanese, Iraqis, Yemenis. I think, unfortunately, I would have to say that the majority of people here are not educated about anything having to do with different cultures and religions. Back home, we focused on history, language, and culture. But here, even college students don't know anything about other cultures. I have friends who took four years of high school Spanish, and now they can barely communicate. So what they know about the world is because

of their families, their environment. We thought about moving, maybe to a different state. Now there are Iraqi communities in New Mexico, New York, Philly, California, Florida, and Texas. But our families are here, both sides, and at least there are other Arab people who can understand you.

Due to increasing Islamophobia and anti-Arab sentiment, Fatima and Sadiq felt a measure of safety living in a mostly Arab ethnic enclave, even if it rendered them "stuck" in Michigan for the foreseeable future. Moreover, because of their IVF cycle, Fatima and Sadiq had twenty unused embryos waiting for them in cold storage in the Arab-serving IVF clinic. When I asked them what they planned to do with their frozen embryos, they had this to say:

SADIQ: I have no idea. I thought about it, but I don't know. I guess they can keep them there.

MARCIA: Would you consider donating some of them to other couples?

FATIMA: No! I don't want to do that. We don't want our kids with someone else.

SADIQ: I like to keep them to myself.

MARCIA: So you're opposed to donation?

FATIMA: I wouldn't say I'm against what they do, especially if people want to do this to save their marriage. But for me, I wouldn't want to do it.

SADIQ: To me, it seems like . . . I can't really imagine giving my kid to someone else and to see it grow up. "This is my kid, and I donated it." Even if it's okay to do, it doesn't seem right to me. Donating the baby to someone else, I don't see that it's a good idea.

MARCIA: Do you know if donation is approved by the religion?

SADIQ: He doesn't approve, Sayyid Sistani [that is, Iraq's major Shia religious authority]. He's the main person we follow.[3]

MARCIA: So, if you have extra embryos, what will you do?

FATIMA: Can you get rid of them?

SADIQ: Yes.

FATIMA: I think we will have to ask our religious person.

SADIQ: You *can* get rid of them.

FATIMA: But we'll have to ask, just to be safe.

Like many pious Muslim couples, Fatima and Sadiq were concerned about the moral acceptability of IVF, relying on the opinions of highly respected

Islamic religious authorities. But their most immediate concern was the unexpected news they had received that very afternoon—namely, Fatima was pregnant, even though none of her IVF embryos had been transferred to her womb in the midst of her life-threatening OHSS emergency.

Although I was happy for this young Arab refugee couple—who had faced a perilous journey and so many subsequent difficulties—I was confused about Fatima's "mystery" pregnancy. Fatima explained to me that the doctor had told them to refrain from sex during the IVF cycle. But, once again, they had thrown caution to the wind. One episode of unprotected intercourse had resulted in an unplanned pregnancy—a "natural" pregnancy that had withstood the rigors of IVF hormonal stimulation and a severe case of OHSS.

As the clinic was about to shut its doors for the weekend, I asked Fatima how she was feeling about the pregnancy. "I didn't know I was pregnant," she explained. "It was a surprise, an unexpected surprise!" Sadiq added, "Oh yeah, it was the lucky nine, the lucky shot!"

Fatima was still feeling sick and distended from the OHSS. Sadiq was still unemployed with no idea where he would find another job. The couple's unpaid mortgage and hospital bills were piling up. But that summer afternoon, Fatima and Sadiq were beaming. They had each other. They had a miraculous pregnancy. And they now had hopes and dreams of a future baby—an American baby, born to Arab refugee parents, on the margins of Detroit.

Introduction: When Arabs Fled

A Legacy of Conflict

THE STORY OF FATIMA AND SADIQ, INTRODUCED IN THE Prologue, began back in 1991, when the United States invaded Iraq in the First Gulf War. In the quarter-century since then, the Middle East has seen unprecedented levels of violence, not only in Iraq but across the region as a whole. Of the fifty violent conflicts occurring around the world in the years 2014 and 2015, three of the most deadly—with annual casualties exceeding 10,000—were in the Middle Eastern countries of Afghanistan, Iraq, and Syria.[1] Saudi Arabia was also at war with Yemen. The Libyan civil war was destabilizing North Africa. More than sixty years of protracted conflict between Israel and Palestine had led in 2014 to a devastating summer war in Gaza. And, by that point, the rise of the so-called Islamic State (also known as ISIS, ISIL, Daesh) in Iraq and Syria was threatening the region—and the world—as a whole.

These incidents of political violence in the Middle East were varied and ghastly in their effects. On-the-ground combat and aerial bombing campaigns involved the use of chemical weapons, barrel bombs, cluster bombs, suicide bombs, improvised explosive devices (IEDs), and drone strikes.[2] Millions of civilians were killed, injured, maimed, and displaced. Thousands of others were imprisoned, tortured, beheaded, raped, and sold as sex slaves. Middle Eastern civilians caught in war zones were facing food insecurity, particularly in Syria, where government-imposed food blockades were causing massive starvation in some villages. Those who were able to escape the region flocked to Europe, leading to the worst humanitarian crisis on the continent since World War II.[3]

This book traces these wars in the Middle East to the Arab refugee crisis in the West—a crisis that began well before the world took notice in 2015. Fatima and Sadiq were among the first wave of Arab refugees to leave the Middle East in the wake of the First Gulf War. The Second Gulf War—also known as Operation Iraqi Freedom—led to a second wave of Iraqis fleeing their country between 2003 and 2011. Since then, the chaos caused by ISIS, which formed in 2013 and which declared itself a "caliphate," or "Islamic State" by June 2014, has fueled the flight of even more Arab refugees[4]—a flight that began in earnest in 2011 with the outbreak of the Syrian civil war. By 2015, more than 4.8 million Syrians had fled their country, primarily to the neighboring Middle Eastern states of Turkey, Lebanon, and Jordan. But not until the summer of 2015—when nightly newscasts began showing the faces of haggard and hapless Syrian refugees, flooding into Europe on foot or in overpacked rubber dinghies—did Western countries begin to respond. German Chancellor Angela Merkel called on her fellow citizens and European allies to "welcome" hundreds of thousands of fleeing Syrian refugees.[5] American President Barack Obama, too, promised to allow 10,000 Syrian refugees into the United States in fiscal year 2016.[6]

However, in the wake of these humanitarian pronouncements, ISIS-inspired terrorist attacks—in Paris, San Bernadino, Brussels, Orlando, Nice, Berlin, and many non-Western countries as well—prompted a new wave of Islamophobia. In his campaign for president, Donald Trump called for a ban on Muslims entering the country, even though no Muslim refugee had ever committed a terrorist attack on US soil.[7] In the midst of growing anti-Muslim, anti-refugee public sentiment, more than thirty US governors took measures to prevent Syrian refugees from entering their home states. One of those was Republican Governor Rick Snyder of Michigan—the state with the largest number of first- and second-generation Arab refugees, including Fatima, Sadiq, and their families.[8]

Given US responsibility for at least some of the violence that has unfolded in the Middle East at the turn of this century, a number of important questions need to be asked. First, does the United States have a moral obligation to offer asylum to fleeing Arab refugees? Second, what are the responsibilities of states such as Michigan to provide refugee resettlement services? Third, has the United States done a good job of resettling Arab refugees who have already arrived, providing them with adequate employment, education, housing, and access to safe and affordable health care?

These are the questions to be taken up in this book, a book that explores why Arabs have fled from war zones, where they have resettled in the United States, and how poverty and discrimination continue to affect their lives as naturalized, although marginalized, American citizens. The fate of Arab refugees in the United States has been Janus faced: on the one hand, most Arab refugees such as Fatima and Sadiq feel grateful to the United States for taking them in and allowing them to aspire for a better life in America, whereas on the other hand, many Arab refugees who began arriving in the United States after the First Gulf War still live lives of utter poverty and hardship. For example, Sadiq worked two jobs before being laid off from his employment in the Michigan auto industry. Fatima almost graduated from a local college before her tuition money ran out. Yet, together, Fatima and Sadiq accrued just enough money to marry, buy a small house, and undertake an expensive IVF cycle. Despite mounting debts and a medical emergency, Fatima and Sadiq achieved their American dream of conceiving a miracle baby together.

To write a book about refugees like Fatima and Sadiq, it is important to begin back in their home countries. Most of the people whose stories are traced in this book fled to Michigan from two Middle Eastern war zones, primarily in Iraq and Lebanon but also from Palestine. Many of the Yemenis in this book, who came to Michigan as poor economic migrants, are no longer able to return home because of a devastating war unleashed in their country by Saudi Arabia and its Gulf allies. In this book, then, we will see how war in the Middle East has destroyed lives, damaged infrastructures, inflamed sectarian tensions, and engendered heinous acts of brutality. War in the Middle East is a tragedy in two parts, with 2011 serving as a critical dividing line. Before 2011, fifteen of the twenty-two nations of the Middle East and North Africa—encompassing 85 percent of the region's total population—had already suffered from protracted conflicts.[9] Then, in 2011, the so-called Arab Spring happened, bringing with it high hopes for democratic transition, peace, and prosperity in the region. Soon, however, those hopes turned into nightmares in several Middle Eastern countries. Three bloody wars emerged in Libya, Syria, and Yemen. The birth of ISIS in Iraq and Syria wreaked havoc on the region as a whole. The US war in Iraq officially ended in 2011, but the violence did not, leading to an ongoing Iraqi refugee crisis. And in Syria, the worst refugee crisis in a single generation transpired in the midst of a brutal civil war, which turned into a regional cataclysm and international humanitarian crisis.

In the next section, I provide a brief history of these pre- and post-2011 Middle Eastern wars. Such a recounting casts a grim light on the causes and consequences of political violence in the Middle East. Unfortunately, in the pre-2011 period, the United States bears considerable responsibility for both war and displacement. This is especially true of the 2003 US invasion of Iraq, which set in motion much of the violence that has followed.

Middle East Wars: A Tragedy in Two Acts

Tragedy Act One: From World War II to War in Iraq

The modern history of war in the Middle East dates back to the end of World War II and can be traced to five critical forces.[10] First was the founding of the state of Israel in 1948, which resulted in a protracted conflict between Israel and Palestine, as well as a series of wars between Israel and neighboring Arab nations. Second were colonial independence movements, especially against the French in North Africa, which led to wars of independence, most notably in Algeria (1954–1962). Third were internecine, sectarian-inflected conflicts, such as the fifteen-year civil war in Lebanon (1975–1990) and the eight-year Iran–Iraq War (1980–1988), launched by Saddam Hussein and his secular Baath regime against the Shia theocracy that came to power in Iran in 1979. A fourth factor was the rise of Islamist movements in the region, leading to wars between more secular and Islamist forces, in countries ranging from Algeria (1991–2002) to Sudan (1983–2005). Finally, the Cold War between the United States and the Soviet Union played out in the Middle East in ways that continue to haunt the region today. When the Soviet Union invaded Afghanistan in 1978, the United States retaliated by supporting the mujahideen, a radical Sunni Islamist fighting force with roots in Saudi Arabia.

In retrospect, US support of the mujahideen against Russia during the Cold War period was a fatal US foreign policy error. As shown in Pulitzer Prize–winning journalist Steve Coll's book, *Ghost Wars: The Secret History of the CIA, Afghanistan, and Bin Laden, from the Soviet Invasion to September 10, 2001*, the CIA secretly sent billions of dollars of military aid to the mujahideen in Afghanistan in a US-supported jihad against the Soviet Union during the eight years of Ronald Reagan's presidency.[11] The mujahideen fighters were the precursors to the Taliban, the group against which the United

States would eventually go to war in October 2001. Furthermore, US military support of the mujahideen nurtured the rise of Osama bin Laden's al-Qaeda, which received substantial training and support from the Taliban in Afghanistan. Thus, when al-Qaeda attacked the World Trade Center and the Pentagon on September 11, 2001, President George W. Bush declared war on Afghanistan a month later.

Whereas the US-led war in Afghanistan, called Operation Enduring Freedom (OEF), might have been justified within the overarching "War on Terror," President Bush's decision to remove Saddam Hussein from power by declaring war in Iraq less than two years later was a military and foreign policy error of disastrous proportions[12]—of a magnitude perhaps even greater than Reagan's support for the mujahideen in Afghanistan. Without a doubt, Saddam Hussein was a brutal dictator of his own people and a warmonger with neighboring countries. Saddam came to power in 1979, the same year as the Iranian revolution. Within his first year in office, Saddam plunged his country into a crippling eight-year war with neighboring Iran (1980–1988), which led to the death of more than a million people. Two years later, Saddam attacked another neighboring country, Kuwait, the small petro-rich nation wedged between Iraq and Saudi Arabia. This marked the beginning of the First Gulf War, as well as thirteen years of UN-imposed sanctions on Iraq. An oil-for-food program was put in place by the United Nations in 1996 to prevent massive starvation in the country. But the sanctions continued to cripple the Iraqi economy until they were removed at the start of the Second Gulf War.

The Second Gulf War—also known as Operation Iraqi Freedom (OIF), or simply the Iraq War—was declared by President George W. Bush on March 19, 2003, in the aftermath of September 11. As would soon be discovered, the Iraq War was based on erroneous intelligence information, which claimed that Saddam Hussein possessed weapons of mass destruction (WMDs), thus posing a threat to US national security. The Bush administration also argued that deposing Saddam would lead to necessary regime change in Iraq, creating a democratic Iraqi government, friendly to US interests.[13] Moreover, neoconservatives in the Bush administration claimed that defeating Saddam Hussein would lead to increased security for Israel and would allow the United States to gain control over Iraq's oil fields, giving the United States an economic upper hand in the petro-rich Gulf region.

In retrospect, the US war in Iraq is widely condemned as a US military and foreign policy failure—perhaps the worst in modern US and Middle

Eastern history.[14] Based on false intelligence—namely, that Saddam possessed WMDs and was linked to September 11—the US military intervention in Iraq increased political instability in the country, leading to a power vacuum that was filled in part by Islamic terrorist organizations.[15] Whereas Reagan's Cold War policy against the Russians led to the rise of the Taliban and al-Qaeda, Bush's Iraq War created favorable conditions for the growth of ISIS, the radical Sunni Muslim organization that now threatens the world through global terrorism.

How did Bush's Iraq War create the conditions for ISIS? First, the war in Iraq unleashed deep-seated sectarian tensions in a country where Sunni Muslims (about one-third of the overall population) had long held political sway over the Shia Muslim majority.[16] US-enforced regime change put two successive Shia-led governments in charge, first under Prime Minister Nouri al-Maliki, then under Prime Minister Haider al-Abadi. Al-Maliki's government in particular alienated Iraq's Sunni population, including many of Saddam's former military commanders, as well as major Sunni tribal factions in the country. Kurds, a non-Arab ethnic group comprising about 20 percent of Iraq's population, also gained a new foothold in terms of power and quasi-independence in the northern regions of Iraq.[17] In other words, the United States threw its political weight behind the Shia and Kurdish factions at the expense of Sunni Arab tribal leaders and members of Saddam's Baath party. In doing so, the United States effectively "blew the lid off" ethnosectarian tensions and rivalries in Iraq—with consequences that have been truly profound not only for Iraq but for the sectarian divisions that have emerged in the region as a whole.

Despite the Bush administration's rhetoric of democratization, the US-led war in Iraq failed to install a strong, stable democracy in the country. In fact, democratization was never a prime motive for the war in Iraq. From the very outset, experts warned that Iraq had no history of democratic traditions or institutions.[18] When the United States invaded Iraq in 2003, Iraq's preexisting political and social conditions made it unlikely that the country would democratize naturally after the US invasion. The United States was also more committed to regime change than to democratization and nation building per se. Self-interest more than altruism guided the US intervention. And so, the US intervention in Iraq resulted in only an incomplete and unstable democracy, unable to counter the political instability in its midst.[19]

This political instability created the conditions for the growth of Islamist groups, most notably ISIS, but also the al-Qaeda faction known as al Nusra Front.[20] The Shia-led governments backed by the United States in Iraq lacked the ability or authority to control these Sunni jihadist groups from forming in the country. These institutional weaknesses in the midst of a highly volatile and unstable political environment were exploited by jihadists. Despite nearly a decade of US military presence in Iraq, Islamist groups were able to thrive on Iraqi soil. By May 9, 2013, they had claimed part of Iraq as a so-called Islamic State.

In his brief but compelling essay, "Terror's Lineage," Algerian journalist Kamel Daoud calls ISIS the "monster," birthed in Iraq by foreign parents.[21] In Daoud's analysis, the "father" of ISIS is George W. Bush's America, especially the disastrous invasion of Iraq. According to Daoud, the US-led war in Iraq was seen as the "rape" of the Arab world. And, because the invasion was based on a lie—namely, the false link between September 11 and Saddam Hussein—it destroyed America's moral superiority and credibility on the Arab street. As for the "mother" of ISIS, Daoud points to Saudi Arabia, a purported US ally. As Daoud argues, Saudi Arabia is a "strange theocracy [that] is simultaneously allied with the West through the Saudi royal family and opposed to the West by an ideology that is the product of a vicious clergy."

The ideology to which Daoud refers is Wahhabism, a particular brand of puritanical, scripturally oriented, fundamentalist Sunni Islam, which is preached and practiced in Saudi Arabia.[22] Wahhabism is conservative and orthodox. It takes a dim view of Shi'ism, the other major branch of Islam, which it considers unorthodox and heretical. In Daoud's analysis, Saudi Arabia is an "ideological factory" for Wahhabism, which is supported by the Saudi state.[23] Saudi clerics are allowed to propagate their vision of the world through books, television channels, and increasingly through social media. The Saudi government spends billions of dollars building foreign mosques and exporting Wahhabi clerics throughout the Muslim world.[24] Saudi Arabia has been the major supporter of Sunni fundamentalist around the world, including the most radical jihadist strains. For example, fifteen of the nineteen September 11 hijackers were Saudis. Today, the largest proportion of ISIS Twitter users, about 25 percent, come from Saudi Arabia.[25] Although the country hosts the most holy sites of Islam for both Sunni and Shia Muslims, Saudi Arabia is also the heartland of a severe and intolerant form of Sunni Islam, which is both jihadist in orientation and virulently anti-Shia.

These Sunni–Shia tensions are currently roiling the Middle East. Although the Sunni–Shia divide is based on theological differences that date back 1,400 years, sectarianism today is more political and demographic than religious in nature.[26] Overall, Sunni Muslim populations are the demographic majority, comprising 85 to 90 percent of the world's 1.6 billion Muslims and at least two-thirds of the Middle Eastern population as a whole. Of the twenty-two nations of the Middle East and North Africa, eighteen are predominantly Sunni, with the countries of North Africa having no indigenous Shia populations at all. Thus, Shia Muslims are the marginalized minority, constituting only about 10 to 15 percent of the world's Muslim population.[27] However, Shia are the majority population in two of the Middle East's largest countries, Iran (more than 90 percent Shia) and Iraq (between 60 and 65 percent Shia). Shias are also the majority sect in the two small Middle Eastern nations of Bahrain and Lebanon. Significant Shia populations also live in Afghanistan, Kuwait, Turkey, the United Arab Emirates, Syria, and Yemen, as well as along the eastern coast of Saudi Arabia, a region rich in oilfields. In other words, in spatial terms, a significant "Shia crescent" extends across the heart of the Middle East, constituting about one-third of the region's total population. However, with the exception of Iran, which is ethnically Persian and Farsi speaking, Shia populations have never ruled, even in those Arab countries with Shia-majority populations.

The US invasion of Iraq changed all this, serving as a crucial "tipping point" in an unstable sectarian balance of power.[28] To wit, the US invasion of Iraq stripped the Sunni-led Baath government of Saddam Hussein of its power and authority, tipping the sectarian scales in favor of the Shia bloc for the first time in Arab history. Putting its political and military weight behind the previously disenfranchised Iraqi Shia population, the US government unwittingly emboldened the region's Shia Muslims to take advantage of this unprecedented historical moment. As explained by political scientist Vali Nasr in his 2006 book, *The Shia Revival: How Conflicts within Islam Will Shape the Future*:[29]

> When American leaders spoke of changing the region's politics for the better after the Iraq war, they were in effect talking about democratizing the old Sunni-dominated Middle East. They gave little thought to the new Middle East that

> is emerging, and have yet to grasp its potential. This Middle East will not be defined by the Arab identity or by any particular form of national government. Ultimately, the character of the region will be decided in the crucible of Shia revival and the Sunni response to it . . . The overall Sunni–Shia conflict will play a large role in defining the Middle East as a whole and shaping its relations with the outside world. Sectarian conflict will make Sunni extremists more extreme and will likely rekindle revolutionary zeal among the Shia. At times the conflict will be bloody, as it strengthens the extremists, swelling their ranks, popularizing their causes, and amplifying their voices in politics, thus complicating the broader effort to contain Islamic radicalism.

A decade on, it seems that Nasr's political predictions could not have been more prescient. Sectarianism underlies the bitter power struggle between Saudi Arabia (a Sunni monarchy) and Iran (a Shia theocracy).[30] It is at the crux of the Syrian civil war, in which Bashar al-Assad's government (led by a Shia minority sect, the Alawis) is being propped up both by Iran (a Shia theocracy) and Hezbollah (Lebanon's Shia militia), in a battle against Syrian opposition forces (Sunni) and ISIS (ardently Sunni).[31] Sectarian hatred is also behind the war that Saudi Arabia (Sunni) has launched, with Gulf Cooperation Council support (Sunni), against the Houthi rebels (Shia) in Yemen.[32] When the Saudi monarchy (Sunni) executed the Saudi cleric Nimr al-Nimr (Shia), Iranians (Shia) retaliated by sacking the Saudi Embassy in Tehran.[33] In short, many of the region's current battles involve unfortunate sectarian enmities—more politically driven than theological in nature—in which the dominant Sunni bloc (with Saudi Arabia being the Middle East's status quo Sunni power) is pitted against the minority Shia bloc (with Iran at the center of this regional rivalry). However, as predicted by Vali Nasr, the Shia have risen up to support each other in a coalition that now includes the governments of Iran, Iraq, Syria, and Yemen, as well as Lebanon's Shia party, Hezbollah.

In a January 2016 *Washington Post* column entitled "America Can't Stop the Sectarian Tidal Wave," political analyst Fareed Zakaria argued that "sectarian struggle now infects almost every aspect of the region's politics. It has confounded US foreign policy and will continue to limit the ability of the United States, or any outside power, to stabilize the region."[34] According to Zakaria, the US war in Iraq was largely responsible for this "sectarian tidal wave." Yet, he urged the United States to stay out of this sectarian battle from this point on, calling it "someone else's civil war."

Tragedy Act Two: From the Arab Spring to Arab Refugees

Sectarianism—and the death, destruction, and displacement it has spawned—is an unfortunate reality in the post-2011 period. This new period of sectarian violence is all the more tragic, because 2011 was a year of great hope for the Middle Eastern region as a whole. On January 14, 2011, Tunisians ousted their corrupt leader, President Ben Ali. On January 25, 2011, Egyptians followed suit, ending the nearly forty-year rule of President Hosni Mubarak within only three weeks' time. By March 2011, peaceful protest movements were in full bloom across sixteen Arab nations, erupting into a hoped-for "Arab Spring."[35]

However, the Arab Spring was short lived, replaced by violence and bloodshed. In Egypt, nearly 900 people were killed in the protests that led to the fall of Hosni Mubarak. In Bahrain, Valentine's Day protests in the "Pearl Roundabout"—equivalent to Egypt's Tahrir Square—were brutally suppressed by the Bahraini government with the help of Saudi forces. In Syria, peaceful protests in Deraa, one of Syria's many Sunni-dominant cities, were crushed by President Bashar al-Assad's government troops. Soon, the bloodshed in Deraa would devolve into a full-scale, sectarian-inflected, externally fueled civil war. In Yemen, protests turned violent by early summer, with a bomb attack on the palace of President Ali Abdullah Saleh, who was severely burned and forced to flee the country. Meanwhile, in Libya, rebel forces overtook the capital of Tripoli by August 2011 with the backing of NATO and US airstrikes. In October, Colonel Muammar Qaddafi was killed in his tribal stronghold of Sirte.[36]

By the end of 2011, then, dictators had been deposed in four of the main Arab Spring countries (Tunisia, Egypt, Yemen, and Libya). But wars had been sparked in three (Syria, Libya, and Yemen). Sadly, five years on, all three of these wars were still raging. At the top of *Foreign Policy*'s top-ten list of "wars to watch" in both 2015 and 2016 was the civil war in Syria, which was connected to the ongoing war in neighboring Iraq via ISIS.[37] This conflated crisis involving Syria, Iraq, and ISIS was a "Tier I" priority, according to the US Council on Foreign Relations (CFR).[38] Focusing especially on Iraq, CFR noted that "intensification of the conflict in Iraq [is] due to territorial gains by the Islamic State of Iraq and Syria (ISIS) and operations by Iraqi security forces, as well as ongoing Sunni-Shia sectarian violence."[39] According to CFR, this situation "directly threatens the U.S. homeland, is likely to trigger U.S. military involvement because of treaty commitments, [and] threatens the supply of critical U.S. strategic resources."[40]

By the time CFR published its influential "Preventive Priorities" report at the end of 2015, ISIS had already threatened US homeland security by inspiring the deadly terrorist attack in San Bernadino, California, which killed fourteen people. By the beginning of 2016, twenty nations around the world had succumbed to seventy terrorist attacks and more than 1,200 deaths linked to, or inspired by, ISIS.[41] In Iraq and Syria, where ISIS was based, the group had perpetrated unspeakable acts of ethnic cleansing—not only against Shia Muslims but also against Christians, Kurds, and other ethnic minority populations, such as the Yazidis. Radically anti-Shia in its ideology, ISIS had fought pitched battles against the Shia-controlled government forces in both Iraq and Syria. In Iraq, government security forces, which were predominantly Shia, had attempted to fend off the spread of ISIS across large swaths of the country.[42] In Syria, the Shia Alawi-led government of Bashar al-Assad was also fighting a pitched battle against ISIS, in part to protect both Shia and Christian minority communities in the country. By the beginning of 2016, it was estimated that Syria's Shia Alawis, constituting roughly 12 percent of the Syrian population, had lost as many as one-third of all men of fighting age.[43] Bashar al-Assad's regime had turned for reinforcement to Shia fighting forces from Iran and Lebanon, as well as from Russia, Syria's long-time ally.

In the midst of this devastating sectarian violence in both Iraq and Syria, thousands of innocent civilians, including women, children, and the elderly, were being killed, including by both Russian and US airstrikes. Although estimates of casualties have been difficult to obtain, the United Nations, as well as various observer groups, estimate tens of thousands of deaths in both countries. A group called the Syrian Observatory for Human Rights (SOHR), which is based in Great Britain, has been documenting the casualties of the Syrian war ever since it began in March 2011. SOHR estimates that, in the year 2014 alone, more than 76,000 Syrians were killed, including more than 3,500 Syrian children.[44] In August 2015, the United Nations issued a report, estimating total Syrian casualties to be around 250,000.[45] But those numbers soon increased because of Russian airstrikes. Between September 2015 and January 2016, SOHR estimated 1,015 civilian casualties from Russian airstrikes, including the deaths of at least 200 Syrian children.[46] By then, reports had also surfaced from the Syrian city of Madaya that many children were starving to death, due to a six-month Syrian government blockade of food and medicine. (Residents were said to be surviving by eating boiled leaves and animal feed.)

In the midst of so much Syrian suffering, Iraq, too, was being shaken by heart-wrenching violence. In January 2016, the United Nations released a sobering report that described the civilian death toll in Iraq as "staggering."[47] Between January 2014 and October 2015, nearly 19,000 Iraqi civilians had been killed; more than 36,000 Iraqis were wounded, and 3.2 million Iraqis were internally displaced, including in the vicinity of Baghdad, where ISIS-inspired violence was spinning out of control. According to the UN report, ISIS "continues to commit systematic and widespread violence and abuses of international human rights law and humanitarian law. These acts may, in some instances, amount to war crimes, crimes against humanity, and possibly genocide."[48]

According to victim and witness testimonies compiled by the UN Assistance Mission for Iraq and the Office of the High Commissioner for Human Rights, ISIS's tactics in Iraq were both brutal and lethal.[49] ISIS had killed and abducted scores of civilians, often in a targeted manner. Many of those abducted were subjected to adjudication by self-proclaimed ISIS "courts," with punishments ranging from stoning to amputation to execution. In its many public executions, ISIS was said to favor gruesome spectacles, including death by shooting, beheading, bulldozing, burning alive, and throwing people off the tops of buildings. Moreover, hundreds of children had been abducted by ISIS for religious "education" and military training. Those child soldiers who fled from the frontlines during fighting were often murdered. Women and children who were captured by ISIS were subjected to sexual violence, sometimes becoming sex slaves for ISIS fighters.

Given these horrors, it is not surprising that thousands of Iraqi civilians had fled their homes in an attempt to evade ISIS. By the end of 2015, the UN High Commissioner for Refugees (UNHCR) estimated that more than 3 million "people of concern" in Iraq were in need of urgent humanitarian assistance.[50] This included more than 1.5 million internally displaced Iraqis, as well as 400,000 Syrian refugees, and 12,400 Palestinians living in long-term, UN-supported refugee camps in the country. According to UNHCR, many Iraqis, Syrians, and Palestinians living in camps were dying from lack of basic food, water, and medical supplies. Reports of human rights violations were also mounting. In many cases, civilians attempting to flee to safety were being arbitrarily arrested or forcibly expelled by Iraqi (mostly Shia) security forces, especially if they were coming from Sunni-dominant tribal areas. By June 2016, an estimated 68,000 Sunni Muslim refugees, mostly women and children, were forced to flee their homes in Fallujah as Iraqi security forces and Shia militias attempted to take back control of the city from ISIS.

Arab Refugees

Given these gruesome realities, it is no wonder that so many Arabs have fled their countries. Indeed, it is fair to say that no other region of the world has suffered so much war and population disruption due to protracted conflict. To reiterate an earlier point, by 2011, fifteen of twenty-two Arab League nations—comprising 85 percent of the region's population—had already suffered from complex emergencies due to protracted conflicts.[51] As a result, by 2011, the Middle East had the largest percentage of migrants in the world, the majority of whom had fled from ongoing conflict, persecution, and political instability by crossing international borders as refugees or by becoming internally displaced persons (IDPs) within their own countries. However, by 2015, those numbers escalated dramatically. In a grim pronouncement on World Refugee Day, the UN High Commissioner for Refugees reported that 65.3 million people were displaced from their homes in 2015, the majority from the Middle Eastern countries of Syria, Iraq, and Afghanistan (as well as Somalia). Conflicts in those countries were responsible for a 10 percent increase in the total number of refugees and IDPs worldwide in 2015—the first year since World War II in which more than 60 million persons worldwide were forcibly displaced.[52]

Historically speaking, Palestine and Lebanon have been particularly emblematic of these violence-related population disruptions.[53] In the case of Palestine, the majority of Palestinians were expelled from their homes during the founding of the state of Israel in 1948–1949. Most Palestinians fled to neighboring Jordan, the only Arab state to eventually grant Palestinians citizenship rights. Palestinians who fled to the neighboring countries of Lebanon, Syria, and Iraq were treated as refugees, most of them living in long-term refugee camps supported by the UN Relief and Works Agency (UNRWA). Of the estimated 11 million Palestinians now living worldwide, 6.6 million are refugees, and nearly one-half million are IDPs in Israel and the Palestinian territories. Nearly one million Palestinians live outside the region, mostly in Chile, but also in a variety of Latin American and Western countries, as well as the Arab Gulf states.[54]

In neighboring Lebanon, nearly one-half million Palestinians live in UNRWA-supported refugee camps in a country that does not allow Palestinians to become naturalized citizens.[55] Thus, it is fair to say that Lebanon has been no safe haven for Palestinians. But, at the same time, Lebanon has often been a dangerous place for the Lebanese themselves. Although significant outmigration from Lebanon began well before World War I,[56] the flight from Lebanon increased dramatically with the outbreak of the Lebanese civil war in 1975. During twenty-five years of protracted conflict, more than one-third of the entire population of Lebanon left the country. Of the estimated 15 million Lebanese worldwide, only about 3.5 million remain in Lebanon today. Nearly 7 million Lebanese live in Brazil alone and nearly one-half million in the United States, where they make up the single largest group of Arab Americans. Lebanese ethnic enclaves are also found in other parts of the world, including most parts of Latin America and the Caribbean, in French-speaking West Africa (particularly Cote d'Ivoire, Sierra Leone, and Senegal), and in Europe, Australia, and Canada. Given the millions of Lebanese who have left their country due to war, it is ironic that Lebanon now hosts more than one million Syrian refugees, comprising nearly one-fifth of the country's total population.

Other parts of the Middle East beyond the Arab world have also experienced massive violence-related outmigration. For example, following the 1979 Islamic revolution, 4 to 5 million Iranians fled their country, primarily to North America (both the United States and Canada), as well as Europe and Australia. When the Soviet–Afghan War broke out in the same year as the Iranian revolution, Iran itself became a safe haven for fleeing Afghan refugees. Nearly 6 million Afghans resettled in Iran and Pakistan in one of the largest refugee flights in modern history. With the US invasion of Afghanistan in 2001, UNHCR began a program to repatriate the majority of Afghans,[57] under the mistaken assumption that US military intervention would somehow bring peace and stability to the country. Although UNHCR assisted 4.7 million of the 5.8 million Afghans who eventually returned home, renewed violence in the majority of Afghan provinces reversed this repatriation process during the 2010–2015 period. By 2014, more than 3 million Afghans had again left the country in a desperate attempt to escape the violence. In 2014 alone, more than 14,277 Afghans were killed. In 2015, that number had more than doubled to 33,165. Given these dangers, Afghanistan continued in its position as the world's top supplier of refugees for the thirty-second year in a row.[58] In fact, one-quarter of all refugees entering Europe in the first two months of 2016 were Afghans, along with one-quarter who were Iraqis and the other half who were Syrians. In other words, Afghans, Iraqis, and Syrians are the three major refugee populations flooding into Europe.

Unfortunately, as of this writing, the United States is still intimately involved in Afghanistan's violence. Although President Barack Obama pledged to remove US troops from Afghanistan by the end of his presidency, he was unable to do so. The US war in Afghanistan had raged on for fifteen years—a state of warfare that some commentators described as "permanent."[59] Despite the displacement of millions of Afghan citizens during this period, the United States took in a mere fraction of the total. For example, only 428—or 0.8 percent of the total refugees admitted to the United States in 2011—were from Afghanistan.[60] Many Afghan men who served as military translators for US forces were left stranded in Afghanistan. Others who made it to America sometimes ended up on the streets, unable to find affordable housing for themselves, their wives, and children. In several cases, US veterans who served in Afghanistan rallied to support their homeless Afghan comrades.[61]

By comparison, the US commitment to Iraqi refugee resettlement was more substantial. The US government was estimated to have spent $1.5 billion on humanitarian assistance to Iraq during the war period (2003–2011). But in 2007, following criticism that Iraqi translators whose lives were in danger were desperately awaiting asylum, the US Refugee Admissions Program (USRAP) began resettling vulnerable Iraqi nationals in the United States.[62] Between 2007 and 2013, more than 200,000 Iraqi nationals were referred to the United States for humanitarian resettlement, mostly from transit camps in Jordan. By 2015, slightly more than half of those asylum seekers—about 110,000 Iraqi men, women, and children—had made it to the United States, where they were placed in every state, including Alaska and Hawaii. However, the largest number were resettled in southern California and in Michigan. In fact, between 2007 and 2013, Michigan accepted more than one-third of the 85,000 Iraqis who entered the country. As a result, two out of every three refugees in Michigan are Iraqi.[63]

Given that the United States has taken in relatively few Afghans but slightly more Iraqis fleeing from wars that the US military started in their home countries, the new question facing the United States is what to do about Syrian refugees. Should the United States take in thousands of Syrian refugees from a war that it did not start? This is the question that came to the fore in the summer of 2015, when UNHCR made the grim pronouncement on July 9 that more than 4 million Syrian men, women, and children had fled their country, creating "the biggest refugee population from a single conflict in a generation."[64] By January 2016, the number of Syrian refugees had swelled to 4.9 million.[65] By then, half of Syria's prewar population of 23 million had either been killed, forced to flee, or internally displaced. By that point, the United States had also spent more than $4 billion on relief efforts for 13.5 million Syrians—or more than half of the country's original population—who had been forced to flee their homes and who were mostly women and children (more than 75 percent). Estimates suggested that 5.5 million Syrian children, either in or out of the country, and mostly under the age of fourteen, were in desperate need of assistance.[66]

Yet, America has invested little in Syrian refugee resettlement, despite President Obama's pledge to take in 10,000 Syrian refugees in fiscal year 2016. During the first five years of the Syrian civil war, the United States admitted only 2,647 Syrian refugees—or exactly .0006 percent of the 4.7 million total.[67] In contrast, 813,599 Syrian refugees had received asylum in Europe, or close to 18 percent of the total Syrian refugee population. Before 2015, only about 220,000 Syrian refugees had applied for asylum in Europe. But by the end of 2015, the total number had risen to more than 900,000, with October 2015 experiencing the highest number of applications for a single month at 159,219.[68] In 2015 alone, 29 percent of the 1.2 million people who applied for asylum in European Union (EU) member states were from Syria, more than from any other country.[69] Of those whose asylum claims were processed, the majority had found homes in Germany (more than 250,000), followed by Sweden (more than 30,000). Having said this, the major burden of the Syrian refugee crisis was not being shouldered by EU nations. Instead, most Syrian refugees had fled to neighboring Middle Eastern countries, primarily Turkey (2.2 million according to official estimates, but possibly as many as 3 million total), Lebanon (1.2 million), and Jordan (650,000), but also Egypt (130,000) and even Iraq (250,000).

Glaringly absent from this list of Middle Eastern host countries were Saudi Arabia and the five petro-rich Gulf Cooperation Council (GCC) nations, including Bahrain, Kuwait, Oman, Qatar, and the United Arab Emirates (UAE). These Sunni-dominant countries have had no history of refugee resettlement, nor do they generally grant citizenship rights to foreigners, even if they are Arabs. Thus, five years on, the Arab Gulf nations had still not accepted any

Syrian refugees, although Gulf-based Islamic charities were providing refugee assistance in other Middle Eastern countries such as Lebanon. Instead, Saudi Arabia and its Gulf allies (Bahrain, Kuwait, and the UAE) had turned their attention to the Houthi Shia rebellion in Yemen, which they decided to suppress through military intervention.[70] Part of an emerging "Salman Doctrine" (named after the Saudi king),[71] Saudi Arabia began launching air strikes in January 2015, effectively beginning a new sectarian-inspired war within the Arab Gulf. According to the UN Office for the Coordination of Humanitarian Affairs (OCHA), 21 million Yemenis—or about 80 percent of the entire population—were in dire need of humanitarian assistance by the end of the year. Already one of the world's poorest nations—with 7 million Yemenis living in hunger as of 2011—food insecurity had more than doubled in the country by January 2016.[72] In addition, 2.5 million Yemenis were internally displaced, and more than 8,000 were killed by Saudi air strikes targeting densely populated urban areas.

This new war in Yemen brought forth a new wave of Arab refugees. By the beginning of 2016, more than 166,000 Yemenis had fled their country, many of them crossing the Gulf of Aden and the Red Sea by boat to the East African nations of Djibouti, Ethiopia, and Somalia.[73] Yet, Somalia itself is no safe haven. Prior to the war in Yemen, approximately 246,000 Somalis were living in Yemen as registered refugees from the long-term civil war in their own country—a war that has made Somalia one of the top three refugee-producing countries in the world.[74] Yet, with the new war in Yemen, the direction of flight between Somalia and Yemen was reversed. Some Yemenis were able to flee to Yemeni enclave communities in South and Southeast Asia, as well as in the West. For example, by 2016, more than 80,000 Yemenis had made new homes in Britain. In the United States, at least 40,000 foreign-born Yemenis were scattered across the country, primarily living in California, Illinois, New York, and Michigan.[75]

Arab Detroit

Michigan might seem like an unlikely home for Yemenis and other fleeing Arabs. With its cold winter climate, flagging auto industry, and widespread poverty—on graphic display with the lead-drinking-water crisis in Flint and the teacher "sick-outs" to protest to dangerously deteriorating public schools in Detroit—this rust-belt state has relatively little to offer to incoming Arab refugees. Yet, over the past fifty years, the greater Detroit metropolitan area has been one of North America's largest Arab receiving grounds.[76] Beginning in the 1950s, exiled Palestinians started resettling in the Detroit suburbs, a pattern that continued among Palestinians over the five ensuing decades. By the 1970s, Palestinians were joined by Lebanese, whose numbers swelled with each passing decade of the civil war. By the 1990s, Lebanese and Palestinians were joined by Iraqis, thousands of whom came as refugees in the aftermath of the First Gulf War. Thus, over half a century, metropolitan Detroit absorbed three major populations of fleeing Arabs—Palestinians, then Lebanese, then Iraqis. By the end of the 1990s, Michigan-based scholars dubbed the city's new ethnic enclave "Arab Detroit," highlighting the importance of one-quarter million people of Arab descent now living in the area.[77]

The demographic contours of this Arab Detroit population have been carefully described by a University of Michigan–based survey team, who in 2003 published the Detroit Arab American Study (DAAS).[78] DAAS was undertaken with active support from the Arab community and funding from the Russell Sage Foundation. The DAAS survey showed that Arabs in the greater Detroit metropolitan area traced their ancestry to four primary sending areas: Lebanon (35 percent), Iraq (32 percent), Palestine/Jordan (12 percent), and Yemen (8 percent). As already noted, most had come during the tumultuous Middle Eastern "war decades" of the 1970s, 1980s, and 1990s. For example, 61 percent of the Lebanese in the DAAS survey had come to Arab Detroit during the twenty-five-year period of civil war and occupation of southern Lebanon (1975–2000). Similarly, 81 percent of the Iraqi Muslims coming to Arab Detroit by the time of the DAAS survey had arrived as refugees from the First Gulf War, a number that exceeded 35,000 by the year 2000.

These Lebanese and Iraqi refugees had settled primarily in Dearborn, the so-called capital of Arab Detroit. As noted in Fatima and Sadiq's story in the Prologue, Dearborn is located on the margins of Detroit, just over the southwestern border of the city. Prior to Arab resettlement, Dearborn's claim to fame was its mammoth Ford Rouge factory, the largest in the state of Michigan. But, by the year 2000, Dearborn had also become famous as a kind of "little Arabia." Beneath the billowing smokestacks of the Ford factory, the streets of Dearborn had become lined with scores of Arab-run businesses, including clothing shops, restaurants, bakeries (Figure 1) and halal meat markets (Figure 2), as well as a multitude of services for Arabic-language speakers, including immigration and legal aid, medical facilities, a refugee assistance

FIGURE 1. Bakery.
PHOTO CREDIT: Justine Hooks.

FIGURE 2. Halal meat market.
This, and the bakery shown in Figure 1, are examples of businesses serving the Arab Detroit community and its culinary traditions.
PHOTO CREDIT: Justine Hooks.

program, and a number of Islamic mosques and schools, including the Islamic Center of America, the largest mosque in the United States.

Although Dearborn is often called the "capital of Arab America," it could be more accurately described as the "capital of Muslim America," or, more precisely, the "capital of Shia Muslim America." Dearborn is home to nearly 80 percent of Arab Detroit's Muslim population, and well over 50 percent of those Muslims are Shias from Lebanon and Iraq. Seventy-five percent of them were born outside the United States, leaving their home countries in the wake of sectarian-inflected violence. As minorities in the Middle East, Shia Muslims are now the majority in Dearborn, a population that has continued to grow because of the Iraq War. Despite initial US government reluctance to take in any more fleeing Iraqi refugees, changes in US immigration policy in 2007 allowed Iraqi refugees to begin entering the country in 2008. By 2008 and 2009, fully one-quarter of all refugees entering the United States were Iraqis, with Arab Detroit taking its full share, nearly as many as the cities of New York, Chicago, and Los Angeles combined.

Interestingly, most of these Shia Muslim Arab refugees eventually apply for US citizenship, a process of naturalization that can take place after a five-year mandatory legal residency period. As shown in the DAAS survey, rates of US citizenship are high in Arab Detroit—80 percent overall—with 84 percent of Lebanese and 80 percent of Iraqis becoming naturalized citizens over time. The only group that does not display such high citizenship rates are Yemenis. According to the DAAS survey, 53 percent of Yemenis in Arab Detroit are citizens, but 46 percent are not. Yemenis are also the least educated group in Arab Detroit, with more than one-third of adults lacking a ninth grade education. As a result, Yemenis are more likely to be monolingual Arabic speakers. Furthermore, 70 percent of all Yemeni households exist on incomes of less than $30,000 per year; 18 percent live well below the federal poverty line on incomes of less than $10,000 per year. In the midst of such poverty, Yemeni families often end up residing in inner-city Detroit, particularly in a former Polish neighborhood called Hamtramck.[79]

Yet, Yemenis are not the poorest Arabs in Detroit, according to the DAAS survey. Fully 82 percent of all Iraqi Muslim families live on household incomes of less than $30,000 per year. Nearly half, or 42 percent, live on household incomes of less than $10,000 per year. Overall, at least one-quarter of all Arab households surveyed by DAAS were earning incomes below $30,000 a year. The three poorest groups were, in order, Iraqis followed by Yemenis then Lebanese.

By March 2011, reported unemployment rates for Iraqis were more than 25 percent, or nearly three times the national average of 9 percent at that time.[80]

To summarize, an overarching sociodemographic profile of Arab Detroit reveals a poor, struggling community of mostly Shia Muslim war refugees from Iraq and Lebanon, as well as a very poor community of Yemeni migrants, all of whom are existing, literally and figuratively, on the margins of Detroit, a deteriorating rust-belt city. A map of Detroit would show three concentric circles: first, a poor, virtually black inner city, circled to the left by a poor Arab Shia Muslim community, and surrounded on all sides by a ring of suburban white affluence. Many middle- and upper-middle-class Christian Arabs live in this outer ring, primarily Iraqi Chaldean Catholics, who consider themselves to be "white" and "non-Arab," according to the DAAS survey data.[81]

Given this ethnic-racial profile, it is not surprising that metropolitan Detroit ranks as one of the most racially segregated cities in the country.[82] Since the 1950s, racial/ethnic segregation in Detroit has increased significantly. As whites have moved to the suburbs, the city of Detroit has become increasingly black, with more than 80 percent of all Detroit residents now African American, according to 2010 US census data. The racial segregation of Detroit is mirrored in the city's economic inequalities. Among US cities with populations above 200,000, Detroit ranked first in the percentage of its population living below the poverty line, at 38 percent. According to a recent United Way report, fully 67 percent of Detroit's families, or more than two-thirds, are living under the federal poverty line or in a state of "ALICE"—asset limited, income constrained, (though) employed.[83] For Arab Americans living in Detroit, the poverty rates are similar, with 38 percent of all families living in poverty and 44 percent of female-headed households doing so. This stands in stark contrast to the predominantly white suburbs of Detroit, where just 5 percent of white residents, 7 to 10 percent of Arab Americans, and 13 percent of African Americans live in poverty.

Beyond the poverty statistics, both blacks and Arabs in Detroit face other forms of discrimination, involving racial and ethnic profiling. For Arabs, the situation became much worse after the terrorist attacks of September 11, 2001, the events that set in motion President Bush's declaration of a "War on Terror," followed by the passage of the Patriot Act, the creation of Homeland Security, and the resulting suspicion, investigation, and profiling of Arab Muslim communities.[84] For Arab Muslims, incidents of racial discrimination, negative stereotyping, and hate crimes have all been well documented following

September 11. For example, the DAAS survey found that 15 percent of Arab Detroit respondents had had a "bad experience" after September 11 based on their ethnicity or religion. These experiences included "verbal insults, workplace discrimination, special targeting by law enforcement or airport security, vandalism, and in rare cases, vehicular and physical assault."[85]

Given this backlash against Arabs and Muslims during the "Terror Decade,"[86] Arab Muslim resettlement in the United States presents a major paradox. On the one hand, America's instigation of, and continuing involvement in, Middle Eastern wars, especially in Iraq, but now also Syria, means that thousands of Arabs have been forced to flee their home countries. A relatively small percentage of these fleeing Arabs have arrived as US refugees over the past decade. On the other hand, once they arrive, these Arab refugees are made to feel unwelcome, facing sometimes bitter discrimination and hostility in an increasingly xenophobic, Islamophobic, anti-Arab, anti-Muslim America. As seen most clearly in the 2016 presidential debates, Arabs and Muslims are publicly vilified as potential "terrorists." Efforts to ban Muslims from entering the country and to close down all mosques reflect a message of distrust, intolerance, and even hatred that is increasingly accepted by the American public.[87] The fact that most Arabs and Muslims are trustworthy and law-abiding individuals—and that not a single refugee, Muslim or otherwise, has ever committed a terrorist act on US soil—seems to have eluded both the media and popular imagination, leaving deeply entrenched caricatures and anxieties that are difficult to overcome. In the wake of the San Bernadino shootings, for example, President Barack Obama's well-intentioned State of the Union message of tolerance and respect for the American Muslim community apparently did little to quell these overarching fears, at least among Republicans.[88]

As a result of these sentiments, the events of the past decade and a half have generally reversed the assimilating efforts of Arab Muslims in America to move from "margin to mainstream,"[89] or to try to "blend in" as an "invisible" (racially unmarked) ethnic minority population.[90] Instead, studies have shown how Arab Muslims increasingly suffer under the power of negative stereotypes. For example, recent studies of Arab and Muslim teenagers in the United States showed that they have been forced to cope with incidents of harassment, prejudice, discrimination, and pervasive Islamophobia and "anti-Arabism"[91] (Figure 3). For Arab Muslim women, wearing the *hijab* (Islamic head covering), and among some women, the *niqab* (facial veil) (Figure 4), has

FIGURE 3. Teenagers at Islamic school (madrasa).
PHOTO CREDIT: Justine Hooks.

FIGURE 4. Woman wearing Islamic headscarf (hijab) and facial veil (niqab). Figures 3 and 4 show examples of Islamic institutions and practices in Arab Detroit, the so-called capital of Muslim America.
PHOTO CREDIT: Justine Hooks.

singled them out for discrimination and harassment. In a study carried out in New York City, women wearing *hijab* were victims of physical violence or the threat of physical violence by being readily identifiable as Muslims.[92] Some were denied access to housing and public services, including health care. A majority of all Muslims in New York City, both Arab and non-Arab alike, reported incidents of targeted discrimination, abuse, violence, police profiling, and harassment directed at them and their children. For Arab Muslim men—who are generally portrayed in US media as untrustworthy, religiously fanatical, oppressive to women, and inherently dangerous—life in America has been especially stressful, not only because of ethnic/religious profiling but also because of the threat of deportation. In one study of sixty-two US Muslim clergymen, imams reported an increase in counseling requests because of male congregants' feelings of stress and discrimination. This was true among all of the imams with Arab-majority congregations, even though none of the imams in the study had received any formal mental health training to deal with their male congregants' psychosocial distress.[93]

In short, life for Arab Muslims in America has not been easy, especially since the beginning of the twenty-first century. Arab Muslims face intersecting forms of oppression and discrimination based on their ethnicity and religion, which are often compounded by their low social class status, their lack of education, and sometimes also by their race, gender, and appearance (especially veiling).

In 2000, Michigan anthropologists Nabeel Abraham and Andrew Shryock published a hopeful volume called *Arab Detroit: From Margin to Mainstream*.[94] In it, they argued that many of the new Arab immigrants coming to Arab Detroit would eventually assimilate into mainstream US society. Yet, a decade on, by the year 2011, they recognized that much of their new-century optimism had been seriously misplaced. In a second edition entitled *Arab Detroit 9/11: Life in the Terror Decade*, they focused instead on the targeting of the Arab Detroit Muslim community, as well as the community's efforts to push back against the heightened surveillance by US law enforcement and government agencies.[95]

Yet, largely absent in both these volumes of *Arab Detroit* were any detailed ethnographic accounts focusing on the daily struggles of new Arab immigrants and refugees from the three main sending countries of Iraq, Lebanon, and Yemen. What were their lives like after arriving in America? What were their major challenges? Was Homeland Security the biggest threat? Or was putting food on the table the daily struggle? What really mattered in the lives of these new Arab Americans who were trying to navigate everyday life in a strange and hostile land?

Reproductive Exile in Arab Detroit

From September 2003 to June 2008, in the midst of the "Terror Decade," I made my way to Dearborn on an almost weekly basis to study the lives of this new Arab Muslim population. My own study began two years after September 11, continued throughout the first four years of the US-led war in Iraq, and, after a six-month pause in 2007 (to conduct a study in the United Arab Emirates), ended with the beginning of the US financial crisis in 2008. By the time of the 2011 Arab uprisings, the 2013 Chapter 9 bankruptcy hearings in Detroit, and the 2015 Syrian refugee crisis spilling into Europe, my own study had already ended. But nearly five years of continuous ethnographic research in the heart of Arab Detroit revealed to me a community of marginally employed, often desperately poor, sometimes uninsured men and women—people whose stories I had not read in the pages of *Arab Detroit*. Indeed, *Arab Detroit* had characterized these people as "boaters"—Arabs "fresh off the boat," according to the derogatory self-stereotypy of the more established local Arab community.[96]

Who were these so-called boaters? In my own study, they were mostly Shia Muslims from Iraq and Lebanon, who had come to Arab Detroit to escape political violence in their home countries. Fatima and Sadiq were typical in this regard—Iraqis who had come to America as teen refugees. Defying any facile stereotype of the "boater" generation, both Fatima and Sadiq had become fully bilingual, managing English with ease and confidence. They were both naturalized American citizens, and both had been gainfully employed. Fatima was also educated, the only woman in my study to have gone to college. Yet, like many of those I met, Fatima and Sadiq were also struggling in other ways. They were both currently unemployed, and Fatima had lost her health insurance when she stopped working. As a low-income couple with no social safety net, they had turned to their religion, particularly a local Muslim charity, for financial assistance. Their own natal family members were too poor to offer any form of financial aid. At the time I met Fatima and Sadiq, they were unable to pay their mortgage or their hospital bills, and they were facing the real threat of bankruptcy and housing foreclosure. They were stuck,

FIGURE 5. Ford Rouge plant.
The Ford Rouge plant—the largest Ford factory in the world—spews pollution over Arab Detroit.
PHOTO CREDIT: Justine Hooks.

pregnant and sick, unemployed and broke. Fatima described this as "the worst time *ever* in both of our lives"—a surprising statement, given that they had both survived several years in the abominable conditions of a Saudi Arabian desert refugee camp.

Many of the stories I heard in Arab Detroit had a similar tone of sadness and despair. My interlocutors spoke to me of war traumas and deaths in the family, reproductive health impairments and physical disabilities, divorces and loneliness, poverty and chronic stress. Infertility, or the inability to have a child, was just one of many struggles that most of my interlocutors were facing. But it was through this lens of infertility that I came to know about their other hardships. In a cultural setting in which marriage and parenthood are mandatory aspects of adult personhood, the inability to become pregnant was a major heartache for most of the Arab Muslim men and women in my study. Poverty and lack of health insurance had prevented most of them from getting access to affordable infertility treatment, especially IVF, an expensive health technology that is rarely covered by health insurance in America.

As described in the Prologue, I met these poor, infertile Arab couples at an Arab-serving infertility clinic in the heart of Dearborn's commercial district, located less than a mile up the road from the massive Ford Rouge fac-

FIGURE 6. IVF Michigan clinic site.
This medical office building, which is located just a mile up the road from the Ford Rouge plant, serves mostly Arab patients.
PHOTO CREDIT: Justine Hooks.

tory (Figure 5). Called IVF Michigan, the clinic is one of the Midwest's largest infertility treatment and assisted reproduction centers, with seven offices located throughout southeastern Michigan and northwestern Ohio. Although the clinic is headquartered in an affluent northern Detroit suburb, IVF Michigan continues to maintain an active office in the heart of Dearborn (Figure 6), headed by an Arab American Shia Muslim physician from Lebanon, who feels a moral responsibility to care for the Arab poor. According to my interlocutors, this physician was "famous"—known for his "good reputation" in the Arab community. Part of his fame, it seemed, surrounded the tender acts of mercy he would occasionally display by offering discounts on the costs of treatment.

Within this Dearborn clinic, I met ninety-five Arab patients—fifty-five men and forty women, most of whom arrived together at the clinic as couples, but some of whom came alone, including eighteen men and four women. Almost half of my interlocutors were from Lebanon (45 percent), with the other half split almost evenly between Iraqis (23 percent) and Yemenis (21 percent). However, I also interviewed a small number of Palestinians (6 percent), as well as one Syrian man, a Moroccan woman, a Bahraini woman, and a woman who was an American Muslim convert.

I spent hundreds of hours in the clinic, usually on Friday afternoons after the main Muslim communal prayer had been held at local mosques around the city. This was also the time when the Lebanese doctor would drive down from IVF Michigan's headquarters to see his Arab patients in the Dearborn clinic. There, he or the clinic administrator (also a Lebanese Shia Muslim woman) would introduce me to patients who were willing to be part of my research project. In 2003, I had just returned from an eight-month study of male infertility in Lebanon, where I had interviewed hundreds of mostly Shia Muslim Arab men. This fact, along with my many years of research in the Middle East, probably served to increase my perceived trustworthiness. Most people agreed to speak with me, and I often spent hours serving as both ethnographer and health educator for this infertile population, especially when men and women shared their medical records with me.

It is important to note that all of the individuals who participated in my study were asked to read and sign an informed consent form, in either Arabic or English. I made it clear that participation in the study was entirely voluntary, as well as confidential. We always met in a back office space, where we would sit together around a small round table. The ethnographic interviews usually lasted about an hour but would sometimes take all afternoon, usually when a couple had much that they wanted to convey to me. Most of the Palestinians and some of the Lebanese men and women in my study spoke English, as did some of the Iraqis. However, most of the Yemenis were monolingual Arabic speakers, and a few of the Yemeni women were also illiterate in Arabic. I conducted about half of the interviews in English and half in Arabic, sometimes switching back and forth between the two languages, as was common practice in the clinic.

For the first three years of my study, I focused primarily on male infertility, asking the men to answer a series of semistructured demographic and reproductive life history questions. However, by the end of year three, I dispensed with the semistructured portion of my study to focus more generally on infertility treatment quests, including any attempts made to have access to IVF. Many perceived barriers to medical care were discussed in these interviews, along with other problematic aspects of being infertile in a community where prolonged childlessness was considered both unusual and socially unacceptable. Because many of my interlocutors were uncomfortable being audio recorded, I also took handwritten notes during all of the interviews, reviewing and transcribing those interview notes and writing extensive case summaries in my computer immediately after my interviews were finished. At the end of my interviews, I always presented each person with a University of Michigan engraved blue-and-gold gift pen, which the men in particular seemed to appreciate. I also provided each person in my study with my University of Michigan business card, in case they ever wanted to reach me.

What was most striking about my ethnographic research in Dearborn was the amount of suffering revealed in the interviews. Reproductive-aged men, most of them in their twenties and thirties, had endured many hardships as political refugees, including the trials and tribulations of war, torture, and persecution in their home countries. As in my earlier study in Lebanon, *il harb*, "the war," figured prominently in men's reproductive narratives. Iraqis in particular feared that their infertility was somehow due to war-related exposures, a theme that will be taken up in later chapters. Most of the men and women in my study had emigrated to the United States under conditions of economic or political duress in their home countries, including all of the Iraqis, who had come to the United States as official refugees. Their lives had been disrupted in significant ways. For example, these men and women tended to be poorly educated because their schooling had been disrupted by war and exile. Most of the women and about one-third of the men in my study were still struggling with the English language. For those who could not speak English at all, their abilities to communicate with US health care personnel were severely restricted. Overall, this population faced many structural barriers to health care access, leading to significant health disparities.

By the end of my study, I came to think of these poor, struggling, infertile Arab refugee couples as "reproductive exiles." Having left their home countries because of war and political violence, most of these couples remain stranded—unable to return to Middle Eastern home countries because of ongoing conflict and fears regarding safety but unable to gain access to infertility services in their "host" country of America. Without exception, all of the men and women were dreaming of making a "test-tube baby" to achieve cultural mandates of adult personhood and parenthood. However, this infertile Arab population faced many "arenas of constraint"—structural, ideological, and practical obstacles and apprehensions—that affected their ability to seek health care of any kind, let alone the high costs of IVF technology.[97]

Overall, this Arab Muslim refugee population was *structurally vulnerable*—a term forwarded by medical anthropologist Philippe Bourgois and his colleagues to highlight the positionality of marginalized populations within class-based systems of economic exploitation and discrimination.[98] Focusing primarily on interactions within the US health care system, Bourgois and his colleagues describe structural vulnerability as an individual's social location within society's multiple, overlapping, and mutually reinforcing power hierarchies (for example, socioeconomic, racial, and cultural) and institutional and policy-level statuses (such as immigration status, labor force participation, access to health insurance), which put a patient's health at risk. Structural vulnerabilities lead to "health disparities," or differences in health status, health environment, and access to quality health care, which lead structurally vulnerable patient populations to have significantly poorer health outcomes than others.[99] Such health disparities are particularly prevalent in the area of reproduction, where they manifest in untoward outcomes such as low birth weight, infant and maternal mortality, increased rates of reproductive tract infections, and high levels of infertility.

In this book, four major areas of health disparity facing the growing Arab refugee population in America are highlighted: first, the lingering health effects of war; second, postwar reproductive health impairments, especially male infertility; third, the lack of access to quality health care services in the United States; and fourth, the virtual exclusion from access to IVF, which is needed to overcome most cases of infertility but which is far beyond the economic means of virtually all of the Arab Muslim reproductive exiles in this study. By linking these issues of political violence, refugee resettlement, structural vulnerability, health disparity, and reproductive exile, my goal here is to provide a crucial and timely scholarly intervention, which renders visible the overwhelming problems faced by many Arab refugees who have come to the United States in their darkest hour of need.

About This Book

Each chapter of this book provides an important piece of this intersectional analysis. In Chapter 1, "Why They Fled: War and the Health Costs of Conflict," I draw on medical anthropologist Merrill Singer's concept of "syndemic" to explore the multiple interlocking comorbidities, or coexisting epidemics, that interact synergistically to cause great human suffering.[100] Chapter 1 zeroes in on what Singer calls "war syndemics," or the interlocking health problems that surface and often kill during times of political violence.[101] Chapter 1 focuses particularly on the war syndemics occurring in Lebanon and Iraq, the two home countries of most of my Arab Detroit interlocutors. Wars in both of these countries generated multiple interacting forms of misery. These are shown in part through the stories of several Lebanese and Iraqi men and women, who arrived in the United States after surviving the horrors of war. As a result, Arab Detroit is not only an Arab ethnic enclave but is also an enclave of traumatized war victims. This chapter highlights the devastating impacts of war on human health, including reproductive health. As we will see, infertility becomes part of the war stories that victims tell.

Chapter 2, "Where They Resettled: Poverty on the Margins of Detroit," paints a bleak portrait of poverty in Arab Detroit, comparing the poverty and discrimination facing black Detroiters with those facing Arab Americans there. In both cases, poverty affects the ability of the city's residents to secure safe housing, stable employment and education, and the means to improve their standard of living. Economic impoverishment and accompanying low social class status are therefore critical problems for many in the city of Detroit, including the recently resettled Arab Muslim refugee population. This chapter thus locates Arab poverty on the margins of Detroit, a city that has gone through paroxysms of economic instability and downturn, accompanied by "white flight" from the city's core.[102] During the years of profound economic recession in Michigan (beginning around 2005), many Arab men in this study lost their jobs, with negative implications for their marriages, family life, and emotional and physical health. It recounts the struggles of those in my study to find jobs, pay rent, and seek health care in a city undergoing rapid economic decline. The chapter also questions the strategies of the US Refugee Admissions Program (USRAP), including the quantity and quality of assistance that it has given to Arab refugees, especially those coming from the country of Iraq. Chapter 2 examines Iraqi refugee resettlement in America overall, asking whether refugee resettlement in economically struggling cities such as Detroit has been a wise decision. As we will see, high rates of unemployment and poverty have taken their toll on Arab refugee health.

Chapter 3, "How They Struggle: Health Disparities and Unequal Treatment," depicts the reproductive health challenges faced by poor Arabs and poor blacks in cities like Detroit, where these marginalized minority populations experience so-called stratified reproduction. Stratified reproduction is the term used by Shellee Colen and then forwarded by medical anthropologists Faye Ginsburg and Rayna Rapp to describe "power relations by which some categories of people are empowered to nurture and reproduce, while others are disempowered."[103] In America, both Arabs and blacks are generally not seen as "deserving" reproducers, given that they are usually stereotyped as being hyperfertile reproducers of too many babies. Arab Muslim couples who are facing infertility problems do not garner sympathy, given contemporary political discourses about the reproduction of "future terrorists." Having said that, infertility is a major reproductive health disparity for both Arab and black populations in the United States. Arab refugee men in particular may face compromised reproductive health, including severe infertility problems that may be related to the stresses, injuries, and toxins of war. This chapter thus focuses on infertility as a reproductive health disparity among Arab men and women. For Arab couples suffering from infertility, IVF costs approximately $12,500 per cycle in the United States, given that only a handful of US "mandate states" subsidize IVF services (and Michigan is not one of them.).[104] Thus, affording IVF is a profound challenge for many infertile and impoverished Arab couples, who are effectively banished from the world of test-tube baby making.

In the final ethnographic Chapter 4, "What They Feel: Reproductive Exile between Moral Worlds," I examine the existential feelings of exile among those in my study who find themselves straddling American secular and Muslim moral worlds in their quests for conception. Islam is "technoscientifically agentive," encouraging Muslims to seek solutions to their suffering. Islamic religious authorities have, in fact, condoned IVF to overcome infertility, leading to the robust growth of affordable IVF services across the Muslim world. However, for all of the Iraqi refugees, as well as for those from Lebanon and Yemen who had fled because of war and poverty, returning to their homelands was usually an impossible dream. For Iraqis in particular, their home country has been decimated by ongoing war, ISIS violence, and a shattered medical system. Thus, this Arab refugee population is essentially exiled to Michigan for the foreseeable future. Many of these Arab refugees have lost everything in their flight from the Middle East to the United States. Although "home" may still mean the home left behind in the country of origin, Arab refugees want to "feel at home" in America. However, as shown in Chapter 4, these feelings are elusive. Because marriage and parenthood are normative dimensions of adult personhood among Middle Eastern populations, reproductive exile may invoke marital crises, as gender interactions within marriage can take a turn for the worse when no children are being born. The relative ease of divorce in the United States places increased pressure on Arab refugee couples to achieve their reproductive goals. Placed in this difficult marital and medical position, some infertile Muslim men and women undertake what I call "reprotravel"—or determined quests for conception between countries and moral worlds.

The Conclusion, "Why America Must Care: The Lives of Arab Refugees," looks to the future, asking what will happen to this structurally vulnerable Arab Muslim refugee population. On the one hand, many of the men and women in my study hoped to build a better future in America, with "diasporic dreams" of going to college, owning a home, starting a small business, and making a family.[105] On the other hand, the United States is an uncertain place for Arab refugees, given the widespread misunderstanding and mistrust on the part of the American public. As a result, the "American dream" may become an "American nightmare" for some of those who have resettled in the United States, hoping for a better life.

Given the ongoing wars in the Middle East and the world's worst refugee crisis since WWII, Americans, including American anthropologists, must take a stronger stand against war and do more to advocate for refugee health and well-being. In the United States, where Iraqi refugees have continued to resettle, and where thousands of new refugees from Syria may eventually enter, we must do our best to attend to their dire needs for health, safety, and economic security, preventing the kinds of poverty, physical and psychological suffering, and resultant poor health outcomes already observed among the Arab refugee populations featured in this book.

Moveover, resettled Arab refugees deserve to build their families in America, especially after all that they have lost. As part of an effort to end reproductive health disparities, an entirely new approach to assisted reproduction in America is needed. This book will end by featuring a new global movement for low-cost in vitro fertilization (LCIVF), which could prevent minority infertility and bring reproductive justice for all.

At the end of the day, this book is about America's moral obligation to help those Arab refugee populations in need. Only because so much war and displacement has occurred in the Arab world does a book like *America's Arab Refugees* need to be written. Directly or indirectly, the United States has caused profound human suffering in the Middle East through its long and ongoing history of military intervention in the Arab world. Making war in the Middle East has come back to haunt the United States in multiple ways, including through the emergence of ISIS. But it is the refugees—not the terrorists—who deserve our utmost attention. This book is dedicated to the plight of Arab refugees everywhere.

1 Why They Fled

War and the Health Costs of Conflict

Syndemics and War Stories

For those of us who have never lived through a war, it is hard to imagine what it would be like. Bombings, sniper fire, land mines, abductions, hunger, house raids, torture, rape, flying shrapnel, lack of water and electricity, imprisonment, loss of life and limb. These are the kinds of horrors that war inflicts on human beings, both combatants and civilians. In the twentieth century, it is estimated that 45 million combatants and 62 million civilians died as a result of war—not only because they were killed outright but because diseases and other forms of death took even more lives than battlefield injuries.[1]

War damages human health in multiple ways, both during and after conflict. The health costs of war tend to co-occur, interacting synergistically to cause "syndemics," or simultaneous epidemics of human suffering. To take but one example, epidemics of malnutrition and infectious disease often go hand in hand during wartime because food shortages and unsanitary living conditions take their toll on human populations, especially those fleeing to makeshift refugee camps. Medical anthropologists Bayla Ostrach and Merrill Singer call these synergistic interactions of war-related morbidity and mortality the "syndemics of war."[2] As they note,

> War, by causing physical and emotional trauma in populations, destroying healthcare systems and social infrastructures, despoiling the environment,

> intentionally or unintentionally causing or exacerbating food insecurity and malnutrition, creating refugee populations, and spreading infections (e.g. through the movement of troops, dislocation of civilian populations, changes in the environment) promotes the development of syndemics.[3]

In this chapter, I explore the syndemics of war in the Middle East, particularly in the two Arab countries of Lebanon and Iraq, where most of the people I met in Arab Detroit had once lived. This chapter takes us back to their home countries, asking: What happened there? What forced these Lebanese and Iraqi people to flee for their lives? As we will see, the health costs of war in both Lebanon and Iraq have been profound, leading to trails of human misery. In Lebanon, for example, the death or flight of more than one-third of the country's entire population led to serious demographic consequences and reproductive disruptions, the results of which are still being felt in that country today. In Iraq, co-occurring epidemics of cancer and birth defects have emerged, likely as a result of wartime environmental contamination.[4] In fact, an ongoing controversy over the US military's use of depleted uranium (DU) in Iraq suggests that war may be literally "toxic," with human health consequences lasting for decades, even future millennia.

In my own study in Arab Detroit, *il harb*, "the war," was on the minds of many of my interlocutors. Nearly one-third of the Lebanese I met, and almost all of the Iraqis, had come to the United States to escape the wars in their home countries. Their war stories, some of which they shared with me, could only begin to convey the human suffering.

Mahmoud

Mahmoud was twenty-six and living in southern Lebanon when Israeli troops invaded his village. Not yet understanding the gravity of the situation, Mahmoud attempted to make an escape in his car, running directly into an Israeli tank. The tank charged his vehicle, pushing it off the road into a deep ravine. Mahmoud was crushed under the weight of his own automobile, sustaining massive internal injuries—a punctured liver and bladder, a broken back, dislocated shoulders, dislocated hips, and the breaking of every single rib in his body. However, Mahmoud was not left to die by the Israeli soldiers, who deposited his broken body in a nearby hospital. Although the doctors predicted that Mahmoud would die on the operating table, he lived. And, after months of painful recovery, Mahmoud's relatives in the United States were able to fly him to America for long-term physical therapy and rehabilitation.

By the time I met Mahmoud in an Arab Detroit IVF clinic, he had resettled in the United States, where he was receiving Supplemental Security Income (SSI) because of his painful disabilities. Still in his mid-thirties, Mahmoud looked like a much older man, silver-haired and walking irregularly with a cane, because one of his legs was now two inches shorter than the other. In private, Mahmoud also told me that he had lost his bladder control and was diagnosed with a very, very low sperm count, making him unable to impregnate his wife of six years.

Mayada

Mayada, who hailed from Lebanon's Greek Orthodox community, was stuck in Beirut's war zone for nearly a dozen years because her parents were unable to secure the resources to escape with their five children and several grandchildren. Mayada did not blame her parents. As she put it, "My parents worked *very* hard, *very* hard to keep us alive." However, their twenty-one-year-old son, who had spent most of his childhood and youth in Beirut's war zone, was eventually shot and killed by a sniper. Within weeks, the family's second eldest child, a daughter aged thirty-four, was also killed by a sniper. Her death was especially painful because she had just been visiting her older sister, who had given birth to a baby daughter. The senseless deaths of two of their five children devastated Mayada's parents, who finally secured passage to Greece for the remaining family members. Following their escape, a family member in the United States sponsored their move to America. They ended up settling in Arab Detroit, along with many other exiled Lebanese who had fled from Beirut's war zone.

When I met Mayada, she conveyed to me how her family was still haunted by the war. Mayada herself was adamant that she would never *ever* return to her home country or put her own daughter in harm's way. She also told me that her mother and older sister were "broken" people, unable to overcome their guilt and anguish. As Mayada explained,

> It's *very* hard for my mother. Those were *her* children, her own blood. All her life was affected by this. Even now my mother still suffers from this, and she takes antidepressant medicines in order to function. But you should see my sister. She looks older than my mom. She's the one who had the baby, and she keeps saying, "If the baby was not born there, she [our sister] would still be doing something; she would still be alive." My sister has severe depression. I told her to go to the pharmacy and get some medicine. Even take a walk around the

block. "Just walk!" But she stays in the house all the time and is very, very sad. Even though we tell her that we have to get over it—"Forget the past"—this happened to her, and she can't live with it. Even if a war stops, a lot of bad memories remain.

Kamal

Bad memories also haunted Kamal, an Iraqi refugee who had become a small business owner in Arab Detroit. Although he was happily married and relatively successful by community standards, Kamal's experiences as a soldier in the Iran–Iraq War, as well as his participation in the Shia intifada against Saddam Hussein, had stayed with him, physically and emotionally, over many years. As Kamal told me,

> I was a telecommunications specialist in the Army. But I was in a tank, *always* in a tank. I saw *everything*! The smells, the dead people. Sometimes we were sleeping with people who were dead in the tanks, injured people, with blood all around. We saw *everything*! So when we see [that] someone is dead, we don't even care. We saw *so many* dead people, *so much* blood. Sometimes, we had to eat with people who were dead beside us. And while we were fighting, Saddam was using chemicals [that is, weapons]. But I didn't smell it. And then we heard that there is [radioactive] uranium everywhere. You know, Marcia? Cancer. *A lot* of people in Iraq got cancer. If you ask anybody here, "You got the flu?," the question there would be, "You got cancer?" Before, it was not easy to use the term *saratan* [cancer]. But now, it's easy to say, "I got cancer." My sister, she had a sixteen-year-old daughter. She died after two months from cancer, liver cancer. She found out, and then she died.
>
> But, Marcia, I want to tell you something about me. I have no problem with sex, no problem with my body. I don't smoke, no drinking. I do exercise every day, and I'm healthy. But I know a lot of [Iraqi] men like me. They don't have kids, and they take a long time to get a baby. I know about fifteen to twenty people like that, here in Michigan. Some are friends of mine. We are all refugees. The 1990 revolution, *we* did it against Saddam! And so we had to live in refugee camps in Saudi Arabia, where the conditions were very bad. It was in the middle of the desert, always dusty, and the water was not good. The tea would turn white because the water was salty, and the soap sticks to your hands.
>
> All of us Iraqi refugees, the same life we lived. The same war. The same camp. The same thing. And we began talking about the subject of [not getting]

babies. I always tell them, "We don't want to be shy [about this] because we *need* a baby! Don't be shy! Go to the doctor. Don't stay at home. Tell him [the doctor], 'I'm sick, and I need to take medicine.'" I know somebody [with male infertility], and he was ready to make a divorce with his wife, and he's young! But I tell him, "Please don't do that! Go to the doctor. Do something!" In Iraq, we lost all our good doctors. But here in America, everything is good. The doctor is good. Technology is good. Medicine is good. But some men, they're embarrassed to say, "I have this problem." It's the *rujula*, the "manhood." But this is wrong.

The Health Costs of Conflict

Mahmoud, Mayada, and Kamal all speak to the damage that war inflicts on human health. Kamal's story in particular points to the syndemic nature of long-term war in Iraq, where death, environmental contamination, cancer, refugeeism, and reproductive disruption are synergistically interconnected in his narrative. In addition, it is clear from these war stories that war disrupts the lives of four different groups of people—those who actually fight wars (combatants, including soldiers and militia members); refugees and internally displaced persons; those left behind (mostly women, children, and the elderly); and health care professionals. Wars create chaos, both personal and social, for individuals and for societies at large. Using the powerful metaphor of "disrupted lives" as a framework for understanding, it is evident that war disrupts human lives on both the individual and societal levels, per the metaphor of disruption forwarded by medical anthropologist Gay Becker:

> In all societies, the course of life is structured by expectations about each phase of life, and the meaning is assigned to specific life events and roles that accompany them. When expectations about the course of life are not met, people experience inner chaos and disruption. Such disruptions represent loss of the future. Restoring order to life necessitates reworking understandings of the self and the world, redefining the disruption and life itself.[5]

Beyond the lives disrupted by war, war militates against the achievement of human health. In a historic conference convened by the World Health Organization (WHO) in the Central Asian city of Alma-Ata, Kazakhstan, in September 1978, health was famously defined in a ten-point charter called the "Declaration of Alma-Ata." Article I of the declaration states:

> The Conference strongly reaffirms that health, which is a state of complete physical, mental, and social wellbeing, and not merely the absence of disease or infirmity, is a fundamental human right and that the attainment of the highest possible level of health is a most important world-wide social goal whose realization requires the action of many other social and economic sectors in addition to the health sector.

In other words, the Declaration of Alma-Ata contends that health is a human right and that the achievement of "health for all" should be an important global priority. However, the declaration ends with a stern warning about the mistaken misdirection of valuable health resources toward military spending. Article X cautions:

> An acceptable level of health for all the people of the world . . . can be attained through a fuller and better use of the world's resources, a considerable part of which is now spent on armaments and military conflicts. A genuine policy of independence, peace, détente and disarmament could and should release additional resources that could well be devoted to peaceful aims and in particular to the acceleration of social and economic development of which primary healthcare, as an essential part, should be allotted its proper share.[6]

In other words, the first and last articles of the Declaration of Alma-Ata point to a fundamental conflict: As long as wars are being waged around the world, global health will never be achieved. Wars make the Alma-Ata goal of "health for all" impossible, not only because of the morbidity and mortality that wars inflict but also because wars lead to a crucial misallocation of funding away from health and toward military spending.

What does war "cost" in terms of human health? War affects population health in six important ways:[7] *physical* (the years of healthy life lost to sickness, disability, and death); *mental* (the increase in psychological disorders resulting from war-related "triggers"); *reproductive/demographic* (the increased reproductive and sexual vulnerability of women, the exodus and death of men, the orphaning of children, and long-term demographic shifts); *social structural* (the loss of social safety nets, increased poverty, and food insecurity); *infrastructural* (the loss of health care infrastructure and medical personnel through random destruction or deliberate targeting); and *environmental* (increased environmental illness from toxic weaponry and waste and breakdowns in sanitation).

How have these six health costs played out in the Middle East, a region that provides numerous salient examples of recent and ongoing conflicts? Because most Arab Detroiters fled from wars in Lebanon and Iraq, it is important to capture the nature of those wars, and the ways in which death, destruction, displacement, and serious environmental degradation deeply affected the population health of both countries.[8] In the midst of such devastation, it is not surprising that thousands upon thousands of Lebanese and Iraqis fled to Arab Detroit and beyond. In other words, to adequately understand the refugees of Arab Detroit, it is important to begin with the wars that forever changed the health and well-being of Arab Detroiters such as Mahmoud, Mayada, and Kamal.

The Costs of Conflict in Lebanon

Lebanon's civil war is officially dated as beginning in 1975 and ending in 1990.[9] Lebanon's war is called a "civil war" because it took place on Lebanese soil between various Lebanese factions—including the Lebanese Army and many religiously based Lebanese militia groups. However, it is important to recognize that there were many external actors who added fuel to the Lebanese fire by providing financial and military support to various local militias. As shown in "War in Lebanon: A Timeline" (in the frontmatter of this book), these external forces included the Palestine Liberation Organization (PLO), Syria, Israel, and the United States, as well as the Soviet Union, Iran, and several European nations.[10] In terms of US involvement, the Lebanese civil war drew US troops to Beirut, where 241 American servicemen were killed in a 1983 bombing attack on US army barracks. This was the single deadliest attack on Americans overseas since World War II, and it led to a hasty withdrawal of all US troops in the following year.

Israel, however, was involved in the Lebanese conflict over many years. In fact, the dating of the Lebanese war from 1975–1990 is somewhat inaccurate, if the twenty-two-year Israeli occupation of southern Lebanon and the western Bekaa region of Lebanon is taken into consideration. Israel invaded Lebanon for the first time in 1978, occupying much of southern Lebanon with the aid of the mostly Christian South Lebanon Army (SLA). In 1982, Israeli forces launched a full-scale invasion in Lebanon, moving north to occupy parts of West Beirut. There, Israel supported Christian Phalangist militia forces in a deadly massacre on two Palestinian refugee camps, Sabra and Shatila, which evoked international outrage.[11]

Eventually, two southern Lebanese Shia Muslim parties, Amal and Hezbollah (the latter backed by Iran), cohered in an effort to resist the Israeli presence in the country. The "liberation" of southern Lebanon and the Bekaa by these two groups took more than twenty years to accomplish, with the eventual withdrawal of all remaining Israeli forces on May 25, 2000, and the subsequent emptying of southern Lebanon's political prisons (such as the infamous Khiam Detention Center). If the presence of Israeli forces in Lebanon (1978–2000) is taken into consideration, then the dating of Lebanon's war expands from fifteen to twenty-five years, including the decade of occupation from 1990 to 2000.

Unfortunately, political violence in Lebanon did not end at the turn of the new millennium. Forty thousand Syrian "peacekeeping" forces, including a well-embedded Syrian intelligence operation, remained in the country until April 2005, when Syria finally withdrew its troops from Lebanon under mounting international pressure. This occurred in the aftermath of the February 14, 2005, assassination of Lebanese Prime Minister Rafik Hariri, which was immediately blamed on neighboring Syria. The Hariri assassination was one of a string of politically motivated assassinations that occurred on a fairly regular basis in Lebanon during the first decade of the new millennium. Also during that period, Israel launched deadly attacks in Lebanon in retaliation for Hezbollah's capturing of two Israeli soldiers. The six-week "summer war" of 2006 led to 1,191 Lebanese casualties, mostly of civilians, and an emergency evacuation of most foreigners from the country.

Five years on, in 2011, Lebanon was again destabilized by the Arab uprisings that swept across the region. The sitting Lebanese government collapsed, and in neighboring Syria the civil war that began in March 2011 spilled over into Lebanon in 2012. By that point, sectarian clashes and border conflicts were beginning to emerge between mostly Sunni Muslim Lebanese factions opposed to the government of Syrian President Bashar al-Assad, and Shia Lebanese forces, including Hezbollah, who declared their allegiance to the Syrian regime. From 2012 on, dozens of Lebanese were randomly killed in suicide bombings and orchestrated attacks in public places, including mosques—an indication of the extent to which the Syrian civil conflict reignited sectarian tensions in Lebanon.

In addition, thousands of Syrian refugees poured into Lebanon. In the first year of the Syrian war, it was estimated that 160,000 Syrians had entered Lebanon, about one-third of them receiving shelter within Lebanese homes. However, two years on, that number had swelled to more than one million Syrian refugees registered with the United Nations—or one in every five people living in Lebanon. In order to staunch this flow, new restrictions were placed on Syrians entering Lebanon as of January 2015, making it much more difficult for Syrians to escape the war.

To summarize, then, Lebanon has had little reprieve from violence over a period of forty years. To date, no truth and reconciliation initiatives, or any clear forms of societal dialogue, have taken place to heal the wounds created by the country's long civil war or to mend the ongoing religious, ethnic, and political divisions in a country with eighteen recognized religious sects.[12] Scant attention has also been paid to how the Lebanese war years affected the health and well-being of the population. Why did so many Lebanese flee for their lives? As will be shown here, during the civil war period (1975–1990) and the subsequent occupation of southern Lebanon (1990–2000), the impacts on health were severe, with a syndemic of war-related problems, the impacts of which are still being felt in the new millennium.

Physical Costs

Living through the Lebanese civil war was dangerous. The war led to the death of an estimated 7 percent of the Lebanese population (including Mayada's two siblings), and to the serious injury of 10 percent of the population (including Mahmoud).[13] Most deaths and disabilities were due to direct violence, as opposed to malnutrition or infectious disease epidemics. But it is important to note that vaccination services were severely disrupted during the civil war, leading to epidemics of childhood diseases, such as mumps, which would not have occurred had child health services been unaffected.

Additionally, in southern Lebanon, an estimated 150,000 unexploded land mines and gun shells have continued to pose a threat to public safety.[14] In a report issued in 2002, the United Nations estimated that 130,000 unexploded land mines still remained in Lebanon, with 188 minefields and 508 other "danger zones" scattered over cultivated fields, roads, and other agricultural lands in a relatively small area of 850 square kilometers in southern Lebanon, as well as in the western Bekaa Valley region. According to the UN report, the Israeli military admitted to having left behind 70,000 land mines and

288 vehicle traps on its retreat from Lebanon in 2000.[15] Thus, 2,714 Lebanese civilians had already been killed or wounded by land mine explosions by the time that the report was issued in 2002. Since then, the UN Interim Force in Lebanon (UNFIL) has managed to clear more than 35,000 land mines and unexploded ordnance (UXO) in southern Lebanon. However, the UN Mine Action Service has continued to press for mine-clearing operations in southern Lebanon because thousands of unremoved land mines continue to represent a deadly public health issue for the country.[16]

Mental Health Costs

The Lebanese war also taxed the mental health of its citizens, in a nation already severely underserved by prewar mental health services. In a country with approximately 3 million Lebanese citizens and nearly 400,000 additional Palestinian refugees, there was only one functioning psychiatric hospital at the time of the war, with fewer than fifty psychiatrists in the country and very few clinical psychologists, the latter mostly working in schools.[17] Thus, Lebanon's national mental health program was in no way prepared to deal with the mental health consequences of the war and occupation.[18] Throughout the war years, the single mental health hospital was full to capacity, with acute psychoses (including schizophrenia, which increased in incidence during the war[19]) accounting for 60 percent of all psychiatric hospital admissions. The Lebanese Ministry of Health recognized that it needed to provide ambulatory mental health services within primary health care centers in Lebanon to "assist the large numbers of displaced persons, the disabled, the bereaved, and so on affected by the war."[20] However, mental health services were not prioritized, given the many other pressing health care, environmental, and infrastructural needs.

The war took its toll on Lebanese mental health in a variety of specific ways. For one, the war led to significantly increased rates of anxiety and depression, as described quite clearly and poignantly in Jean Said Makdisi's war memoir, *Beirut Fragments*.[21] Many Lebanese citizens who stayed in the country during the war coped on a daily basis through psychotropic self-medication, available through a black market in such tranquilizers as Valium. Even after the war ended, many Lebanese adults continued to use antidepressants and antianxiety medications, such as Xanax and Prozac, even though few obtained these medications through psychiatric visits and prescriptions. In one of the few studies on the mental health of former prisoners and political detainees, more than half of those who had been imprisoned in southern Lebanon's notorious Khiam Detention Center reported ongoing psychological distress; more than three-quarters (77 percent) reported current use of psychotropic medications, even though few of these individuals were under the regular care of mental health personnel.[22] In addition, substance abuse problems, with both alcohol and drugs, increased significantly during the war period. Narcotics production of both opium and heroin was estimated to have tripled during the war years. About 8,000 to 10,000 young Lebanese became addicted to drugs during the war, a number that increased to approximately 24,000 young drug addicts in the immediate postwar period.

From 2002 to 2003, a group of Lebanese researchers carried out a study called the Lebanese Evaluation of the Burden of Ailments and Needs of the Nation, involving detailed health-related interviews with nearly 3,000 Lebanese adults.[23] The researchers asked study participants about their experience of war-related trauma, such as being a civilian in a war zone or being threatened by a weapon. They found that one in four Lebanese had experienced one or more mental health disorders at some point in their lives, with major depression being the single most common disorder. The researchers estimated that, by the age of seventy-five, about one-third of the Lebanese population would experience one or more mental health problems. Exposure to war-related events increased the risk of developing an anxiety, mood, or impulse-control disorder by sixfold, threefold, and thirteenfold, respectively. Yet, despite the significant prevalence of war-related mental health problems, only half of those interviewed with a mood disorder had ever received any professional help; treatment rates for other mental disorders were even lower. The average delay in treatment ranged from six years for mood disorders to twenty-eight years for anxiety disorders. In other words, despite a significant burden of war-related psychological distress in Lebanon, few Lebanese were receiving help for their problems.

Reproductive/Demographic Costs

The sociodemographic impacts of the Lebanese civil war, in terms of reproductive and population health, were also profound. Up to 30 percent of the Lebanese population emigrated out of the country during the war period on either a short-term or a permanent basis. For example, the population of the country was estimated at 3.2 million in 1976 but only 2.7 million by 1990, a population decline of more than 15 percent.[24] Overall, it is estimated that nearly 19 million Lebanese now live outside the country. Many in the Lebanese diaspora refuse to return because of the country's ongoing political instability.

Many of those who left the country during the war years were young men, whose families feared for their lives as potential military and militia conscripts. As with wars in general, women, children, and the elderly were left behind in Lebanon, leading to unprecedented demographic disruptions. Age at first marriage was significantly delayed (to 27.5 years for women and 30.9 years for men), close to the oldest average ages at first marriage in the world and the highest in the Arab world.[25] As a result of high male outmigration and high male mortality during the war, many women who were left behind were unable to marry, with demographic imbalances of marriageable males to marriageable females estimated at 1:7 or even 1:11. Women without partners (either through lack of marriage or through husband's death or absence) meant that the number of female-headed households in Lebanon increased dramatically during the war, one of the highest rates of female household headship ever recorded.[26] Many children were also left without both parents due to war-related casualties. The orphan population in Lebanon skyrocketed during the war years, with the majority of orphans being raised in religious and charitable institutions throughout the country.

In addition, reproductive health suffered during the war, as shown in my own study conducted in Lebanon in 2003.[27] There, I collected reproductive life history interviews from 220 men, the majority of whom were Lebanese and had lived through the civil war and Israeli occupation. Detailed information was collected about these men's exposures to war-related events, including participation in the war as a combatant; civilian residence near sites of heavy bombing; war-sustained injuries to self and to other family members; experiences of kidnapping, torture, or imprisonment; and displacement from home. Through my study, I was able to determine that exposure to one or more war-related events significantly increased a man's odds of being infertile. The men who had suffered the harshest exposures to war (through combat, kidnapping, torture, and displacement) were the most likely to suffer from infertility problems. Heightened male infertility problems, coupled with the death and outmigration of so many young Lebanese men, have been devastating for the future reproduction of the Lebanese population as a whole.

Social Structural Costs

In addition, the men I interviewed in Lebanon almost uniformly reported high levels of stress. In the aftermath of war, Lebanese men and their families faced economic and labor uncertainties, which in many cases contributed to their poverty.[28] At the time of my study, unemployment figures in Lebanon ranged from 12 to 25 percent, making at least one-third of the Lebanese population at risk of poverty. Overall, the war in Lebanon was damaging to the economy, with debts in 2003 estimated at $32 billion, or 180 percent of gross domestic product (GDP)—a budget deficit to GDP ratio reaching 16.6 percent.[29] According to a 2002 sustainable development report,

> Lebanon witnessed during the last few years additional pressures due to a dramatic drop in economic growth, which reflected negatively on the class structure by a widening of the social gap: a destitute majority, a very small class of the extremely wealthy and a dramatic reduction in the middle class. Studies indicate that around 61.9% of the Lebanese households fit in the low-income bracket, and that 12.9% are in the below 70 U.S. dollar per capita group. The decline of the middle class is due to economic stagnation and soaring unemployment. Studies indicate that unemployment rates reached 21% in the year 2001.[30]

This postwar poverty in Lebanon was reflected in poor health care. With approximately 40 percent of the Lebanese population lacking any form of medical insurance, even the minimal fees charged by nongovernmental organizations such as the Red Cross and Red Crescent were beyond the financial reach of more than 80 percent of the Lebanese population.[31] The war-related loss of social safety nets in Lebanon made obtaining primary health care an impossibility for many impoverished Lebanese families, including when they were ill or injured.

As shown in the work of Lebanese American anthropologist Suad Joseph,[32] Lebanese families were forced to rely heavily on their own kinship networks to sustain them throughout the war years and in war's aftermath. Family aid constituted a vital social safety net, literally rescuing other family members in times of need. Even in the postwar period, many families in Lebanon faced acute stress, particularly in economically hard-hit low-income urban and rural communities. Lebanese anthropologist Jihad Makhoul and her colleagues describe the "unraveling" of the Lebanese family as reflected in child welfare.[33] Through collection of Lebanese children's life stories, they showed that family violence, including child abuse, was a recurring theme.

High rates of child labor were also linked to early school attrition in these struggling Lebanese families.

According to Makhoul and her colleagues' research, family hardship and child labor were common not only among low-income Lebanese households but also among Palestinians living in refugee camps throughout Lebanon. Lebanon is home to more than 400,000 Palestinians, some of whom took refuge in Lebanon in 1948 and others who came to Lebanon via Jordan in 1970. More than half of these Palestinians reside in the twelve registered refugee camps run by the UNRWA program. Others live in unofficial camps on the fringes of Lebanese communities.

Palestinian refugees in Lebanon lack many basic citizenship rights. They are considered a special type of foreigner and must carry refugee identity cards; they are restricted from traveling to foreign countries; they are limited to menial labor due to prohibitions on the practice of more than seventy-five different forms of occupation; and they are prohibited from significant improvement in their homes, which are viewed by the Lebanese state as temporary residences.[34] Accordingly, most Palestinians in Lebanon live in abject poverty, in poorly built homes with little or no ventilation. The only formal medical services available to the Palestinian refugee population are run by UNRWA but tend to be seriously overtaxed and underfunded.[35]

In short, Palestinians in Lebanon face abhorrent living, working, and health care conditions. They are an unwanted refugee population in Lebanon who are widely blamed by some segments of Lebanese society for helping to incite (through PLO activity) and then perpetuate the Lebanese civil war. Thus, this refugee population within Lebanon suffers significant problems of poor health and discrimination on many levels. Yet, without return rights to Palestine, they have nowhere else to go and are unlikely to leave Lebanon in the near future.[36]

Infrastructural Costs

One of the major infrastructural costs of the Lebanese civil war was the growth of urban slums and squatter settlements, including of both Palestinian refugees and of Lebanese IDPs, primarily from the Israeli-occupied south. Beirut, the capital city of Lebanon, thus became home to a number of Palestinian refugee camps, as well as substantial slums, hastily built by mostly southern Lebanese Shia Muslim migrants as they poured into Beirut during the war period.

In addition to uncontrolled urbanization and the growth of an urban slum population, Lebanon's physical infrastructure was severely damaged by the civil war. As noted by WHO,

> Fifteen years of civil war caused massive destruction to the country's infrastructure, estimated at $US 500 million. Electricity, water and telecommunication systems, as well as the road network, were severely damaged. Coupled with this destruction, there has been a rapid deterioration in the quality of life of the people, in the areas affected in particular and in the whole of Lebanon in general.[37]

Some of this damage occurred directly to the health care infrastructure. Public health care facilities were either destroyed or left to deteriorate during the war period. Although there were once nineteen government hospitals in different districts of Lebanon, most of them became completely inactive during the war period, due to a lack of basic supplies and equipment as well as the necessary medical personnel.

Health care staff left Lebanon in large numbers during the war. Although some physicians returned after the war ended, salary levels remained so low in the early postwar period (for example, $1000 to $2000/month) that many doctors were forced to seek employment in the private health care sector. As a result, Lebanon now has among the highest ratio of private doctors per capita in the region. Although this partially offsets the erosion in the public health sector, "It has not contributed to a meaningful improvement in healthcare in general," according to WHO.[38]

Environmental Costs

The long Lebanese war also took its toll on the environment. In an article entitled "The Ecological Crisis in Lebanon," environmental scholar Fouad Hamdan begins: "Lebanon is experiencing an ecological crisis that is the result of decades of uncontrolled and unregulated development and nearly sixteen years of civil war."[39] Indeed, the war years were devastating to Lebanon's environment on many levels. Perhaps the worst war-related environmental scandal involved the illegal importation of toxic waste. Namely, in 1987, during a period of intense intersectarian fighting, an Italian company shipped 2,411 tons of toxic waste in 15,800 barrels and 20 containers to Lebanon—taking advantage of "the chaos of the civil war, in a deal hammered out with a Lebanese firm and supervised by members of the now-disbanded militia, the Lebanese Forces."[40] When the deal became known in 1988, public outrage in

Lebanon forced the Italian government to promise to return the toxic material to its own shores. However, only 5,500 of the 15,800 barrels (about one-third) were returned to Italy, with more than 10,000 barrels and 20 containers of a "deadly cocktail of toxic materials" remaining in Lebanon.[41]

Although the Lebanese government tried to cover up the toxic waste scandal, the Mediterranean office of Greenpeace continued to pursue the issue, arguing that all of the remaining waste should be returned to Italy. In December 1996, the Lebanese Ministry of Environment finally adopted a regulation banning the future import of all hazardous waste into Lebanon, including for the purposes of recycling. However, public documents showed that there were at least five sites in Lebanon still heavily contaminated by the toxic waste from Italy, including a quarry, with the potential to spread tons of contaminated soil all over Lebanon.[42]

In general, protecting the environment has not been a priority of the Lebanese government. Hamdan notes that the Lebanese Ministry of the Environment, established after the war, is "small and badly equipped, without an effective professional staff."[43] Instead, the Lebanese government has focused all of its funding and rebuilding efforts on the infrastructure (that is, electricity, roads, telecommunications, water systems, and the tourist center of downtown Beirut). Such "visible" efforts to restore Lebanon's prewar beauty are easier to publicize than environmental cleanup. However, as Hamdan concludes,

> The time has come for Lebanese authorities to use their historic opportunities to rebuild Lebanon on a sound environmental basis. They must acknowledge environmental problems, set sound environmental strategies, and work with NGOs [nongovernmental organizations] and Lebanese citizens to ensure the country's health and prosperity in the new century.[44]

Unfortunately, environmental issues have continued to plague Lebanon. In 2015, the country experienced an eight-month "trash crisis," with 8,000 tons of waste lining Lebanon's streets and filling as many as 800 makeshift landfills.[45] The crisis began in July 2015, when government officials closed Lebanon's largest Naameh landfill, which had been a major site of dumping since the end of the civil war. The landfill closure was partly a response to a popular environmental movement called "You Stink," which mobilized community members to protest the significant health hazards posed by the Naameh landfill. However, closure of the nation's largest landfill occurred at the same time as the expiration of the government's contract with Lebanon's waste-management company, Sukleen. As a result, trash was neither collected nor deposited in the landfill, leading to veritable mountains of trash building up on city streets and vacant lots. Although the trash was eventually removed by early 2016, the public health costs of eight months of standing garbage on city streets—as well as the air pollution and release of potential carcinogens caused by illegal trash burning and incineration—have yet to be determined.[46]

As of this writing, the environmental pressures on Lebanon are compounded by the presence of more than one million Syrian refugees in the country, which has increased the population by 20 percent. In a report in the British medical journal *The Lancet*, the Syrian refugee crisis has been called a "Lebanese–Syrian crisis," because "Syrian refugees put pressure on the Lebanese health-care system and economy, and Lebanon's hosting capacities are overstretched."[47] In a study conducted by a Lebanese medical NGO among 90,000 displaced Syrians in 2013, half of them were suffering from contagious skin diseases due to lack of adequate hygiene; more than one-quarter were suffering from gastrointestinal illnesses due to unsanitary food preparation and contamination; one-fifth were suffering from respiratory diseases, including potentially deadly acute respiratory infections among children; and 7 percent of children were malnourished. Thirteen percent of adult refugees were diagnosed with mental illnesses attributable to war trauma and displacement.[48] As the authors of the study concluded, "In view of this Lebanese–Syrian crisis, surely the international community needs to find a solution to the Syrian crisis; meanwhile, we need an emergency plan for the Syrian refugees."[49]

Sadly, the Syrian refugee crisis has spilled over to many other neighboring Middle Eastern countries, including Iraq, the country to be featured in the next section. What have thirty-five years of perpetual war done to the people of Iraq? As in Lebanon, long-term war in Iraq has been utterly devastating on many levels. But unlike Lebanon, Iraq's war story is one in which the United States is deeply implicated.

The Costs of Conflict in Iraq

Iraq has suffered from the syndemics of war in every decade from the 1980s forward. Its modern history is arguably even more tragic than Lebanon's. As shown in "War in Iraq: A Timeline" (in the frontmatter of this book), the Baath Party rose to power in Iraq in 1963, with Saddam Hussein eventually becoming president in 1979. Within his first year in office, he declared war on Iran (on September 22, 1980). The deadly Iran–Iraq War lasted more than eight years—making it the longest conventional war between two countries in the twentieth century. The Iran–Iraq War is said to have cost as many as 1.25 million lives, although recent demographic analyses suggest a significantly lower death toll.[50] Still, Kamal's war story—which is replete with dead bodies—bespeaks the brutality of the Iran–Iraq War, which "scarred both countries deeply, with horrific fighting at the battlefront and long-range missile attacks on cities."[51]

Only two years after that war ended, Saddam Hussein invaded another neighboring country, Kuwait, on August 2, 1990, this time inciting the wrath of Kuwait's Western allies. The United States and a coalition force of approximately thirty nations invaded Iraq in January 1991 in a six-week war that led to Saddam Hussein's surrender. The costs of the First Gulf War to Iraq as a nation far outlasted the rather short duration of the conflict. Most important, the UN Security Council imposed economic sanctions on Iraq for its aggression on its neighbors. During a thirteen-year period (1990 to 2003), Iraq faced restrictions on importation of all items except essential medicines.[52] Not until December 1996 was an Oil-for-Food Program initiated by the UN Security Council in an attempt to alleviate major sanction-induced medicine and food shortages in the country, which had led to increases in hunger and starvation.

Ironically, the UN sanction period did not end until the United States declared war on Iraq on March 19, 2003. The Second Gulf War was led by the United States in coalition with Great Britain as well as smaller military contingents from a variety of allied nations. Although President George W. Bush declared "mission accomplished" on May 1, 2003, this hasty proclamation was decidedly premature. The US-led war in Iraq dragged on for another eight-and-a-half years, requiring a major troop "surge" of 30,000 US military personnel in 2007 in an attempt to decrease the heavy coalition and civilian casualties and to increase internal security.

Officially, the Iraq War ended with the withdrawal of US combat troops from the country on December 18, 2011. However, as described in this book's Introduction, the war sparked an ongoing sectarian conflict in the country, one that US military forces could neither prevent nor contain. Most ominously, the Sunni insurgent group calling itself the "Islamic State of Iraq" had emerged by 2009, declaring its allegiance to al-Qaeda. However, by 2013, the Islamic State group had splintered from al-Qaeda, morphing into the Islamic State of Iraq and Syria (ISIS). By 2014, the ISIS insurgency in Iraq had escalated into a true civil war. As of this writing, ISIS continues to wage a full-blown sectarian war in both Iraq and neighboring Syria, where it is engaged in a pitched battle with government military, Shia militias, and Kurdish forces. Both the United States and Russia have been drawn into this new battle with ISIS, primarily from the air, via Russian bombing campaigns and US aerial drone strikes. In retaliation, ISIS has gone "global," inspiring terrorist attacks in Europe, the United States, and in many other nations around the globe.[53]

What has this ceaseless violence done to the Iraqi people? To be more specific, how has public health in Iraq been cumulatively compromised by thirty-five years of relentless war, the debilitating UN sanction period, the paranoid brutality of Saddam Hussein's regime, two US-led invasions of the country, and the ghastly sectarian civil war that has unfolded? Here, I examine what is known about the public health costs of war in Iraq, focusing especially on the second US-led war, which lasted from March 19, 2003, to December 18, 2011.[54] I place special emphasis on two major public health controversies—first, the "body count," or the number of Iraqis who have died since 2003; and second, the US military's use of depleted uranium (DU), a radioactive substance with potential long-term impacts on Iraqi health.

Physical Costs

The most important impact of war in Iraq has been the high death toll. Since the United States invaded Iraq in 2003, thousands upon thousands of Iraqis have died, mostly as a result of war-related violence. This Iraqi "body count"—or the number of war-related casualties—has been, and continues to be, a highly controversial issue. On the one hand, no one can precisely say how many Iraqis have been killed because estimates vary greatly and the accuracy of information coming out of Iraq is uncertain. However, another problem surrounds the US military's total refusal to engage in Iraqi death toll estimates. Early on, US General Tommy Franks, who led the 2003 US invasion of Iraq and the overthrow of Saddam Hussein, famously stated, "We don't do body counts."[55]

As a result of US coalition indifference to the Iraqi death toll, a number of academic research groups and human rights organizations rallied to undertake their own estimates of wartime casualties in Iraq, as well as to demand US coalition accountability in this regard. Within the first three years of the US invasion of Iraq, three major Iraqi death surveys were carried out but with different methods and, hence, divergent results.

The first major study was carried out by a research team affiliated with Johns Hopkins Bloomberg School of Public Health, Columbia University School of Nursing, and Al Mustansiriya University School of Medicine in Baghdad. It was published in the October 29, 2004, issue of the highly regarded British medical journal *The Lancet*.[56] In the *Lancet* study, a cluster sample survey of mortality was undertaken throughout Iraq by a team of courageous Iraqi epidemiologist-physicians during the month of September 2004, in the midst of heavy fighting. Using these survey data, the risk of death was estimated to be 2.5 times higher after the March 2003 invasion of Iraq when compared to the preinvasion period. Two-thirds of these violent deaths were reported in one cluster in the heavily bombarded city of Fallujah, even though violent deaths were widespread throughout the country. Sadly, most of the violent deaths reported were of women and children and were mainly attributed to coalition forces, particularly air strikes by US forces using helicopter gunships, rockets, and other forms of aerial weaponry. The *Lancet* authors estimated, conservatively, that more than 100,000 excess deaths had occurred during the first year and a half of war in Iraq, mostly violent deaths among the vulnerable civilian population. Thus, they concluded that there was "little excuse" for the dearth of body count tallies by coalition forces, and they called on an independent authority, such as the WHO, to confirm their findings.

Challenged almost immediately by the US military on the epidemiological methods used to calculate mortality risk, the same group of authors rallied again to update their original survey. The second *Lancet* study was based on another cross-national cluster survey carried out between May and July 2006 and published in the October 11, 2006, issue of *The Lancet*.[57] It showed that the number of people dying in Iraq had "continued to escalate." Forty months postinvasion, the survey team estimated 654,965 excess Iraqi deaths as a consequence of the war, the vast majority of which, 601,027 in total, were due to violence, primarily from gunfire but also from car bombings. They estimated that, across Iraq, approximately 2.5 percent of the population had died as a result of the US-led invasion.

Interestingly, these *Lancet* data were challenged again but this time by a group of Iraqi researchers, who, supported by the WHO, formed the Iraq Family Health Survey (IFHS) Study Group. Through a nationally representative sample of 9,345 Iraqi households, the IFHS group conducted its own survey of violence-related morality, which it published on January 31, 2008, in the highly regarded American medical journal, *The New England Journal of Medicine*.[58] According to the IFHS study team, only 151,000 Iraqis had died due to violence in the period from March 2003 through June 2006, or less than one-quarter of the total reported in *The Lancet*. Still, the authors concluded that war-related violence was a primary cause of adult death in Iraq and the leading cause of death among males ages fifteen to fifty-nine.

Given these discordant results—approximately 650,000 Iraqi deaths reported in the British *Lancet*, versus 150,000 reported in the American *New England Journal of Medicine*—additional studies were carried out in Iraq over time. An international research team calling itself the University Collaborative Iraq Mortality Study conducted another national cluster sample survey of 2,000 randomly selected Iraqi households. On October 15, 2013, they published their results in a highly regarded joint US-UK publication called *PLOS Medicine*.[59] Unlike *The Lancet* and *The New England Journal of Medicine* studies, this study focused on cumulative Iraqi mortality over the entire period of US military intervention (2003–2011). According to the cumulative estimates, approximately 500,000 Iraqis had died from the war over time. More than 60 percent of deaths were due to violence, and approximately 30 percent were due to indirect causes, including the collapse of the Iraqi health care system and the destruction of other crucial infrastructure, such as sanitation, transportation, and communication.

This massive death toll continues to be monitored through an international project called "The Iraq Body Count" (IBC). IBC is now the world's largest public database of violent deaths occurring since the beginning of the US invasion. Designed by an independent US/UK coalition of academic and peace activists, the database is continually updated using cross-checked reports of deaths from a variety of recognized sources within Iraq, such as mortuaries, hospital records, media reports, NGO records, and official figures provided by the Iraqi Ministry of Heatlh.[60] The IBC count includes civilian deaths caused by coalition military action as well as insurgent and terrorist attacks. It also includes excess civilian deaths caused by the breakdown in law and order that has led to increased criminal activity in the country.

Accordingly, over more than a dozen years, from 2003 to 2016, IBC reports that approximately 251,000 deaths have occurred in Iraq due to direct war-related violence among both civilians and combatants. Of these, more than half—or between 159,869 and 178,644—are of Iraqi civilians. IBC data show that the Iraqi death toll has fluctuated from year to year. For example, during the first three years of the US invasion, the death toll increased from twenty deaths per day in 2003 to thirty-six deaths per day in 2005. By 2007 and 2008, the Iraqi death toll surged with the US troop surge. But then it receded during the final three years of the US military occupation. However, by 2013, in conjunction with the emergence of ISIS, civilian casualties began to escalate again. According to IBC reports, the Iraqi civilian death toll was 4,622 in 2012; 9,851 in 2013; 20,030 in 2014; and 16,115 in 2015. By 2015, IBC was calling the massive death toll in Iraq "a catastrophic normal."[61]

As of this writing, Iraq is one of three countries—along with Syria and Afghanistan—where more than 10,000 war-related deaths are occurring annually. Compared to the 4,491 cumulative deaths of US military personnel during the entire 2003–2014 period,[62] the Iraq body count is at least fifty-five to 110 times higher than the American body count, depending on which death toll estimate is used. Put matter-of-factly, the United States started a war in Iraq that has been truly deadly. This high death toll continues to this day, with thousands of innocent Iraqi lives being taken.

Mental Health Costs

Given the ongoing Iraqi death toll and the unknown numbers of Iraqis who have been wounded, kidnapped, or exposed in other ways to the horrors of war, it is not surprising that Iraq is suffering from a mental health crisis.[63] Four major violence-related conditions predispose populations to mental health disorders—torture, exposure to mass violence and death, displacement, and living life in a climate of fear, violence, and disruption.[64] All of these conditions are highly prevalent in Iraq, but the country's mental health infrastructure was in no way prepared to handle this mental health crisis. For example, in 2003, when the war began, Iraq's population of approximately 24.5 million was served by only 100 psychiatrists, a single inpatient psychiatric hospital in Baghdad (with 1,300 beds), a number of outpatient psychiatric centers in a few universities, and a small number of private clinics in the main cities.[65] In addition, mental health services to treat the victims of torture were entirely inadequate, even though more than half of all households in some areas of Iraq had a family member who had been tortured under Saddam Hussein's brutal regime.[66]

However, with the US invasion, mental health disorders skyrocketed. Early reports emerging from Iraq during the first three years of the war showed that Iraqis were suffering increased rates of anxiety and depression as well as a

35 percent increase in cases of posttraumatic stress disorder, particularly in urban neighborhoods where major battles and explosions had taken place.[67] As in Lebanon during the civil war, Iraqis were reported to be self-medicating through increased alcohol and substance abuse, particularly the use of psychotropic medications such as sleeping pills and tranquilizers, which were available without physicians' prescriptions. In one clinic, 60 percent of the depressed patients had become addicted to psychotropic medications; such medications were preferred over alcohol, were easier to obtain, and were considered a more discreet way to cope with mental health problems among this largely Muslim population.[68]

However, these reports were largely anecdotal. Virtually no reliable data were available on the mental health status of Iraqi citizens who were living through the war or whether they were able to have access to mental health treatment services. Although extensive studies began to be undertaken on the mental health consequences of deployment in Iraq for US and UK armed forces and their family members,[69] the war-related mental health problems of Iraqis themselves remained largely unstudied and uncertain.

To remedy this situation, a national mental health needs assessment was carried out in Iraq in 2006 and 2007 by the aforementioned Iraq Family Health Survey (IFHS) Study Group. With support from WHO's World Mental Health (WMH) Survey team, IFHS conducted the Iraq Mental Health Survey (IMHS), a study involving a nationally representative sample of 4,332 Iraqi adults, age eighteen years and above.[70] The IMHS was conducted in all regions of Iraq, including Anbar Province and Iraqi Kurdistan. Not surprisingly, the IMHS findings were sobering. High levels of psychological distress were found among the Iraqi population, with one in five women and one in seven men—or nearly one-fifth of the entire Iraqi population (18.8 percent)—suffering from some type of recognized mental disorder over the course of a lifetime, especially those Iraqis who had been exposed to one or more traumatic events. Not surprisingly, anxiety disorders were the most prevalent condition, followed by mood disorders, especially major depression. Almost 70 percent of those Iraqis with recognized mental disorders also reported suicidal thoughts, even though fewer than 10 percent had received any form of treatment. For the youngest age group, ages eighteen to thirty-four, the risk of developing any mental health disorder was significantly elevated, with the odds of posttraumatic stress disorder (PTSD) being 5.3 times higher than for the oldest generation (ages sixty-five and above). These data likely underestimated the levels of psychological distress in Iraq because Iraqis who were homeless or displaced, too ill to be interviewed, or living in areas too dangerous to be surveyed were excluded from the study.

The IMHS study focused on adult mental health. But the mental health of Iraqi children was also cause for concern. An early report in the *British Medical Journal* claimed that the vast majority of Iraq's 13 million children had experienced some form of psychological trauma because of the war,[71] with at least one-half million of these children in serious need of psychological treatment.[72] Later reports emerging in 2006 from Baghdad, Mosul, and Nassiriya found that 14 to 37 percent of Iraqi children and adolescents showed symptoms of PTSD.[73] In Mosul, where the rates of PTSD were highest, less than 10 percent of ill children had received any form of treatment.

According to WHO, mental health disorders are now the fourth leading cause of ill health among Iraqis, starting in children as young as five years.[74] Thus, WHO has been working closely with the international aid organization, Médecins Sans Frontières (MSF), and the Iraqi Ministry of Health to develop a new mental health system for Iraq, one that relies primarily on psychological counseling rather than the use of psychotropic medications. As described in the MSF report, "Healing Iraqis: The Challenges of Providing Mental Healthcare in Iraq," an attempt is being made to integrate mental health treatment services into primary health care centers in the country.[75] The program includes training of new psychological counselors, telephone helpline services, and working to overcome the stigma still associated with mental illness. However, the ongoing conflict in Iraq has hampered health care provision overall, especially in areas of violent ISIS insurgency.[76] Among Iraqis seeking mental health treatment from MSF, almost half of all cases of psychological distress are violence related.[77] Thus, building a mental health infrastructure in Iraq has been an extremely challenging task and will remain so until sectarian violence abates across the country.

Reproductive/Demographic Costs

In addition to Iraq's mental health crisis, the reproductive and demographic consequences of war in Iraq have been shattering. Overall, Iraq has experienced a dramatic increase in excess maternal and child deaths—a reflection of the fact that more than one-third (36 percent) of the total global burden of maternal death, child death, and stillbirth exists in countries that have ongoing armed conflicts.[78] In Iraq, the US invasion began after thirteen years of

UN sanctions and embargoes, which had already significantly undermined maternal and child health. UN agencies estimated that one out of every eight children in Iraq died before the age of five; one-third were malnourished; one-quarter were born underweight; and one-quarter did not have access to safe drinking water in a country where almost half of the total population consisted of children.[79] These devastating figures reflected overall food insecurity. In 2003, 18 million out of 24.5 million people in Iraq lacked secure access to food; thus, child malnutrition rates were high in a country where malnutrition was once rare before the UN sanction period was imposed in 1990.

The years of the Second Gulf War did little to improve overall child health in the country. During the war period, under-five child mortality in Iraq was among the highest in the Middle East.[80] A deadly syndemic of malnutrition and infectious disease combined to take its toll on Iraqi children. In a study conducted in Baghdad among three- to five-year-old children, nearly one-fifth were malnourished, with the highest rates in unsafe neighborhoods where adult family members had already been killed.[81] Moreover, WHO statistics showed that the three major killers of young children in Iraq were preventable infectious diseases, including pneumonia, diarrhea, and measles.[82] Although measles is a vaccine-preventable illness, disruptions in vaccination supplies and delivery meant that many Iraqi children were never vaccinated.

According to the "Dirty War Index"—a measure of "undesirable" civilian and child deaths occurring during war—15 percent of the "undesirable" deaths that occurred in Iraq from 2003 to 2008 were among women and children.[83] The only bright spot in Iraq's overall maternal and child health profile during that time involved maternal mortality. Deaths of Iraqi women during childbirth diminished significantly during the war because international aid agencies made significant efforts to assure safe passage to hospitals and to prevent childbirth-related mortality.[84] However, a concomitant increase in infant mortality and birth defects among babies born to Iraqi mothers suggests that war has still taken an insidious toll on maternal and child health across the country.[85]

Social Structural Costs

By the end of the US war period, 4.7 million Iraqis—or approximately 15 percent of Iraq's total population—were estimated to have been displaced, meaning that Iraqis were among the world's largest refugee population.[86] However, since January 2014, forcible displacement of 3.2 million more Iraqis has occurred as the result of ISIS violence.[87] Accordingly, there are now approximately 8.7 million Iraqis in need of humanitarian assistance.

War-related death and displacement in Iraq have had both demographic and social structural consequences, in a society where the nation itself is literally being torn apart. To reiterate one of the main messages of this book, the US invasion of Iraq unseated, and then fueled, bitter sectarian tensions and violence on a level that was totally unprecedented (and unwittingly unpredicted by George W. Bush's administration).[88] The US invasion of Iraq paved the way for sectarian violence, which has, in turn, led to the flight of refugees, the internal displacement of millions of Iraqis, and the increasing impoverishment and immiseration of the Iraqi population as a whole.

In a report called "Uncertain Futures: The Impact of Displacement on Syrian Refugee and Iraqi Internally Displaced Youth in Iraq," the international aid organization Save the Children documented the suffering of Iraqi youth, ages fifteen to twenty-five, in a country where nearly half of the population of 34 million is under the age of nineteen.[89] The majority of internally displaced Iraqi youth said that they saw no future for themselves in Iraq. Most had faced extended educational disruptions, heightened concerns about violence, and a lack of job opportunities. Most also expressed feelings of hopelessness and discrimination, both at the hands of NGO workers and on the part of regional governments. Among male displaced youth, the possibility of joining an armed group was compelling—less a reflection of ideological persuasion than of poverty and young men's felt needs to receive a salary and provide for their families, especially when their fathers had been killed. Save the Children's report concluded on a sobering note:

> The dangers of ignoring this displaced youth population in Iraq are stark. With poor access to safe and quality support services, many of these youths face a variety of hardships such as isolation, insecurity, psychological distress, extended disruption of education, heightened protection risks, exploitative working conditions, desperation and hopelessness. This presents a worrying situation for the future of Iraq. Indeed . . . community leaders are worried that disaffected youth, with few positive options, will fuel tensions and violence for decades to come.[90]

As summarized in the Save the Children report, the future of Iraq is, indeed, "uncertain." With millions of Iraqis displaced and thousands continuing to die, it is unclear how Iraq will hold together as a nation and what will eventually become of today's youthful generation, stuck in a conflict not of their own making.

Infrastructural Costs

Just as war has taken its toll on the Iraqi people, it has also devastated the country's infrastructure. Nearly a decade and a half of perpetual violence has damaged roads, communication systems, potable water supplies, sanitation treatment systems, and the power grid, the latter playing out in frequent electricity shortages. Quite paradoxically, the United States has spent billions of dollars in Iraq attempting to reconstruct what it has destroyed. From fiscal year 2003 to 2012, this "destruction-reconstruction" effort cost $60.45 billion—an amount four times the sum committed to Iraq by America's allies and nearly twice the amount spent (in today's US dollars) for the reconstruction of Germany after WWII.[91] Between its two wars in Iraq and Afghanistan, the United States has spent more than $1.4 trillion, including $160 billion on reconstruction alone. Thus, it is fair to say that the war in Iraq cost thousands of Iraqi lives, as well as billions of US taxpayer dollars.

For Iraqis, the cost of damaged infrastructure has played out in high rates of injury. In a study entitled "Injury Burden during an Insurgency: The Untold Trauma of Infrastructure Breakdown in Baghdad, Iraq," a team of American and Iraqi physician-epidemiologists conducted a survey of 1,172 households in Baghdad regarding injuries sustained during a three-month period in 2009.[92] They found that injuries were far more frequent than fatalities in the study population. Most of these injuries resulted from the conflict-induced breakdown of Iraqi infrastructure, rather than from direct violence. Thus, the "untold trauma" of the war involved unintentional injuries sustained from electric shocks, falls in rubble, unintentional explosions, and accidental gunshot wounds.

Unfortunately, the medical infrastructure to handle such emergencies was severely compromised. Prior to the US invasion, the Iraqi health system had already been seriously undermined by the UN sanction period. It was estimated that the Iraqi Ministry of Health was able to meet only 10 to 15 percent of the country's medical needs, due to embargoes on essential medicines and supplies.[93] However, the 2003 US invasion destroyed medical infrastructure itself—including an estimated 12 percent of Iraq's hospitals and primary care centers.[94] As with infrastructure reconstruction in Iraq, the United States and other international funders spent millions of dollars attempting to reconstruct

Iraq's medical facilities. Thus, by the time of the 2011 US withdrawal, approximately 240 hospitals and 1,200 primary health care centers were operating in the country.[95]

Having said this, ongoing violence in the country—including the deliberate targeting of physicians and the looting of health care facilities—has continued unabated, contributing to instability in the overall medical environment. This has been especially true of the progressive loss of qualified health care personnel from Iraq. Many experienced physicians and ancillary medical staff have either died during the war or left the country, leading to significant gaps in coverage and quality of health care services. In a study of more than 400 Iraqi refugee doctors in Jordan, these exiled physicians cited many obstacles to health care delivery in Iraq and reasons they had fled. Among the difficulties they faced in Iraq were construction of barricades limiting free access to health facilities; significant shortages of medicines, including critical drugs such as insulin; lack of functioning medical equipment, supplies, and laboratory facilities; loss of ancillary staff, including skilled health care workers such as nurses and technicians; and outright violence against physicians, including targeted assassinations. Many of their colleagues had succumbed to violent deaths, and those who had not were often afraid to practice medicine outside of their own homes.[96] Of those physicians interviewed for the study, nearly half had already left Iraq by 2006, whereas others had been displaced within the country before eventually fleeing to Jordan. Few of these Iraqi refugee physicians had plans to return.

In short, the disruption and targeting of health services in Iraq has become a brutal weapon of war, as it has in neighboring Syria.[97] Although the Geneva Convention aims to protect medical spaces and health care workers from interference and attack during armed conflicts, Iraq provides a glaring example of Geneva Convention violations. Medical neutrality has not been achieved or sustained in Iraq during wartime. This ongoing targeting of Iraqi physicians and health care facilities represents a major violation of international humanitarian law.

Environmental Costs

Of all the destruction set in motion by the US invasion of Iraq, the one with the longest-term health consequences may have to do with contamination of the environment. Both the First and Second Gulf Wars in Iraq left a toxic residue called depleted uranium (DU). Uranium itself is a naturally occurring heavy metal that is found in very low concentrations in Earth's soil and oceans. Hence, trace amounts of natural uranium are found in drinking water and food, and the average daily human intake of uranium is about 1 microgram per day.[98] However, natural uranium is mined and processed to create highly radioactive "enriched" uranium, which is used in nuclear reactors and in nuclear weapons. The waste product of the uranium enrichment process is "depleted" uranium, or DU, which is about 60 percent more radioactive than natural uranium. Like lead, nickel, and other heavy metals, DU is chemically toxic to humans.

DU has been used since 1959 in the US munitions industry because it is 65 percent denser than lead, it has a high melting point, it has a tensile strength comparable to most steels, and it ignites when it fragments. Thus, the US military has called DU the "silver bullet" for destroying enemy tanks. DU is also the "silver shield" to armor US tanks against enemy fire. However, when DU explodes, it creates "a fine, respirable size dust that contaminates an impact site and presents a hazard to combat troops and civilians."[99] This DU dust in the environment has a radioactive decay chain lasting 4.5 billion years, thereby posing long-term health risks to exposed populations.

DU first emerged as a social, political, and scientific issue after the First Gulf War. It is estimated that nearly 900,000 DU rounds (more than 286,000 kg) were fired in Iraq by US and British troops during the First Gulf War. Thus, interest in DU initially focused on its relationship to health problems reported by US and UK veterans, including what came to be known in the veteran activist community as "Gulf War syndrome."[100] In a ten-year follow-up study of American veterans who were hit by "friendly fire" and thus had DU shrapnel embedded in their bodies, researchers showed that higher-than-normal levels of uranium continued to be excreted in these veterans' urine over time and that elevated urine uranium levels were associated with perturbations in reproductive hormones, especially increased prolactin levels (which can cause male infertility and erectile dysfunction). Some evidence of neurological and genetic damage was also discovered in this small group of DU-affected veterans.[101] However, because no major health problems were evident, the US military continued to use DU munitions in the Second Gulf War with impunity. According to the US General Accounting Office, approximately 6 billion DU rounds were fired by US armed forces in Iraq during the first three years of the Second Gulf War.[102] Approximately 80 percent of those rounds were estimated to have missed their targets and thus were deposited relatively intact in the local environment, presenting a potential long-term hazard as they oxidized and migrated into soil and water.[103]

What are the potential health effects of this massive release of DU into the Iraqi environment? This is a question that is being vociferously debated in the scientific and environmental, if not the military, communities. At the start of the Second Gulf War, WHO released a report entitled "Potential Impact of Conflict on Health in Iraq," which suggested that DU might be related to reports of increased cancers, birth defects, and renal diseases in the Iraqi population.[104] As noted in the report, "Epidemiological studies are needed to investigate such increases and explore all possible causal factors."[105]

Since then, a series of studies have been carried out in the heavily bombarded city of Fallujah, which sustained some of the worst damage by US forces. Nearly a decade on, epidemiological studies show high rates of congenital malformations (15 percent of all births); higher than expected rates of cancer, especially leukemia and lymphoma, including in children; higher than expected rates of infant death, when compared to infant mortality rates across the region; and an anomalous sex ratio in children under age five, suggesting that genetic damage was sustained in the zero to age four cohort.[106] Hair samples taken from the parents of children with congenital anomalies in Fallujah show the statistically significant presence of enriched uranium in mothers' bodies. According to the study authors, "These findings suggest the enriched uranium exposure is either a primary cause or related to the cause of congenital anomaly and cancer increases. Questions are thus raised about the characteristics and composition of weapons now being deployed in modern battlefields."[107]

Whether birth defects, cancer, and reproductive problems among US and UK male veterans (as well as Kamal and his infertile Iraqi refugee friends in Arab Detroit) will eventually be linked to the US military's use of DU in Iraq is uncertain. Despite WHO's initial efforts to raise the DU question for public health, the agency has become mired in a DU controversy, which is playing out in the pages of *The Lancet*. Namely, in 2012, WHO supported an Iraqi government survey of 18,800 Iraqi mothers that, contrary to the aforementioned studies, found "no clear evidence to suggest an unusually high rate of congenital birth defects in Iraq."[108] This WHO-funded study has subsequently been questioned on methodological grounds in the pages of *The Lancet* by those researchers whose studies demonstrate DU's reproductive toxicity.[109]

This controversy has also been picked up by media in the United Kingdom and the Middle East, although less so in the United States. Al Jazeera—the major Middle-East news organization based in Doha, Qatar—has warned of "war's legacy of cancer" in Iraq and the worrying malformations among "Fallujah babies," tying these epidemics to "two US-led wars in Iraq," which have "left behind hundreds of tonnes of depleted uranium munitions and other toxic wastes."[110]

Whether DU proves to be a major reproductive toxicant and environmental carcinogen in Iraq has yet to be proven definitively. However, environmental toxicologists are already warning of the potential long-term health effects. As with the Iraq body count, activists have accused the US Department of Defense of gross negligence in failing to account for DU's human and environmental toxicity. Summarizing the situation quite fairly, Dan Fahey, a long-term analyst of the DU controversy, concludes,

> DU munitions are neither the benign wonder weapons promoted by the Pentagon propagandists nor the instruments of genocide decried by hyperbolic anti-DU activists. While the political effects of using DU munitions are perhaps more apparent than their health and environmental effects, science and common sense dictate it is unwise to use a weapon that distributes large quantities of a toxic waste in areas where people live, work, grow food, or draw water.[111]

The fact that many Iraqis *are* living, eating, and drinking in zones of known DU contamination is a serious cause for concern. If DU turns out to be as toxic as some experts suspect, then future generations of Iraqis, living in places like Fallujah, will be the unwitting inheritors of the radioactive legacy of US military intervention. In short, a single toxic substance—DU—may constitute war's most lasting effect.

Conclusion

As should be clear from the examples of both Lebanon and Iraq, when it comes to war, there are no public health victories—only syndemics of misery that may take generations to overcome. War is bad for human health and well-being on multiple levels, including the six dimensions highlighted in this chapter. The public health effects of war are immediate and direct (for example, death in combat). But, even more significantly, the public health effects of war are long term and indirect (for example, environmental toxicity). As shown in the case of DU in Iraq, many of the long-term health effects of war are still not well understood, and may take generations to uncover.

Clearly, the current wars in the Middle East and the lingering effects of earlier wars continue to haunt and disrupt the lives of millions of people. War has been a cause of profound human suffering in both Lebanon and Iraq, the two countries featured in this chapter and from which most Arab Detroit refugees, including Mahmoud, Mayada, and Kamal, have fled. In the next chapters, we will hear the war stories of other refugees in Arab Detroit, who attribute their reproductive health problems and their psychic suffering to the legacies of war and to the ongoing problem of survivors' guilt.

Violent conflicts have disrupted many innocent lives across the Middle East, destabilizing the region as a whole and militating against the well-being of the region's citizenry. Overall, the pursuit of war in the Middle East precludes the possibility of "health for all," which was the utopian goal of the Declaration of Alma-Ata. If the achievement of global health is to become a worldwide reality in the twenty-first century, then it behooves us to assess the public health costs, as well as the political costs, of war and to agitate for peace in all the war-torn societies of the Middle East.

2 Where They Resettled

Poverty on the Margins of Detroit

From Iraq to Michigan: A Tale of Two Engineering Students

In Arab Detroit, there are thousands upon thousands of Iraqi refugees. They began arriving in 1992 after the First Gulf War and were joined by a second wave that started in 2008. Some of these refugees came directly to Michigan from the Middle East, as assigned by the US Refugee Admissions Program (USRAP).[1] However, others took circuitous routes, finding a permanent home in Arab Detroit only after an initial placement in another state. Some of these refugees came with their families, whereas others did not. This was especially true for young Iraqi men, many of whom fled from Iraq alone. Some were fighters, some assisted US forces as translators and guides, and others were civilian noncombatants. Many were lucky to make it out of Iraq alive.

So it was with Ali and Ibrahim, two Iraqi engineering students, both Shia Muslims, who fled from Iraq to avoid certain death. Ibrahim was a fighter, joining the Shia intifada to overthrow Saddam Hussein after the First Gulf War. Ali was a noncombatant who had been religiously trained in one of Iraq's famous Shia seminaries. Coming from different cities in southern Iraq, the two men did not know each other. Nor did they become acquaintances in the growing Iraqi refugee community in Arab Detroit. But their lives were similarly scarred by war and by a haunting sense of survivors' guilt. Although they were comparatively lucky to have made it to America, their lives as refugees in the United States were not easy, as their stories of pain, suffering, hardship, and longing will show.

Ali

When I first met Ali, it was a cold, overcast spring day in Michigan, the kind where people were still wearing their winter coats. I arrived in the Dearborn IVF clinic on a Friday afternoon, a time when Muslim men sometimes presented at the clinic alone after the Friday communal prayer. I was told by clinic staff members that a man had come to the clinic especially to meet me after he had read my study ad posted in the clinic's waiting area. This volunteer was Ali. As I was soon to discover, Ali was a religiously trained Iraqi Shia Muslim *shaykh* who had once studied theology and jurisprudence while also obtaining a master's degree in engineering. This tall, substantial man—standing well over six feet tall, in a black suit and white dress shirt, with a closely trimmed beard—was an imposing figure. Yet, as we sat together in a private space in the clinic, it became clear that Ali was actually a broken man, with a life story that could only be described as quite tragic.[2]

Ali had been born in southern Iraq to a large family of six sons and six daughters. In the early years of Iraq's Baathist political regime, even poor Shia families were able to educate their children under the social welfare system. So Ali and all his brothers were sent to the University of Baghdad, where they studied to earn master's degrees in engineering. However, before they attended college, Ali and his brothers had studied in a Shia madrasa in the holy city of Najaf, where Ali had learned to read and interpret the Qur'an. He graduated as a Shia cleric in 1985, six years before the First Gulf War, an event that would change his life forever.

When US troops invaded Iraq in early 1991, the US government armed both the Shia Muslims in southern Iraq and the Kurds in northern Iraq, encouraging them to rise up against the regime of Saddam Hussein. Ali's religiously trained family members did not fight but were caught in the postwar dragnet. Targeted by Saddam's regime for being "religious" Shia Muslims, Ali and two of his brothers were sent to prison. The two brothers—both *shaykhs*, both engineers, and both young fathers of two children—were killed, news that blinded their elderly father, according to Ali. Ali survived his three years of imprisonment, but he was brutally beaten and tortured in a small cell, a "dark dungeon," where he lived from 1991 to 1994. On his unexpected release, he fled to neighboring Syria, then to Lebanon, where the large Shia

Muslim community took him in on a temporary basis. Soon thereafter, he was granted political asylum in the United States and was resettled as a refugee in Arizona.

In Arizona, Ali met his future wife, Nadia, also a resettled Iraqi refugee. Ali and Nadia loved each other and were physically passionate, sometimes making love two to three times a day. This was partly intended to conceive a child, which both of them ardently desired. However, Ali had been born with a medical condition, undescended testicles, which should have been surgically corrected when he was still an infant (to bring the undescended testes down into his scrotum). By the time he entered college, Ali realized that something was wrong. So he sought a doctor's advice and was told to undergo semen analysis. "That was in 1983, twenty-two years ago, when I did my first test in Iraq and they found no sperm," he said. "That day was very sad, very sad. The doctor explained, 'No, nothing!' and I cried." Although Ali had undergone a corrective testicular surgery, called orchiopexy, when he arrived as a refugee in Lebanon, he also underwent a testicular biopsy, in which small samples of his testicles were removed in an attempt to find any existing sperm. Again, no sperm were found.

Still, Ali did not give up hope. When he married Nadia, he believed that some future scientific discovery in the United States might cure him. For example, he had read about a football player in California who had injured his testicle but who had purportedly undergone a testicular transplant from his brother. Ali wondered if this was a common procedure (it is not), for he hoped that some similar form of testicular repair might restore his own fertility.

Meanwhile, Ali's wife Nadia was becoming desperate to have her own children, given the scrutiny of her childlessness in the growing Iraqi refugee community in Arizona. Although she loved her husband, she loved children even more, telling Ali, "I *need* a baby." Eventually, Nadia exercised her right to divorce within the American judicial system, leaving Ali after three years of marriage. She remarried quickly, to another Iraqi refugee, and became the mother of two children. Out of love and compassion for her first husband, she continued to call Ali to check in on him, letting her young children speak to their "uncle" on the telephone.

To mend his broken heart, Ali moved to the much larger Iraqi refugee community in Arab Detroit. There, he knew no one, but he found easy employment as a clerk in a Lebanese-owned gas station. In his job, he earned $500 per week, barely enough to cover his rent ($700 per month), his food

($300 per month), his car payments and gasoline ($300 per month), and the $200 monthly remittances to his elderly disabled parents in Iraq. Ever since he fled Iraq, Ali had not worked either as an engineer or a Muslim cleric, the two professions for which he was highly trained.

However, Ali's biggest problem in life was his inability to remarry. "There are lots of women in Iraq," he said, "but they all want children. There is no Iraqi woman who does not want to be a mother." Ali was not opposed to marrying a divorcee or a widow with children, even if she was an American. During our conversation, Ali asked me if I was married ("Yes"), and then if I could help him to find an American wife. "My health is very good," he explained. "Every day, I wake up with an erection. I am *strong*. My sex drive is very good. But for the past six years in America, I've not used it. I *need* a wife. I need one *now*. Any wife, American or Iraqi, Muslim or not. It doesn't matter to me. Can you help me?"

I told Ali that I would contact a friend, a widowed Sunni Muslim woman with children, who also hoped to remarry. Meanwhile, I asked Ali if he was allowed to masturbate to relieve his sexual tension. "No, this is *haram* [religiously forbidden]," he explained. "I cannot do this." Instead, he told me, the semen was being released "naturally," through nighttime emissions, which were occurring once or twice each week.

During that afternoon's office visit, Ali had been advised by one of the clinic staff to consider using sperm donation. "It's difficult," Ali confided to me afterward. "In Iran, Ayatollah Khamene'i says it's *halal* [religiously permitted]. But it's a problem. For example, if the [infertility] problem was from your husband, would you get donor sperm? It's hard. I love science, but it is very difficult for me to accept this [donor sperm]. After [the doctor] suggested this, my self-feeling was very bad. My psychological state is now very bad."

I left the Dearborn clinic on that cold spring afternoon feeling very sorry for Ali and his plight. As promised, I contacted my widowed friend to see whether she would be interested in meeting up with Ali as a prospective husband. However, as a devout Sunni Muslim woman, she could not imagine herself being married to a devout Shia Muslim cleric. She declined my offer of an introduction to Ali, who, even though he was a highly educated engineer and Shia *shaykh*, was considered infertile, unmarriageable, and ostracized. Indeed, in my final conversation with Ali, he described himself to me as *miskiin*, a "poor one," in every sense of that term.

Ibrahim

Shaykh Ali had never fought a war in Iraq, although he suffered tremendously in war's aftermath. Ibrahim, on the other hand, had been a freedom fighter. As a young engineering student in Basra, Ibrahim had joined the Shia resistance, participating in the intifada to remove Saddam Hussein from power. Ibrahim was shot in the pelvis, and spent four months in a Basra hospital after surgery to remove the bullet fragments. But, shortly following Ibrahim's release, Saddam's forces crushed the Shia-led uprising, and Ibrahim fled to Saudi Arabia with thousands of other Shia resistance fighters. There, he spent six full years in an isolated, desert refugee camp, the conditions of which were appalling. However, it was back in Iraq that Ibrahim's family faced Saddam's revenge. Ibrahim's older brother, the father of four young children, was taken from his home by soldiers. As Ibrahim lamented, "I lost my brother because of me. After I left, they took him. He has four children, and they never heard from him again."

Ibrahim could not go back to Iraq, so he applied for admission to the United States as a refugee. Already thirty years old, Ibrahim had experienced sexual intercourse only twice in his life, both times back in Basra before the First Gulf War. With his arrival as a refugee in St. Louis, Missouri—also home to a large Bosnian Muslim refugee population—Ibrahim soon discovered the "open" sexual environment of the United States. With his good looks and decent English skills, which he had acquired during his college years in Iraq, Ibrahim was considered attractive by American women. Thus, he began having numerous sexual liaisons, a fact that he confessed sheepishly. "I am blaming myself. My libido is high, and maybe I 'spent' all of my sperm back before marriage, because I had an active sex life. I don't know, sometimes. I did what I did, but it wasn't right . . . Maybe God wants to punish me."

Ibrahim then went on to describe how he had once loved a young American woman back in Missouri. But the steering wheel on a U-Haul truck he was driving locked in place, causing the truck to crash and killing his American girlfriend in the passenger seat. Ibrahim spent a year in a St. Louis hospital with multiple fractures. But the death of his girlfriend caused Ibrahim significant stress and feelings that he was now responsible for the loss of two loved ones.

During his recuperation, Ibrahim spoke to his father back in Iraq. "Why do you have such a tough life?" his father asked him. "You need to settle down." The family began looking for an Iraqi wife, one who would be willing to move to America to be with Ibrahim.

After his release from the hospital, Ibrahim eventually moved, first to Arizona, then to Dearborn to be part of the larger Iraqi refugee community. There, he began thinking about marriage, and he let his family intervene. This is how Ibrahim met Amina, his younger sister's friend and a high school chemistry teacher in Basra. Amina and Ibrahim courted for several months by long-distance telephone calls, before he eventually traveled to Jordan to meet her and sign the marriage contract.

Although it took several months, Amina eventually joined Ibrahim in Dearborn as his wife. But after a year of living together, with sex almost every day, Amina was not getting pregnant. Haunted by his sexual past, Ibrahim suspected that he might be infertile. So he came alone to the Dearborn IVF clinic, where he underwent a semen analysis.

I happened to meet Ibrahim soon after he had received the devastating news of his very low sperm count. Ibrahim lamented to me, "I was shocked. I cried, 'cause I want a baby. I feel upset. I feel like I'm not a normal person. She [Amina] is the strong one. She said, 'I don't care, as long as I have you. We do our best, and that's it.' But, especially among Arab people, I feel like I'm not a man. It's a bad feeling. I don't know where it comes from, but I feel this."

At this point, I wanted to offer Ibrahim some kind of solace, so I told him, "But it's just a medical condition like any other condition." He then replied, "Well, this helps to calm me down. I *am* beginning to feel like that—like some people are born and don't have nice hair. It's just something I'm born with."

Whether Ibrahim truly believed that his male infertility was a medical condition and not God's punishment for his past, it was telling that he was seeking medical therapy when I met him, hoping to "activate" his sperm production by taking medication. Although the Lebanese doctor could offer him no such miracle cure, Ibrahim was attempting to achieve reproductive success. His most ardent desire, he told me, was to become the father of one or more test-tube babies.

To that end, Ibrahim was trying to make some money at a local Arab-owned computer firm, while also finishing his computer science degree at a local community college. However, he made only $1,500 a month—not enough to cover his household expenses, plus remittances his large Iraqi family expected him to send back to the home country. His employer offered no health insurance, so he had also been uninsured for the past four years.

When Ibrahim was told that he would need a $15,000 cycle of intracytoplasmic sperm injection (ICSI)—the variant of IVF designed to overcome male infertility—he was shocked. "I *could* do it if it costs $5,000," he explained, "because I might be able to save the money or borrow the money from a friend. But $15,000, no way." Unless and until Ibrahim's fortunes somehow changed, there would be no way for Ibrahim to achieve fatherhood—or a sense of atonement for his feelings of survivor's guilt or punishment by God for having sinned.

Miskiin—On Being Structurally Vulnerable

Ali and Ibrahim were among the many Iraqi refugees I met in Arab Detroit. Most had fled from the First Gulf War. But by the time I completed my five-year study, the second wave of Iraqi refugees was beginning to join this existing refugee community. Because of my study's focus, all of the Iraqi men I interviewed were infertile, perhaps as a result of war and its toxic effects. And whether married or single, almost all of these men were struggling financially. Some had little to no education and thus no English skills, which posed significant obstacles to their employment. Even those with university degrees, such as Ali and Ibrahim, were un- or underemployed and usually working for hourly wages in menial jobs that had little or nothing to do with their earlier professional training. In most cases, these Iraqi refugees were no longer receiving any benefits from the US government. This included health insurance, which had expired within their first few months of US residency. Iraqi refugees like Ibrahim who had been injured during the wars, or were torture victims like Ali, were receiving little if any medical care or mental health counseling, despite their significant physical and psychological wounds.

As seen in Ali's and Ibrahim's stories, both men were struggling to make ends meet, with little hope of fashioning a future family life in America. As Ali summed it up, he was *miskiin*—a poor man—a term which, in its polyvalent Arabic meaning, conveyed both Ali's economic deprivation as well as his engulfing sense of misery and misfortune. Sadly, Ali was not alone in his plight. Most of the men and women I met in Arab Detroit were eking out subsistence lives in the midst of the worst US economic recession to hit Michigan, a rust-belt state with a crumbling auto industry. In other words, the notion of *miskiin* applied quite broadly to my study population of Iraqi refugees.

On a conceptual level, the Arabic notion of *miskiin* equates quite well with the analytical trope of "structural vulnerability," forwarded by Philippe Bourgois and other medical anthropologists to describe the populations they study. These include, among others, undocumented Latino migrant day laborers in California;[3] Puerto Ricans living in hypersegregated, inner-city neighborhoods along the East Coast corridor;[4] homeless injection drug users in San Francisco;[5] pregnant street youth in Berkeley, California;[6] and impoverished men and women living with stigmatizing mental illnesses and disabilities in New York City.[7]

According to Bourgois and his colleagues, structural vulnerability is defined as "a positionality that imposes physical/emotional suffering on specific population groups and individuals in patterned ways," and that is "a product of class-based economic exploitation and cultural, gender/sexual, and racialized discrimination."[8] Domains of structural vulnerability include one's financial status, legal status, educational level, language ability, residence, food access, social network, and whether the environment in which one lives exposes a person to risks (toxins, violence, drug use) and/or discrimination (based on national origin, accent, religion, skin color, and the like).[9] Structural vulnerability is also about access to health care—or lack thereof—and how ill health is thus a product of one's social location, especially exclusion from public services and basic legal rights. Structural vulnerability encompasses notions of "worthiness," or whether those in positions of power, such as health care providers, perceive a structurally vulnerable individual to be deserving of respect and quality care. When such interactions connote "undeserving-ness"[10]—namely, that vulnerable people are somehow responsible for their own plight—then individuals in these structurally vulnerable positions may begin to internalize their "externally generated depreciated status" in ways that impinge on their own embodied subjectivities and psychological well-being.[11]

Unfortunately, structural vulnerability and depreciated subjectivities are part and parcel of the Iraqi refugee experience in the United States. Resettled in the very country that caused their displacement and suffering, Iraqi refugees in the United States have been met with deep suspicion as Muslim "others" and thus have not generally been welcomed into American society with open arms. In addition, they have not been adequately supported by the US government in both the resettlement process and beyond and are therefore an impoverished population.

The remainder of this chapter thus poses three important questions about the experience of Iraqi refugee resettlement. First, where have Iraqis been resettled in the United States, and how has this resettlement process unfolded? Second, how have Iraqis fared in Michigan, one of the primary states for refugee resettlement? Finally, how has Michigan's economic recession—and particularly the financial collapse of Detroit—affected this structurally vulnerable refugee population? As I will argue, Detroit is a less-than-ideal destination for fleeing Arabs, many of whom end up being trapped in an impoverished American city.

Iraqi Refugees: A Resettlement Story

Although recent attention has focused on the refugee crisis in Europe, it is important to remember that America is the land of immigrants. To this day, the United States remains the world's top resettlement country for refugees.[12] US Citizenship and Immigration Services (USCIS) defines a refugee as "any person who is outside his or her country of nationality who is unable or unwilling to return to that country because of persecution or a well-founded fear of persecution."[13] Asylum seekers (also known as asylees) share this official USCIS definition with refugees, but asylees are already physically present in the United States or at a US port of entry when they apply for resettlement, whereas refugees are not. Both refugees and asylees are considered "vulnerable" populations because they are fleeing from repressive, autocratic, or conflict-embroiled nations.[14] However, the admissions processes and agencies responsible for these two groups differ.

As previously noted, the agency responsible for refugee resettlement in the United States is called USRAP. USRAP was formed in 1980, when Congress passed the Refugee Act. This act amended the Immigration and Nationality Act of 1952 and the Migration and Refugee Assistance Act of 1962 and thus represented the first comprehensive amendment of US immigration laws. The Refugee Act invested USRAP with two specific goals: first, to provide a permanent and systematic procedure for admission of refugees "of special humanitarian concern" to the United States; and second, to coordinate federal assistance to absorb these new refugees in a uniform and comprehensive manner, thereby meeting their resettlement needs and promoting their self-sufficiency.[15]

Within the first year of the Refugee Act's passage, nearly 240,000 refugees were admitted to the United States, primarily from Vietnam, Laos, and Cambodia in the aftermath of the Vietnam War.[16] The next highest influx of refugees, approximately 142,000, arrived in the United States in 1993. These refugees were primarily Bosnian Muslims, who were fleeing from the Balkan Wars, as well as the first wave of Iraqi Shia Muslim refugees, of which both Ali and Ibrahim were a part.

After 1993, US refugee admissions quotas declined steadily, as Congress, in consultation with the US president, decreased the number of refugees to be accepted on an annual basis. Perhaps because of post-September 11 xenophobia, the years between 2003 to 2007 marked the nadir in US refugee admissions. For example, only 1,603 Iraqi refugees were admitted to the United States in 2007, despite heavy war-related casualties and high levels of Iraqi displacement to both Jordan and Syria.[17] Critical of this very slow response to the growing Iraqi refugee crisis, human rights groups and refugee advocacy organizations began pressuring the US government to increase the overall refugee admissions ceiling. These groups argued that the United States had a particular moral and humanitarian responsibility to Iraqis—especially to the many Iraqis, numbering in the tens of thousands, who had aided the United States during the war but who remained in harm's way. In 2007, Ryan Crocker, the US Ambassador in Baghdad, called on President George W. Bush to guarantee safe haven to all those Iraqis who had served with US forces, including as interpreters, guides, and drivers, among other functions.[18]

Finally, in 2007, five years into the war, Congress shifted its refugee policy, agreeing to increase overall refugee admissions by 10,000 to accommodate the growing Iraqi refugee population. In fiscal year 2008, 13,823 Iraqi refugees entered the United States, more than eight times the number admitted in 2007. Table 2.1, "Iraqi Refugee Admissions to the United States (2007–2015)," reflects this increase.[19] By 2013 and 2014, Iraqis were the largest single group of refugees being admitted to the US, comprising 28 percent of the total. Overall, 125,970 Iraqis entered the country between 2006 and 2015, representing one-fifth of all incoming refugees.[20]

Yet, in the grand scheme of things, these numbers were still small. An estimated 4.7 million Iraqis—or approximately 15 percent of the country's total population—had been displaced from their homes during the US war years (2003–2011).[21] However, less than 3 percent of this displaced popula-

TABLE 2.1. Iraqi refugees admitted to the United States (2007-2015).

Fiscal year	*Number admitted*
2007	1,608
2008	13,823
2009	18,838
2010	18,016
2011	9,388
2012	12,163
2013	19,488
2014	19,769
2015	12,676
	Total number 125,769

tion made its way to America by January 2015. Moreover, in qualitative terms, those Iraqi refugees who arrived in the United States were not well received. In a detailed 2009 report entitled "Refugee Crisis in America: Iraqis and Their Resettlement Experience," the Human Rights Institute at Georgetown University Law Center described Iraqi refugees as a "forgotten" population, one that was not "faring well."[22]

As the Human Rights Institute report pointed out, the 1980 Refugee Act charged USRAP with the important role of refugee provision—namely, insuring "the basic needs (including food, clothing, shelter, and transportation for job interviews and training) for each refugee resettled."[23] In the early years, USRAP fulfilled this important provisioning role. Even in the midst of a prolonged US recession, Vietnamese refugees who arrived in America in the 1980s were fed and housed and given up to thirty-six months of cash assistance and other forms of support. The goal of the USRAP program in the post–Vietnam War era was to help resettle these vulnerable Southeast Asian refugees and to facilitate their self-sufficiency through a focus on sustainable forms of employment. Because of these early investments, the Vietnamese refugee population in America was able to achieve measurable gains in upward mobility. For example, by 2007, the median household income among Vietnamese Americans was $54,871; 41 percent of Vietnamese Americans had some college education; 27 percent had at least a bachelor's degree (only half a percent below the national average at that time); and only 3.2 percent of Vietnamese American households were receiving public assistance. In other words, USRAP's initial model, which provided three full years of government support, laid the foundation for the Vietnamese to become a "model minority"—proving that refugee integration and achievement was possible in the aftermath of a US-led war.

Unfortunately, welfare reform measures enacted during the Clinton era affected USRAP for the worse. As the agency came to be modeled on domestic antipoverty programs, including Temporary Assistance to Needy Families (TANF) and Medicaid, USRAP refocused its efforts on short-term refugee assistance, leaving aside the earlier aim of long-term support so that refugees could become self-sufficient. Iraqi refugees, arriving in the wake of these domestic policy reforms, were no longer the beneficiaries of US government largesse. What Vietnamese refugees had received in the 1980s, Iraqi refugees did not in the 2000s. The more than 125,000 Iraqis who entered the United States in the height of the economic recession encountered a greatly curtailed USRAP program, one that inhibited Iraqi refugee resettlement and led to widespread poverty in this structurally vulnerable population.

As outlined in great detail in the Human Rights Institute report,[24] ten major "systemic flaws" in USRAP policies and procedures created an untenable situation for Iraqi refugees arriving in the US over the past decade. The systemic flaws are as follows:

Planning and Coordination

USRAP's presettlement processing takes little account of the postsettlement needs of individual Iraqi refugees and their families. The USRAP focus is on the numbers of refugees resettled, rather than attention to individual refugee's social histories, which could affect their resettlement placement. Overall poor planning and coordination mean that some states receive adequate refugee funding, whereas other locales with large numbers of refugees are constantly underfunded, with their refugee agencies and caseworkers constantly pressured to deliver more assistance with limited means.

Cash Assistance

Amendments to the USRAP program mean that refugees no longer receive three years of government support. Today, the maximum allowable period for cash assistance is only eight months, after which refugees are left to fend for themselves. Total amounts of cash assistance are also inadequate, ranging from just 17 to 40 percent of the federal poverty line. Thus, an Iraqi family of six receives only $2,500 to cover living expenses for the first ninety days, and a single adult receives only $425, or less than $5 a day for the first three months. Refugees who do not already have relatives in the United States to house them are also at an extreme disadvantage. Sometimes their cash assistance is redirected to pay for the first month's rent. Because the levels of cash assistance are so low and last for only eight months (or until the refugee finds a job, whichever comes first), many newly arrived Iraqi refugees face extreme economic hardship in their first year of resettlement and beyond.

Sustainable Employment Opportunities

Like the Vietnamese before them, resettled Iraqi refugees typically have a strong desire to work and to support their families. But USRAP no longer provides them with the necessary tools to secure sustainable employment. Employment services are provided either by state agencies or by voluntary (often faith-based) organizations called "VolAgs" (for "voluntary agencies"). These agencies are often underfunded and have too many cases to handle. As a result, Iraqi refugees do not receive enough assistance in their job searches, leading to widespread unemployment in the Iraqi refugee community. Cases of homelessness are not uncommon, including among female-headed Iraqi refugee families with young children (including those whose husbands or fathers have died). Overall, USRAP has failed to promote sustainable employment for Iraqi refugees, of the kind that would lead to their eventual self-sufficiency. In desperate situations, some Iraqi refugees have returned to their country of first asylum (usually Jordan), rather than to face unemployment and homelessness in America.

Recertification and Vocational Training

Some Iraqi refugees, such as Ali and Ibrahim, had been educated in Iraq or had other forms of vocational training. However, USRAP's focus on immediate employment before the eight months of cash assistance runs out means that VolAgs and employment agencies push Iraqi refugees toward low-paying jobs, irrespective of the refugee's prior educational accomplishments or professional training. As a result, those with engineering backgrounds, like Ali and Ibrahim, as well as physicians, lawyers, and other highly qualified professionals, are rarely given the opportunity to recertify and practice their actual professions. Even Ali, trained as a Shia cleric, was unable to pursue his religious vocation in the United States, working instead as a low-paid gas station attendant.

English Language Training

Refugees who arrive with English language skills, such as Ibrahim, tend to have higher incomes, as do refugees who receive English as a second language

(ESL) services. US regulations set aside specific funding for ESL courses and require that they be provided in a maximally available manner, in a means that is culturally and linguistically compatible with a refugee's language and cultural background. However, in reality, newly arrived refugees must often wait months before classes are offered, with the quality of language instruction often being poor. As a result, the vast majority of incoming Iraqi refugees do not receive adequate ESL training, meaning that Iraqi adults, especially women who do not work outside of the home, never learn to speak the English language fluently.

Reasonable Transportation Options

Iraqi refugees often end up being resettled in communities with poor public transportation services. Because their cash assistance is so limited, few Iraqi refugee families are able to purchase cars, and obtaining a US driver's license is both complicated and expensive. As a result, Iraqi refugees must often rely on public transportation, despite poor public transportation services in many communities. USRAP provides no guaranteed transportation services for Iraqi refugees, even those who are seeking employment and need rides to reach their job interviews.

Medical Care

Just as refugees receive only eight months of cash assistance, they are also cut off from Refugee Medical Assistance (RMA) after eight months. This lack of sustained medical coverage is extremely problematic, given that 25 to 41 percent of registered Iraqi refugees have an "important medical condition" when they enter the country, according to a UNHCR report.[25] In other words, many Iraqi refugees arrive in the United States with preexisting health conditions, including both physical and mental health problems. Initial medical screenings are required for all refugees within the first year of their arrival. But, once the eight months of medical insurance runs out, refugees may be reluctant or financially unable to have access to medical services. For adult refugees with dependent children, extended medical coverage can be obtained through Medicaid. But this is not available to childless refugees such as Ali and Ibrahim, who lose their medical coverage within their first year in America. Although all US citizens and lawful permanent residents (that is, green card holders) were entitled to medical coverage under the Affordable Care Act during the Obama administration, Iraqi refugees often could not earn enough money to afford this purportedly "affordable" health insurance option.

Treatment of Mental Health Issues

Many Iraqis qualify for refugee status in the United States because they have been traumatized by violence, including torture. According to one UN study, 20 percent of Iraqi refugees were the victims of torture or traumatic violence; 75 percent of Iraqi refugees were affected by bombings; 75 percent knew someone who had been killed; and 80 percent had witnessed a shooting.[26] As a result, it is estimated that about 70 to 75 percent of Iraqi refugees enter the United States with mental health issues, ranging from insomnia to anxiety to depression to PTSD. Yet, the only mandatory mental health assessment occurs at the refugee's initial health screening, when mental health issues may be unreported and overlooked. Although the Torture Victims Relief Act is designed by the federal government to provide refugee mental health services, it is chronically underfunded. As a result, few Iraqi refugees, even those with serious mental health disorders, end up receiving adequate treatment.

Tracking of Secondary Migration

Although Iraqi refugees are placed in resettlement communities across America, they often end up relocating to Arab ethnic enclaves, as seen in the stories of both Ali and Ibrahim. So-called secondary migration reflects the fact that refugees may not thrive in their initial placements and thus seek a larger Arab diasporic community to lean on for support. Postresettlement mobility is a common trend.[27] Yet USRAP has not developed a sufficient mechanism for tracking secondary migration. Many Iraqi refugees literally become "lost in the system," with no transfer of their case information from one state agency to another.

Long-Term Self-Sufficiency

Finally, and most important, USRAP has a legal obligation to "extend protection to the most vulnerable refugees, promote their long-term self-sufficiency, and support their integration."[28] Whether USRAP has actually fulfilled this obligation to Iraqi refugees has been seriously questioned by the Human Rights Institute. A decade on, data suggest that the USRAP's efforts, modeled on domestic antipoverty programs, have actually failed to work in the best interest of Iraqi refugees and to promote their long-term self-sufficiency.

A study carried out by the US Centers for Disease Control and Prevention (CDC) suggests that the USRAP program has failed to protect Iraqis and to promote their long-term well-being. The CDC is the US federal agency charged with tracking the public health of immigrants, refugees, and migrants in this country. The CDC has attempted to assess the health and well-being of the Iraqi refugee population through a survey conducted in the three most populous resettlement states of Michigan, California, and Texas, as well as the second-tier resettlement state of Idaho.[29] One of the major limitations noted by the CDC survey team was the problem of actually finding the Iraqi refugee population in these states. Given significant rates of secondary migration, state agencies partnering with CDC in its study often had outdated contact information for Iraqi refugees. The CDC study team also noted that local partner agencies most invested in longer-term job training and placement of Iraqi refugees tended to have the most current contact information.

Despite the difficulties of finding participants for the study, the CDC survey team was able to administer 366 surveys to Iraqi refugees across the four states. The majority of study participants were male (60 percent), ranging in age from eighteen to eighty-four years. All of those surveyed were literate in either English or in Arabic, given that the survey was self-administered. Almost 90 percent had been living in the United States for more than one year. Seventy percent were married, 20 percent were single, and 10 percent were widowed or divorced. More than half of the participants were undereducated, having finished only elementary or middle school in Iraq. Thus, the majority spoke Arabic as their primary language (86 percent) and cited their inability to speak English as a major deterrent to their employment. Stunningly, more than two-thirds (67 percent) of those surveyed were unemployed, excluding the less than 5 percent who were of retirement age.

Most of the Iraqi refugees interviewed were married with dependent children; thus their families qualified for Medicaid. As a result, more than three-quarters (77 percent) were insured, mostly through Medicaid or some other state health assistance program. Nonetheless, the CDC survey uncovered high levels of "unmet healthcare needs."[30] Sixty percent of those surveyed had at least one chronic condition (mostly hypertension or diabetes), and 37 percent had two or more chronic conditions. Approximately half of those surveyed reported anxiety, depression, or emotional stress, and about one-third were assessed by the CDC as being at risk for PTSD. Yet more than half (55 percent) of study participants reported delaying or not seeking treatment for a medical problem within the past twelve months. Not having enough money to pay for treatment was the most common reason given, among both insured and uninsured Iraqis. Other common reasons given for treatment delay were having no interpreter and no transportation and not knowing where to go.

In summary, the CDC's report on Iraqi refugee health, like the Human Rights Institute report before it, found that resettled Iraqi refugees are not faring well, including in the states with the highest percentages of Iraqi refugees. Other studies on the health status of Iraqi refugees support the CDC findings.[31] They all point to a "vulnerable" population, at high risk for both chronic diseases and mental health problems. Although the CDC's Division of Global Migration and Quarantine mandates that all refugees undergo a medical examination within a year of arrival,[32] insuring the long-term health and well-being of the Iraqi refugee population over time has not been a priority of USRAP. A decade on, the Iraqi refugee community in America faces high levels of unemployment, poverty, and ill health. This is true in the state where the Iraqi refugee crisis has hit home with the greatest force.

Michigan's Iraqi Refugee Crisis

Michigan has been the bellwether state when it comes to the Iraqi refugee crisis—absorbing not one but two major waves of fleeing Iraqis. During the 1980s, in the decade before the First Gulf War, only about 7,500 Iraqis arrived in the United States. They were mostly Iraqi Chaldean (Catholic) Christians, who had been emigrating from Iraq to the United States throughout the twentieth century. Settling primarily in the state of Michigan, the more than 120,000 Iraqi Chaldeans prospered there, with more than 60 percent owning at least one business in the Detroit environs.[33] However, it is important to point out that Iraqi Chaldeans came as immigrants, not refugees. Thus, their situation was quite different from the mostly Shia Muslim Iraqis, who began to arrive in great numbers after the First Gulf War. Of the 68,000 Iraqi refugees who arrived in the United States during the 1990s, Michigan took in approximately 35,000, or more than half.[34] As a result, Arab Detroit's Iraqi population grew exponentially during the 1990s, along with the Lebanese population, which grew by more than 30 percent in the wake of the Shia Muslim exodus from southern Lebanon. By 2005, the US Census Bureau's American Community Survey showed that both the Iraqi and Lebanese populations in Arab Detroit had grown significantly but that Iraqis now outnumbered the Lebanese, at 39 versus 31 percent of the overall population.[35]

This dramatic increase in Iraqis in Arab Detroit between the early 1990s and the early 2000s represented Michigan's first Iraqi refugee crisis. But in 2007, with the congressional lifting of the Iraqi admissions ceiling, the second

TABLE 2.2. Where have Iraqis been resettled (2006–2015)?[a]

Level	*Number of refugees*	*States (in alphabetical order)*
1	10,000–25,000	California, Michigan, Texas
2	1,000–9,999	Arizona, Colorado, Florida, Georgia, Idaho, Illinois, Kentucky, Maryland, Massachusetts, Missouri, North Carolina, New York, Ohio, Oregon, Pennsylvania, Tennessee, Utah, Virginia, Washington
3	100–999	Alabama, Connecticut, District of Columbia, Indiana, Iowa, Kansas, Louisiana, Maine, Minnesota, Nebraska, Nevada, New Hampshire, New Jersey, New Mexico, North Dakota, Oklahoma, Rhode Island, South Carolina, South Dakota, Vermont, Wisconsin
4	1–99	Alaska, Arkansas, Delaware, Hawaii, Mississippi, Montana, West Virginia

[a] Note that Wyoming is the only state that did not resettle any Iraqi refugees.

wave of the Iraqi refugee crisis began to hit the shores of Lake Michigan. By 2008, Michigan had become one of three states—along with California and Texas—to receive thousands of "second-wave" Iraqi refugees. Over the next seven years, 17,582 more Iraqis were resettled in Arab Detroit, at a rate of about 2,500 per year.[36] Michigan was second only to California, where 23,140 Iraqi refugees were resettled in San Diego and the nearby community of El Cajon. Houston, Texas, took in the third largest group of 10,853 Iraqi refugees.[37]

Given the size of this second wave of Iraqi refugees—125,000 entering the United States over seven years, at a rate of about 18,000 per year—USRAP did its best to spread Iraqi refugees over all fifty states. However, as shown in Table 2.2, "Where Have Iraqis Been Resettled (2006–2015)?," the numbers ended up being quite uneven. Some second-tier states such as Idaho, which was one of the CDC's study sites, took in more than 1,000 Iraqi refugees. But most states took in significantly fewer. For instance, Wisconsin (the state of my birth) accepted 984 Iraqi refugees, followed by Connecticut (the state of my residence), which took in 923. However, other Midwestern and New England states resettled far fewer Iraqi refugees. For example, Iowa and Indiana, in the Midwestern heartland, took in 572 and 471 Iraqis, respectively, while Rhode Island and Vermont, both small New England states, took in 172 and 169. Forty-six Iraqi refugees ended up in Alaska (although whether they stayed there is uncertain), while four were placed in Hawaii, the state of President Obama's birth.[38]

In other words, Michigan was the only major Midwestern state to take responsibility for the second Iraqi refugee crisis. By 2015, Michigan was one of the six top refugee-receiving states in the country, along with California, New York, and Texas (that is, the three most populous US states), as well as Ohio and Arizona.[39] Although Arizona is often regarded as a site of Mexican immigration, it took in the fourth largest number of Iraqis refugees, resettling nearly 7,000 in the Phoenix area between 2006 and 2015.

Both Ali and Ibrahim had spent time in Arizona— Ali being initially placed there, and Ibrahim moving there of his own accord after his initial placement in Missouri ended in a long hospital stay. However, both men became secondary migrants, choosing to start their lives anew in what they imagined to be the prosperous and supportive community of Arab Detroit. As seen in their stories, however, Detroit, Michigan, hardly turned out to be an ideal destination. Both men were quickly sucked into the vortex of poverty that was sinking Michigan's Iraqi refugee population as a whole.

By 2003, at least one-quarter of all households in Arab Detroit were surviving on annual incomes of less than $30,000 a year. However, Iraqi refugees were by far the poorest group. Fully 82 percent of all Iraqi refugee households were surviving on incomes of less than $30,000 per year, and nearly half, or 42 percent, lived on household incomes of less than $10,000 per year.[40] In 2003, the federal poverty line for a family of four was $18,400. But because Iraqi families tended to have more than two children, surviving on less than $10,000 a year meant that most Iraqi refugee families were living in abject poverty. Unemployment was an underlying cause. By then, more than 25 percent of Iraqi men living in Arab Detroit were unemployed, or nearly three times the national average.[41]

These figures are very much in line with what I found in my own study in Arab Detroit. Mean monthly salaries reported by all of the men in my study—including Iraqis, Lebanese, Yemenis, and Palestinians—were $2,420, which equated to annual salaries of $29,000 on average. However, the median monthly salary was only $2,000, and the modal monthly salary (the most common figure) was much lower, at only $1,500 a month. Thus, most men were making less than $18,000 a year, and many had experienced or were currently facing periods of unemployment.

Among the Iraqi men specifically, $1,750 was the average monthly salary. But this figure reflects the fact that three Iraqi men in my study had done relatively well for themselves, including two who owned small businesses (barbershops and a small computer firm). If their monthly earnings were removed from the average, then the monthly salary figures for the rest of the Iraqis in my study were much lower, at only $1,165 per month, or about $14,000 per year. Most of the Iraqi men held very low-wage positions in the industrial and service sectors. The single most common occupation was that of gas station attendant, the only job that Ali could find, despite his engineering and clerical training. Like Ali, most of the Iraqi men were manual laborers, who moved from one minimum-wage job to another. As one man told me, "I've held all kinds of jobs in my life," while another stated, "I know many different kinds of work." For example, one man had first worked in construction but then became a truck driver when he lost his construction job. Eventually laid off as a trucker, he then worked irregularly as a mechanic before finally learning how to cut men's hair in an Iraqi-owned barbershop. Similarly, Sadiq, whose story was told in the Prologue, had begun his working life in the Kawasaki factory in Lincoln, Nebraska. But when his family moved to Arab Detroit, he worked as a baker, then an auto factory worker, then a gas station attendant, before finally being laid off altogether. His wife Fatima was also the only Iraqi refugee woman in my study to have ever worked or gone to college. Overall, Iraqi refugee women in my study spoke so little English that it was almost impossible for them to acquire jobs, even when their husbands became unemployed.

Forty percent of the Iraqi men in my study were, in fact, unemployed when I met them, although all of them had once held blue-collar jobs as drivers, electricians, mechanics, construction workers, and factory workers, often in the auto-related fields. Unemployment was a hard pill to swallow for most Iraqi men, and some became sullen, leaving their wives in the difficult position of undertaking job searches to keep their lives afloat. For example, I met Marwa, who was diabetic and suffering from an infertility-related condition called polycystic ovary syndrome (PCOS). Her husband, Ghaffar, was an unemployed taxi driver. Unable to afford health insurance and ineligible for Medicaid because they had no dependent children, Ghaffar and Marwa could not pay for the medications necessary to treat Marwa's diabetes and PCOS. As the Michigan economy deteriorated further with each passing month, Ghaffar eventually stopped his job search, prompting Marwa to seek help at several of the local refugee assistance agencies. But as she told me, "The last time I went in, I told them I don't have Medicaid, my husband is not working, and he really wants to. I told them, 'give me any paper to fill out' [to find a job, or receive health insurance], and they just said, 'Go online and see for yourself.'"

It was not that refugee assistance agencies were being callous. Two local social service agencies—the Arab Community Center for Economic and Social Services (ACCESS) located in Dearborn and the Arab American and Chaldean Council (ACC), whose Social Service Division was located in the Michigan Department of Human Services and thus had twelve satellite offices in a tricounty area[42]—were organized specifically to meet the needs of the local Arab community. Several faith-based VolAgs—particularly Catholic Charities of Southeast Michigan and Lutheran Social Services of Michigan, which was later renamed Samaritas—also had refugee assistance programs. So did the US Committee for Refugees and Immigrants (USCRI), which operated an office in Detroit and was focused on Iraqi refugee resettlement.[43]

The core problem was the Michigan economy. There were simply too few jobs readily available, especially those centered in the dominant auto industry. Whereas the number of local jobs receded, the refugee population continued to expand, leading to a huge surplus labor problem. Thus, refugee caseworkers were sometimes hard-pressed to offer viable job opportunities, even though their case files continued to pile up. In fact, so many refugees had arrived in the state that caseworkers were having trouble keeping up with the new referrals.[44]

In their case, Marwa and Ghaffar were not recent refugees. Like Ali and Ibrahim, they were secondary migrants from the state of Arizona. Thus, the caseworkers who had handled their initial resettlement were in Arizona, not Michigan. In Michigan, Marwa and Ghaffar were simply part of the floating "forgotten population" of Iraqi refugees, who had no work, no health insurance, and no social safety net.

Not surprisingly, these were desperate times for many of the men and women in my study. Because so few of the women worked, it was the men who bore the weight of unstable employment and ensuing poverty on their shoulders. Men were surprisingly candid with me about their low salaries, their menial jobs, and their economic duress. They referred to their "hard lives," with "no benefits," and "very, very low incomes." They described themselves as "very poor," "almost jobless," and "lower class." The Michigan economy was characterized as "down," "really bad," or as one man put it, "It is nothing. The auto industry is the base of the US economy, and if it is down, then everything is down."

Besides trying to support themselves in Michigan, many of the Iraqi men felt some responsibility for their family members, who were stuck either in Iraq or in refugee camps in Jordan. Their inability to send back remittances weighed heavily on their shoulders. For example, Ibrahim told me that he was experiencing significant stress over his inability to support his family back in Iraq:

> Of course, I'm missing my family, but I've got a lot of stress lately, just about money. They think I have this money, but I don't. I have to make money for the family back there, especially because they think that you didn't do well if you can't send back money. Like me, I had to leave college in Iraq. I came with half an education. I'm starting over. But they don't understand this. They don't know what America is like. It is not just a land of money. Even my wife, when she was living in Iraq, she thought this. But now that she's here, she sees what it's like. She was a chemistry teacher there, but there is no way for her to start working here. We couldn't get her a job because we would have to get her degree translated, and she doesn't speak English that well. Honestly, we would both move back to Iraq if we could, but we know that will never happen. So I just live with the stress. I think all this stress is why I have an ulcer.

Like Ibrahim, many of the Iraqi men I met faced economic duress. A few vignettes capture how they characterized their struggles.

Basim

Basim was thirty-one years old, originally from a village outside of Baghdad. Basim and his wife were resettled in Hartford, Connecticut, where he found a job in a plastics manufacturing firm. "But the smell of the plastics was *so bad,*" Basim told me. "I thought maybe I became sick from that. My eyes hurt so much from that material. I hated my job because of those smells." Desperate to change his situation, Basim moved himself and his wife to Dearborn, where some relatives had already resettled. Jobs there were scarce, so Basim began working as a busboy. At $350 a week, clearing tables was the only job that Basim could find. By the time I met Basim, he had worked as a busboy for nearly seven years, making $1,400 a month, which amounted to $16,800 annually. Although Basim prided himself on being a good Iraqi cook, he had never risen from busboy to chef at any of the Middle Eastern restaurants where he had worked, partly because he spoke so little English.

After eight childless years of marriage, Basim was diagnosed with male infertility at the IVF Michigan clinic in Dearborn. There, the doctor took pity on him and enrolled Basim in a clinical trial so that he could receive his hormonal medications for free. But, by that time, Basim's wife had had enough.

She requested a divorce from her infertile husband, and, just like Ali before him, Basim felt obliged to free her.

"I'm still happy to be here," Basim told me shortly after his divorce. "But I'm not happy with my life, because I have so many problems. When we came from Iraq, I just wanted to have a good life with my wife. But we were poor, and she was never happy because of the problems over children. And because I don't have money, we couldn't do any treatment. I came here [to IVF Michigan] six times with my wife, but it cost too much [to do ICSI], and I don't have money, so she gave up on me."

Rashid

Rashid, who was thirty-two years old, was one of the "lucky ones." On his resettlement in Dearborn, he found a steady job in the auto industry. Working in the shipping department of an auto parts factory, Rashid earned $24,000 a year, an amount that he surmised made him "lower middle class," rather than "really poor" like so many other Iraqi men. Still, he told me about his economic troubles. "I work to pay my bills. I have to pay the rent, the electricity, the phone, the doctor bills, the food. It's hard. I'm struggling, but I have to pay them."

Rashid was honest about his work situation. "Nobody really wants to work; it's just to make ends meet. If you really like your job, then it would be more interesting. But most of the people I know, we are just working for the money. I always think that I could end up unemployed, so I thank God that I have a job to pay my bills. I'm not hating my job, but I always wish that I'm rich," even though he added wistfully, "I will never have that chance."

Ghazi

Ghazi was thirty-six and had lost both of his parents in the war. Like the other Iraqi men I met, he was infertile and had just been told that he would need to pay $10,000 to cover the cost of ICSI. When I met Ghazi, he was in a state of shock. "To be honest with you, that's a huge problem. I'm very poor, to be honest with you. I will never, ever be able to afford that."

At that point, Ghazi pulled back his winter coat to show me the oil-stained shirt he wore each day as a gas station attendant. "I make $8 an hour, and then they take the tax out. I can barely pay the bills. I have too many problems. Can you please tell the doctor to take care of me?"

•••

Of course, there was little I could do to help cover the costs of treatment for Ghazi or for Rashid, Basim, and the other poor Iraqi men I met. Their lives of poverty in Arab Detroit, their lack of access to affordable treatment, their inability to function well without fluent English skills, and their lack of strong social safety nets made them structurally vulnerable in many ways. They lived in the shadow of the Ford Rouge auto factory but were rarely afforded the benefits of stable auto industry employment. By the mid-2000s, Detroit's auto industry was also in free fall, taking the local economy with it.

Despite Detroit's downward spiral, thousands more Iraqis began entering the city in 2008—this time not in Dearborn but in the northern Detroit suburbs of Southfield and Sterling Heights.[45] Robert Guttersohn—a freelance journalist and also an Iraq War veteran—questioned the wisdom of placing new Iraqi refugees in a state where they would only be met by "economic hardship."[46] In an article on "Michigan's Iraqi Refugee Crisis" published in the Detroit *Metro Times*, Guttersohn explained,

> Affordable housing is elusive. Refugees are without pay stubs, credit, and very little savings, if any at all. They receive an initial, one-time assistance of up to $1,125 from the federal government, but most of that is eaten away by initial necessities . . . Most can find employment within the first four to six months, but it's often for low wages. According to the Department of Human Services, Michigan's refugees (70 percent of whom are from Iraq) who found work through its employment program last year were paid on average $8.81 an hour.[47]

As Guttersohn pointed out, the economic conditions facing second-wave Iraqi refugees were much worse than the first wave, because Michigan's economy had declined precipitously, even though public assistance for refugees had remained the same. By the time Guttersohn published his article, the city of Detroit had been forced to declare Chapter 9 bankruptcy. Filed on July 19, 2013, this represented the largest municipal bankruptcy in US history, both in terms of the size of the city and the size of its debt, which was estimated at $18 to $20 billion.[48] This "once great" city—as journalist David Maraniss characterized the place of his birth—was now a city in shambles.[49] To wit, former Detroit mayor Kwame Kilpatrick was sentenced to twenty-eight years in federal prison on multiple felony counts of fraud and racketeering, which were deemed partly responsible for Detroit's financial decline.[50] Detroit's population size had also plummeted—from a peak of 1.8 million in the 1950s, to fewer than 700,000 by 2016, the lowest level since 1850, or before the Civil

War.[51] Moreover, the city's physical infrastructure was collapsing. In an article on Detroit's urban blight, the *New York Times* described the tens of thousands of dilapidated, abandoned buildings; the thousands of vacant, trash-filled lots; and the hulking remains of decrepit factories in what it described as a "hollowed-out city."[52] In reality, so many Detroit structures were either boarded up, burned down, or falling apart that it looked like the city itself had been through the Iraq War.

Detroit's Geography of Despair

In his 1978 presidential address to the Association of American Geographers, prominent black geographer Harold M. Rose used the evocative phrase "geography of despair" to describe Detroit and other major American cities where impoverished black populations were suffering.[53] Four decades on, little has changed. In fact, in measurable terms, the city of Detroit has sunken into even deeper despair. Three major reports, released consecutively between 2014 and 2016, characterize Detroit as a city of almost irredeemable poverty.

The first report, issued by the United Way in September 2014, showed that 1.5 million Michigan families could not afford to meet their basic needs, including food, housing, and health care.[54] Forty percent of Michigan households were either living below the poverty line, or in a state of "ALICE"—that is, asset limited, income constrained, but employed. However, Detroit was suffering the most, with two-thirds of its population (67 percent) living in these economically dire straits. As Ken Toll, a southeastern Michigan United Way representative put it, the report "sheds some light on a terrible reality that some area families are facing. It questions the American dream, and if we're setting up families to achieve it."[55]

A year later, in September 2015, the US Census Bureau issued its report on the state of American poverty. According to the Census Bureau, Detroit was now the most impoverished major city in the United States, with 39.3 percent of its residents living below the federal poverty line. In Detroit, the median household income was only $25,074, or less than half of the national average of $53,657.[56] In addition, Detroit's poverty rate was about 10 percent higher than all other major cities, with the exception of Cleveland, Ohio, where the 39.2 percent poverty rate was almost identical to Detroit's.

The following year, in April 2016, the Brookings Institution released another sobering report. This one focused on "concentrated poverty," or the share of poor residents living in extremely poor neighborhoods, where census tract results showed more than 40 percent of residents living below the federal poverty line.[57] As explained in the report, these neighborhoods are characterized by other intersecting problems, including poor schools, high dropout rates, weak job markets, high crime rates, food insecurity, environmental pollution, lack of access to health care, poor physical and mental health outcomes, and lower life expectancy.[58]

According to the report, Detroit scored highest among the nation's twenty-five largest cities in its rate of concentrated poverty, with one-third of all Detroit residents (32 percent) living in such census tracts.[59] This 32 percent rate represented a fivefold increase from 2000, a rate nearly three times the national average, and more than twice the rate of other large cities with high poverty areas, including Chicago, Houston, Miami, and St. Louis. Moreover, concentrated poverty in Detroit was not limited to the inner city. Instead, it was found throughout a six-county region, including the Detroit "suburbs" of Dearborn, Southfield, Sterling Heights, and Warren, where many Arab families live. Overall, concentrated poverty was much more prevalent in Detroit's minority communities. Whereas only 14.8 percent of white Detroit area residents lived in areas of concentrated poverty, nearly half of all African Americans, or 49 percent, lived in such areas, according to the Brookings report.[60]

Taken together, these recent reports speak to the metrics of despair in the city of Detroit. There, a ring of suburban white affluence surrounds a large, impoverished metropolitan area, where both Arabs and blacks live in working-poor and concentrated-poverty neighborhoods. When coupled with other forms of structural vulnerability and discrimination, such poverty cripples the ability of Detroit's minority populations, both Arab and black, to seek higher education, improve their standards of living, have access to affordable housing and health care, and secure their basic survival needs.

The slow demise of the auto industry, which began as early as 1960, has continued to take its toll on the city of Detroit, as autoworkers of all ethnic backgrounds continue to lose their factory jobs.[61] Increasingly, unemployed Arab and black families in Detroit have been forced to rely on the US welfare system to supplement meager family wages, with negative implications for family structure (for example, increased rates of divorce and single parent households), as well as reported health.[62] A study released in April 2016 in the highly respected medical journal *Journal of the American Medical Association* showed that the poorest residents in southeastern Michigan have a life expectancy significantly lower than the poorest residents of other major metropolitan areas.[63] For example, the poorest residents in Detroit live on average six years less than the poorest residents of New York City.

Moreover, many of the poorest residents of Detroit are so poor that they remain "trapped" in their impoverished neighborhoods. As one Detroit poverty activist put it, "We're seeing on the ground in Detroit, people are trapped. It makes it harder for people to leave. Those with access and means are moving out, leaving behind those who can't leave."[64]

This feeling of entrapment—of being "stuck" in a place with so little to offer—is highly relevant to Detroit's Arab refugees. Forced to flee from their home country, they have ended up in Detroit's geography of despair, where the US government has subsequently abandoned them. Having seen in this chapter how Iraqi refugees have been left to fend for themselves on the margins of Detroit, we will see in the next chapter how their struggles continue in the US health care system. As with African Americans before them, Arab refugees who suffer from reproductive health problems face daunting challenges and unequal treatment in a fee-for-service medical system that is pitted against them.

3 How They Struggle

Health Disparities and Unequal Treatment

Intersectionality

Just as the first wave of Iraqi refugees began flooding into Arab Detroit, a new theory was entering the academic world. It was called *intersectionality theory*, as articulated by black feminist legal scholar Kimberlé Crenshaw. In her article entitled "Demarginalizing the Intersection of Race and Sex: A Black Feminist Critique of Antidiscrimination Doctrine, Feminist Theory and Antiracist Politics," Crenshaw argued that feminist theorists, legal scholars, and social justice activists needed to understand the intersection of oppressions facing black women in US society. To wit, black women experience not only gender discrimination but also racial discrimination; these two axes of discrimination intersect in insidious ways to marginalize and disempower them.[1] Thus, according to Crenshaw, efforts aimed at overcoming *either* gender discrimination *or* racial discrimination will fail to account for the multiplicative and interlocking effects of oppression based on gender/race in black women's lives.

A decade on, black sociologist Patricia Hill Collins adopted this intersectional theoretical framework in her seminal volume, *Black Feminist Thought*. Like Crenshaw, Collins argued that oppression cannot be "reduced to one fundamental type."[2] Race, class, and gender oppression often intersect, as do oppressions based on sexuality and nation of origin. In her book, Collins explicitly expanded intersectionality theory to include the intersecting oppressions faced by other Americans, such as Puerto Ricans, Asian Americans, gays and lesbians, those with disabilities, and "other historically identifiable groups."[3] She introduced the term *matrix of domination* to refer to the organizational structures, power hierarchies, and interpersonal domains through which intersecting oppressions are enacted, thereby producing social injustice in historically marginalized communities.[4]

In addition, Collins introduced the powerful trope *controlling images* to refer to the stereotypical portrayals of people who are oppressed and objectified. According to Collins, "Intersecting oppressions of race, class, gender, and sexuality could not continue without powerful ideological justifications for their existence."[5] Concerned primarily with representations of black women in American society, Collins identified a number of insidious negative stereotypes, including the contented "mammy," the controlling "matriarch," the lazy "welfare queen," and the promiscuous "jezebel."[6] According to Collins, challenging these controlling images—and the binary thinking that goes along with them (for example, white/black, male/female, superior/inferior)—has been one of the major themes and contributions of black feminist thought.

Perhaps most important from a cross-cultural perspective, Collins added a transnational dimension to intersectionality theory, arguing that oppression is also linked to national origin and powerful nationalist ideologies.[7] For example, she pointed to the oppression facing diasporic communities in the United States, such as poor black women forced to migrate from the Caribbean to support their families. She also argued that intersectionality theory was relevant to women of color in other national settings. Presaging the political debates that would occur with the global migrant crisis more than a decade later, Collins worried about xenophobic nationalism—"the belief that closer ties exist among members of the nation than with outsiders; a sense of difference from groups around them; and a shared hostility toward outsider groups."[8]

Although forged in the intellectual milieu of US black feminism, intersectionality theory has become relevant to other marginalized groups facing different forms of oppression. Moreover, intersectionality theory has been adopted by scholars in multiple fields, including sociology, psychology, social work, and public health. Although intersectionality theory has appeared less often in anthropological scholarship, this framework has been advocated by Leith Mullings, former president of the American Anthropological Association and a black feminist scholar. Mullings explores the intersections of gender, race, and class in a volume of essays on the subject,[9] as well as in her CDC-funded study on the stresses facing poor and middle-class black women in Central Harlem.[10] More recently, Mullings has teamed up with feminist public health scholar, Amy Schulz, to apply intersectionality theory to the analysis of health problems facing poor minority communities,[11] particularly blacks and Latinas. Schulz's own work focuses on the many stressors facing poor black women in the city of Detroit, where concentrated poverty, food deserts, lack of social support, and perceived discrimination take a serious toll on women's physical and mental health.[12]

Arab Lives and Black Lives in the United States

Following Mullings, Schulz, and other scholars of gender and health, I have been deeply inspired by intersectionality theory in my own scholarship and teaching. Although I acknowledge my own relatively privileged position as a white American feminist and Yale professor, intersectionality theory matters to me greatly, and I have written about it in a number of published essays.[13] Here, I hope to highlight the ways in which an intersectional framework is highly relevant to my study in Arab Detroit, which, as shown in Chapter 2, is located in the heart of a desperately poor, predominantly black American city.

In this section, I want to compare briefly the intersecting oppressions faced by *both* poor Arabs and poor blacks living in Detroit, and in the United States more generally. Although acknowledging that blacks and Arabs have very distinct social histories in the United States—one of brutal slavery among blacks, versus forced migration and refugeeism among Arabs—I hope to reveal some underappreciated commonalities between these historically marginalized minority groups. Blacks and Arabs continue to face insidious forms of discrimination, as well as racial/ethnic profiling. These intersecting forms of oppression literally seep into the body, thereby affecting the physical, social, and reproductive well-being of both communities in ways that are harmful to both human health and dignity.

Poverty

To begin, most Arabs and blacks endure lives of poverty in cities like Detroit. Although a significant percentage of Arabs and blacks have achieved middle-class status or even higher,[14] many members of both groups are poor, with families existing near or below the US federal poverty line. Economic impoverishment and accompanying low social class status are major problems for both of these ethnic minority populations in the landscape of America. Both groups have been affected by changes in the urban industrial workforce and the outsourcing of US factory jobs to foreign countries. Both groups have been forced to rely on the US welfare system to put food on the table and to have access to health care. Such dependence is associated with negative implications for both family structure and family well-being.[15] Overall, poverty affects the ability of Arabs and blacks to have access to affordable housing, seek higher education, improve their standard of living, and receive quality health care, including for chronic health conditions.[16]

Health Disparities

Both Arabs and blacks in the United States face significant "health disparities"—which are defined by public health scholars as the differences in health status, health environment, and access to quality health care, which lead certain populations to have poorer health outcomes than others.[17] Health disparities imply inequities—namely, that unequal, unjust, and unfair conditions lead to poorer health outcomes among racial and ethnic minority populations.[18] At the beginning of the new millennium, the US Institute of Medicine (IOM) issued a landmark report on health disparities called *Unequal Treatment*.[19] The report called on the US medical community to address this pressing public health issue. Yet, over the ensuing decade, health disparities have not been redressed in the United States, for either Arab or black populations.[20]

In terms of health environment, both Arabs and blacks tend to be concentrated in urban industrial centers, where they are exposed to environmental toxins through occupational exposures, higher ambient air pollution, and toxic waste disposal in their neighborhoods.[21] Urban food deserts, coupled with the oversupply of fast-food chains in poor neighborhoods, lead to nutritional deficiencies as well as obesity. Both Arabs and blacks currently suffer from the so-called epidemic of obesity in the United States, which is linked to other chronic health conditions, including diabetes, hypertension, stroke, and cardiovascular disease. Several recent studies of Arab refugees in the United States show that obesity is now a major problem, one that is associated with higher rates of diabetes and hypertension.[22] Studies have also shown that Arab immigrants and refugees are more likely to rate their health as "fair" or "poor"; this is especially true among Arab immigrants and refugees who do not speak English.[23]

Reproduction

Health disparities are also manifest in the area of reproduction. Major reproductive health disparities include higher rates of low–birth weight infants, neonatal and child mortality, reproductive infections and cancers (such as of the breast and cervix), and associated maternal mortality. Reproductive health disparities have been widely documented in black communities in the United States, as shown in a number of poignant ethnographic studies.[24] Infertility, too, is a well-documented health disparity in the black community, as shown in a National Institutes of Health (NIH) report on this subject.[25] Infertility may precipitate a social crisis for black men and women who are childless and whose very social identities may be determined by their ability to reproduce. For black men and women, "losing the option of procreating and parenting" because of infertility may be devastating.[26] In the only ethnographic study ever conducted on the experiences of infertility among black women, infertility was typically suffered in "silence and isolation," according to the study's author, Rosario Ceballo, a social psychologist at the University of Michigan.[27]

Infertility is also a devastating problem for Arab couples, who are culturally expected to have children early within marriage. For Arabs, both men and women, children are a source of social status. For Arab men in particular, social power is achieved through the birth of children, especially sons, who will perpetuate patrilineal kinship systems into the future. Thus, Arabs are pronatalist, deeming the birth of children to be a major social attribute and a source of joy.[28] Not surprisingly, Arab families in the United States have larger numbers of children in the household and younger age structures than the US population at large.[29]

This kind of pronatalism is also found in black communities in the United States, where the birth of children is highly valued, as are the contributions of children to family life.[30] Even in conditions of poverty, ethnographic studies show the degree to which black women prioritize their motherhood roles and strive to create better futures for their children.[31] The same can be said of many poor black fathers, who, when present, have been found to be more involved in the socialization and parenting of their children than are impoverished white fathers.[32]

Religion

Both Arabs and blacks may turn to their religions, be they Islam or Christianity, to make sense of their suffering, including when they are infertile. The

Islamic scriptures describe infertility as a God-given condition, thereby providing an edifying religious rationale for why some individuals are infertile while others go on to have sons or daughters.[33] However, alternative modes of family formation, including both child adoption and the use of reproductive third parties (for example, surrogates, sperm donors), are controversial in Islam, given that the known lineage of each child is considered a religious mandate. Without recourse to adoption or third-party reproductive assistance, infertile Arab Muslim couples generally have no other way of becoming parents except through medical treatment, which is encouraged in Islam as a religious obligation.[34]

In contrast, both adoption and fostering arrangements are allowed legally and religiously among most Christian communities, including the main denominations of the black church. However, in the sole ethnographic study of infertility among black Americans, neither legal nor informal adoption were popular solutions for childlessness, especially among husbands.[35] Instead, women who were interviewed spoke about their religious faith as the means by which they had endured their experiences and survived without children. Such religiously based coping has been described for other health conditions in the black community,[36] including for those suffering from HIV/AIDS.[37]

Health Care

Both Arabs and blacks may regard the US health care system with some degree of suspicion and distrust.[38] For Arabs, including recently arrived refugees, language barriers, illiteracy (in both English and Arabic), and lack of Western understandings of the body and its physiology may represent major barriers to negotiating health care, especially for those with little education or from rural areas.[39] Furthermore, many Arab women (and their husbands) may be uncomfortable receiving health care from a male physician because of cultural notions of modesty.[40]

For black patients, problems with the health care system may be different and may be related to a long history of racism documented within US medical care,[41] as reflected in the IOM *Unequal Treatment* report.[42] In the reproductive realm, black women may lack trust in their health care providers to deal with their reproductive complaints effectively and without prejudice.[43] Lack of trust is mirrored in other areas of high-tech medicine, including organ donation and the use of advance directives involving life support.[44]

Racism and Discrimination

Such distrust is clearly linked to general histories of racism and discrimination against both Arabs and blacks within US society. Although a long history of racial discrimination, negative stereotyping, racial/ethnic profiling, and hate crimes can be documented for both groups in the United States,[45] the events of September 11, 2001, reversed the generally assimilationist efforts of Arabs to "blend" into white US society as an "invisible" (and racially unmarked) ethnic minority population.[46] Today, both Arabs and blacks are vilified by a significant percentage of white Americans—as reflected in popular support for President Donald Trump, who stated his opposition to the rights of multiple minority groups during his presidential campaign.

Many Americans evidently regard Arab/Muslim and black men as particularly dangerous, untrustworthy, and oppressive. These stereotypes include images of male hypersexuality and hyperfertility. Arab/Muslim men are seen as polygamous fathers of children from multiple wives, harkening back to Western Orientalist fantasies of the harem.[47] Similarly, black men are often portrayed as "informal" polygamists, spawning offspring with multiple unmarried sexual partners (as well as spreading HIV/AIDS to them).[48] The very possibility that Arab and black men might be trustworthy, loving, law-abiding citizens—who may want to conceive and nurture children as responsible father figures[49]—seems to have eluded both the media and popular imagination. The result is deeply entrenched controlling images of Arab and black men that are difficult to overcome.

Although the "Black Lives Matter" movement has poignantly and powerfully begun to address the racial profiling and untimely deaths of young black men at the hands of a mostly white US law enforcement establishment,[50] no such movement has taken hold in American society to defend the rights of Arab/Muslim men, who have been under heightened law enforcement surveillance ever since 9/11.[51] Calls for a blanket "Muslim ban" in the post-ISIS era reflect the degree to which Muslim men are feared as potential "terrorists" by most Americans. It may not be an overstatement to claim that Muslim men are now *the* most feared minority group in American society—more feared for unpredictable terrorist violence than young black men are for everyday street violence and less trusted as rightful members of US society overall.

In short, both Arabs and blacks now experience the intersectional effects of oppression, including poverty, racism, discrimination, and vilifying stereotypes that make Arab men and black men seem unpredictably but inevitably dangerous. Sadly, Arabs now share with blacks their poor health status *and* the combination of fear and prejudice displayed by many white Americans. As I will argue in the next section, this fear also extends to reproduction—namely, the perceived threat that these disdained minority groups will over-populate America with too many "black and brown" babies.

Minority Infertility and Reproductive Racism

In America, Arabs and blacks are confronted by a not-so-subtle eugenic logic, in which their reproduction is condemned and they are prevented from using the "hope technologies" that allow white infertile couples to become loving parents.[52] As already noted, many white Americans see Arabs and blacks as being "hyperfertile" and undeserving of further children. Thus, in the United States, governmental health care subsidies have been focused heavily on *reducing* the fertility of minority and low-income populations, rather than improving their fertility. For blacks in particular, the focus on birth control over infertility treatment provides evidence of the ways in which black women's reproductive needs continue to be denigrated and ignored—one of many salient examples of what black legal scholar Dorothy Roberts calls the "killing of the Black body" throughout US history.[53] Indeed, Roberts argues that many public policies have deliberately punished black women precisely *for* having children.

It is not surprising, then, that public images of infertility hardly ever include black women, or any women of color (such as Latinas, Native Americans, or Arab Muslims).[54] For most Americans, the term *infertility* conjures up images of wealthy, white, well-educated couples seeking high-tech medical interventions. A skewed master narrative dominates perceptions of infertility in the United States, such that views of infertility are deeply inflected by race and class filters. Medical and social science scholars have helped to maintain and perpetuate this dominant narrative by conducting research with the most readily accessible study populations: namely, white economically privileged couples attending infertility treatment clinics.[55] This is true even among anthropologists. Of the five ethnographic volumes devoted to infertility and assisted conception in the United States, all have documented the struggles of white professional couples to become the parents of biologically related children.[56] As a result, ethnic minorities' experiences of infertility and its treatment in America—including their attempts to access IVF—are almost entirely missing from the anthropological record.[57]

Yet, as recognized by both the IOM and NIH, infertility prevalence rates are higher among ethnic minority populations and are part and parcel of the overall picture of health disparities that continue to plague minority communities in the United States.[58] In America, couples who are less well educated, lower income, and from underprivileged minority backgrounds are more likely to struggle with infertility, yet less likely to seek highly specialized medical services.[59] As shown in a number of national studies, acquiring medical services for infertility in the United States is associated with older age, a college education, a high income, and a Euro-American white racial background.[60] Even in Massachusetts, the state with the most comprehensive mandated insurance coverage for infertility and IVF, couples who seek infertility care tend to be highly educated, upper-middle class professionals, largely from Euro-American white backgrounds. In one study, 60 percent of patients attending an infertility clinic in Boston had annual household incomes over $100,000, compared with only 18 percent of the state's population overall.[61]

This well-documented US profile of highly prevalent minority infertility, coupled with starkly unequal access to treatment, represents a case par excellence of what medical anthropologists Faye Ginsburg and Rayna Rapp, following Shelee Colen, have defined as stratified reproduction—or "the arrangements by which some reproductive futures are valued while others are despised."[62] In US society, fertility is valued differently according to race and class. Accordingly, ethnic minority populations' fertility desires are marginalized; their infertility and accompanying suffering remain invisible; and the barriers they face in gaining access to appropriate infertility care index the unwantedness of their babies. Such stratified reproduction has been critically questioned by black feminist scholars Nsiah-Jefferson and Hall:

> Members of minority communities have an equal or even greater need for programs to treat infertility, but . . . these needs have not been defined as a legitimate concern and . . . treatments are generally not available to low-income women, who are disproportionately nonwhite. Going beyond this clear mismatch between the needs and services available, the . . . issue for low-income women and women of color comes down to the social construction of infertility as a "social problem." Why have the infertility problems of minority communities been ignored?[63]

The very invisibility of minority infertility—not only in infertility scholarship, media representations, and infertility clinics but in the social construction of the infertility "problem" itself—bespeaks not only stratified reproduction but outright *reproductive racism* in American society. Racist assumptions about the hyperfertility of minority populations serve to justify the invisibility of minority infertility and its treatment. Such reproductive racism affects both Arabs and blacks and is especially devastating given the high value placed on parenthood and children in both of these minority communities. Although Arab and black women may carry the greatest social burden of infertility when they lack the visible signs of pregnancy, Arab and black men, too, may suffer over their own infertility and childlessness, particularly because infertility and impotency are popularly conflated and paternity may be seen as bound to manhood.[64]

In short, infertile Arabs and blacks in the United States are members of what medical sociologist Sarah Franklin calls the "rising reproductive underclass."[65] Arabs and blacks face unequal access to infertility treatment, especially because IVF is notoriously expensive. Indeed, as we will see in the next section, America is the most expensive place in the world to make a test-tube baby.

IVF and Unequal Treatment

The history of IVF in the United States has been well documented.[66] Namely, after the birth of Louise Brown, the world's first IVF baby, in England in 1978, IVF began to be practiced in the United States in the early 1980s, with the birth of America's first IVF baby, Elizabeth Jordan Carr, in 1981. A decade later, in 1992, the Fertility Clinic Success Rate and Certification Act (FCSRCA) was passed, charging the CDC with the major task of collecting IVF clinical data on an annual basis. Since then, this mandatory CDC surveillance system has documented the increasing number of IVF clinics in the country, the number of IVF cycles performed annually, and each clinic's overall success rates.

In 2013, the period covered by the last published CDC report, there were 467 American IVF clinics reporting to the CDC. Together, these clinics performed 160,521 IVF cycles, resulting in 53,252 live births and 66,691 infants (including twins and higher-order multiples). Exactly 33 percent, or one-third, of all IVF cycles performed that year resulted in the birth of at least one "take-home baby."[67] Furthermore, these babies represented 1.6 percent of all infants born in the United States in 2013, including 18.7 percent of all multiple births (twins, triplets, and higher).[68]

Although these numbers may seem impressive, the fact remains that only about half of all infertile American couples needing reproductive assistance are able to seek medical help, and less than one-quarter (22 percent) actually obtain it.[69] Ever since the beginning of IVF in the United States, so-called unmet demand for IVF remains high.[70] It is estimated that only about 25 percent of the "optimal" number of IVF cycles are being performed annually in the United States,[71] given that approximately 1,500 couples per million population are infertile and in need of reproductive assistance.[72]

So why do relatively few infertile Americans obtain IVF services? The answer is cost. In 2002, when the first study of the health economics of IVF was conducted, the mean cost of a single IVF cycle in the United States was $9,547—or nearly one-third of the average per capita income in the United States that year, which was only $33,360.[73] Five years on, the mean cost of an IVF cycle had increased almost 25 percent to $12,513. This figure is more than three times the global average of $3,518 per IVF cycle and nearly double the cost of IVF in Hong Kong, which at $6,361 per cycle is the second most expensive country in the world.[74] Beyond cost per cycle, the actual cost of making a test-tube baby in the United States is much higher, at $41,132 per live birth. This is because IVF often requires costly repetition to achieve a successful pregnancy.[75]

Unlike Israel or most Western European countries, where IVF cycles are subsidized for infertile citizens as part of national health care plans, the United States offers no such IVF coverage. Fifteen US states have passed laws mandating that IVF services be offered to infertile couples, but only eight of those states provide mandatory IVF insurance coverage.[76] These so-called "mandate states" cluster on the East Coast, and include Connecticut, Massachusetts, Maryland, New Jersey, and Rhode Island. Massachusetts is by far the most generous mandate state, funding an unlimited number of IVF cycles for infertile Massachusetts residents.[77] Arkansas, Hawaii, and Illinois also mandate insurance coverage for IVF, but the coverage in both Arkansas and Hawaii is quite limited. Thus, in reality, insurance covers the costs of IVF in only six US states, five of them on the East Coast corridor, in addition to the state of Illinois. In most states, including Michigan, infertile patients must pay for IVF out of pocket, at the average cost of $12,513 per cycle.

In this private, fee-for-service IVF landscape, American couples may find it very difficult to afford IVF, even those coming from the middle class. However, high unmet demand for IVF is most apparent among disadvantaged minority populations, who have much lower rates of IVF utilization.[78] Although mandate states such as Massachusetts provide equal treatment for minority couples, the hidden costs of IVF—such as the need for transportation and days lost from work—prevent many poor minority couples from having access to IVF services.[79] Furthermore, the passage of the Affordable Care Act (ACA), also known as Obamacare, did little to ameliorate ethnic and racial disparities in IVF access.[80] Under Obamacare, IVF and all related reproductive technologies were considered ineligible for insurance coverage because they were considered "elective" procedures for a non–life-threatening condition. In short, even Obamacare did nothing to help infertile minority couples achieve their parenthood dreams—which is sadly ironic, given how much the nation's first black president has clearly cherished his fatherhood role.

Infertility Struggles in Arab Detroit

Given this overall scenario, it should come as no surprise that infertile couples in Arab Detroit can rarely afford the costs of IVF. Arab couples' inability to pay for IVF is usually heartbreaking for them because most Arab couples ardently desire children soon after marriage. It is important to reemphasize how much parenthood is valued in Arab societies. It is viewed as the route to full adult personhood, as the ingredient for happiness and commitment within a marriage, as the key to social acceptance in the community, and as the only guaranteed path to future immortality. Children are treasured and beloved by their Arab mothers as well as their Arab fathers. Arab parents generally extoll the virtues of their children as the absolute joys of their life, their very reasons for living. Thus, the inability to conceive a desired child represents a major reproductive blow, a source of great anguish and existential pain. Saad and Hala, a young couple whose families had fled from southern Lebanon and who had subsequently met and married in Arab Detroit, articulated the heartache of their infertility struggle.

Saad and Hala

Saad and Hala were still in their mid-twenties when I met them, but they were already experiencing the devastation of infertility. Saad was one of the only men in my study who had graduated from college. But his bachelor's degree in biology from a Jordanian university had done little to help him secure a good job in the local Arab Detroit labor market. Although he was not a blue-collar worker, Saad held a low-wage position as a bank teller, earning less than $19,000 a year.

Like most of the men in my study, Saad was infertile, deeming his condition to be "from God" and thus beyond his individual control. "Definitely, I can feel like it's a problem; because I'm a man, and especially because of the Arab nature, it's difficult to accept," Saad explained to me. "But after that, I thought about why this is happening, and I decided that God chose me to be like this. From that religious viewpoint, it's a test for me, and hopefully I'll be patient and faithful."

Although Saad's religious beliefs provided solace, he still felt that he needed children, a conviction shared by Hala. I asked them about their ideal number of children, and they were adamant about the virtues of a large family:

> SAAD: I'd like a lot! Six or more.
>
> MARCIA: Really?
>
> SAAD: Yeah, we love kids. Both of us, we love kids. And we're planning to have kids.
>
> HALA: We come from big families. Actually, they're seven, and we're ten—five girls and five boys. And I'm the same as my mom; I like kids.
>
> SAAD: I like a big family! To teach them, to send them to school. One doctor, one lawyer, one engineer, and one detective to work with the government. And for the girls, one pharmacist and one doctor.
>
> MARCIA: Wow!
>
> SAAD: I'm serious! That's what we're planning. I love kids.

At this point, Saad went on to describe why children are important to all Arabs:

> Arabs are more joined to their families than anywhere else. That's the Arab nature. You love your kids, your nephews and nieces and cousins' kids. You *relate* with them. You love your own kids more than your nephews, but you love your nephews more than your neighbor's kids. You feel much more for those who are related to you. That's why, when you've got a bigger family, you count on your kids. If you only have two kids, they will always be busy. But if you have seven

> kids, you will find someone to take care of you. This is a strong reason to have a great big family, all helping each other.
>
> Kids also make a marriage stay. Even if you want to keep your life together, you don't want to come home to an empty house. Kids will make it [a marriage] more related, more joined, something to do together. We love each other, but in the Arab nature, it's something very important, in Arab life. When you see your children growing up, you will say, 'This is the result of our marriage. They're growing up side by side.' If any two people get married, this is what Arabs want. I have a [non-Arab] female manager at my bank, and she says she never wanted kids. She preferred to have a dog. A dog is not giving her a hard time like a kid, where if it's sick, she has to take it to the doctor. But here, and in the Middle East, you get married to have a family. The children, that's why you're getting married. To make a family, to have kids.
>
> If you don't have kids, there will be pressure—*very much* pressure! It will start from yourself, and then people will ask you, 'Three, four years, and you don't have children?' They feel like it's a problem in your personality. You can't tell them that you're trying to solve it, but it didn't work. They're going to talk to you about the reason, what happened, why it happened, and so on. Honestly, if you don't have kids, you're willing to try anything!

In Saad and Hala's case, "trying anything" meant taking out a $10,000 bank loan to fund a single cycle of IVF (actually ICSI, as Saad was the infertile partner). Saad's Blue Cross Blue Shield insurance did not cover the costs of ICSI, except for the most basic blood work. Together, Saad and Hala described their decision to take out a bank loan, and the ICSI cycle that followed, in this way:

> SAAD: We *tried* to do something. In Islam, we're encouraged to try all the possible medical solutions. So we did in vitro fertilization [technically ICSI]. She had nine eggs, but one died. After the sperm injection [into the eggs], six lived. Then we took two [embryos], and the other four died before they could be frozen. They were dead. But, with the two left, we did in vitro fertilization. After a month, three weeks after in vitro, the other two [embryos] died in the uterus. So the pregnancy test was negative. To be honest, this made me feel really bad, because we're young and healthy, so this shouldn't fail! It's pretty depressing, in fact. We just found out last week, and now we need to get away from here because we told everybody she's pregnant, and now she's not. How

are we going to tell everyone she's not? I just want to forget about what happened! Everything was going good, and she was doing the blood tests two times a week. And actually, before we did the surgery [ICSI], we thought she was going to be pregnant, 99 percent! That's why we were surprised when they told us she's not pregnant. This is a real surprise for me! And we told people she was pregnant, but not that we are doing surgery [ICSI].

HALA: When I was taking the medicines [hormonal stimulants], I felt the same thing as pregnancy. I was throwing up, and my family said, "It looks like you're pregnant." And we said, "Okay."

SAAD: So the question we have is: Why these two babies—these two eggs, two zygotes—why didn't they attach to the uterus? We're very young, healthy, and had two good-looking embryos. So why didn't they attach?

MARCIA: Well, for any given IVF cycle, the success rate is less than 40 percent.

SAAD: But the doctor gave us self-confidence, like we can get pregnant 100 percent.

MARCIA: Well, the chances increase if you do repeated cycles.

SAAD: But that depends on money. It's the cost, mostly, the first factor you can think about.

HALA: It cost $10,000. I was happy to spend this, but after what happened . . .

SAAD: Now, to be honest with you, I can't raise this kind of money. My two concerns are: first, the money, and second, my wife. The procedure we've gone through, it's not that easy of a procedure. It has lots of physical effects. I don't get hurt from them. The only thing I have to do is taking sperm [through masturbation]. But she takes medicines, and they take the eggs from her through surgery. So I feel sorry that my wife has to go through that. That's my major concern, more than the money. But now, probably because of the money, we can't do it again. To tell you the truth, the doctor deducted a couple of thousand [dollars]. He helped us, to be honest. But I don't know if he can do that again.

HALA: I told Saad, when they told me I'm not pregnant, "I feel like something has taken me up, up, up, and now I've just been pushed down, down, down." I feel heartbroken.

SAAD: I feel *really* sorry that the two [embryos] are dead. You really feel like they're your babies, that this is something really related to you, because they are a *part* of you.

HALA: But I told Saad to just keep it between us. It's a *private* part of our life. We can't tell our families what happened, because it's top secret.

MARCIA: Why is that?

SAAD: Because of the Arab nature, we haven't told anybody, even our families. It's the Arab nature to have a big mouth. First, they will look at an in vitro baby differently. They will look at the child badly—even more than they will look at me [badly for being infertile]. I don't have a problem to tell anyone, "This is because of me. This is my [infertility] problem." But everyone will look at me badly. My family will look at me sadly. Others will say, "Blah, blah, blah . . . they can't have babies." And they'll feel sorry for my wife.

HALA: That's why we're going to keep it secret.

SAAD: In the Arab community here in Dearborn, they need to have a more open mind, so that we can say everything with no shame.

MARCIA: What do you think you'll do next?

SAAD: Wait—that's all we can do. But even if I can somehow make the money, the second one [ICSI] will be hard. God forbid it fails; then what? It's better to have no kids, instead of just giving money to a doctor for nothing. *We* are the ones who will suffer.

HALA: I used to work part-time in a day care. When you're in your twenties, you have more energy to take care of little kids. So this is why we want to have babies when we're young. You don't want to be old and have back pain and hypertension. At that point, you'll need someone to take care of you! When you're young, you have more energy and patience. But I quit this work to have my *own* children. I went through all that, and Saad helped me, but now there's nothing. No money and no children.

War Stories of Male Infertility

Sadly, Saad and Hala's story was fairly typical of the couples I met, all of whom were struggling to make a baby. Moreover, most of the infertility problems stemmed from husbands like Saad. Although infertility is popularly construed as a female reproductive health problem, more than half of all cases of infertility worldwide involve a so-called male factor. This is especially true in the Arab world, where at least 60 to 70 percent of all cases presenting to IVF clinics involve male infertility.[81] Male infertility entails four distinct conditions: oligozoospermia (low sperm count), asthenozoospermia (poor sperm motility, or movement), teratozoospermia (poor sperm morphology, or shape), and azoospermia (total lack of sperm in the ejaculate, although sperm may be present inside the testicles). Sometimes these conditions co-occur; for example, a man may have oligoasthenozoospermia (low sperm count and poor motility).

Male infertility problems are often genetic in origin, involving microscopic deletions of the Y chromosome. These kinds of male infertility problems are neither preventable nor curable, and they are chronic, lasting over the course of a man's lifetime. In the Middle East, these genetically based forms of male infertility are widespread, probably due to cultural practices of consanguineous (cousin) marriage, which results in a significantly increased risk for genetic defects.[82] Among Arab men, behavioral factors may also be linked to male infertility, especially consumption of tobacco, the ingredients of which are toxic to sperm.[83] Although Saad had never been a smoker, fifteen of the infertile men in my study were heavy smokers, either in the past or in the present. Three had been told by physicians to quit smoking to improve their sperm profiles, but only four had managed to do so. One two-pack-a-day smoker, who had been smoking since his youth in Lebanon sixteen years earlier, told me, "I think I should quit. I know it's no good for me. But I *like* smoking." Similarly, an Iraqi refugee, who had once been a prisoner of war, had developed a two- to three-pack-a-day smoking habit, which had lasted for twenty-nine years. "There is no way for me to quit," he said, "because I love it. I will only stop smoking when I die."

For these men, who had been exposed to war, war-related stress (and subsequent coping mechanisms such as smoking) or toxins in the environment could have negatively affected their fertility. Public health reports from Lebanon provide ample evidence of the negative impact of war-related exposures on men's fertility profiles, especially lowered sperm counts.[84] Similarly, chemicals used in the wars in Iraq, including DU, may have posed harm to men's reproductive health, as shown in a long-term study of British veterans from the First Gulf War, who had higher rates of infertility and longer periods to conception.[85] As the British study authors opined, "Theoretically at least, exposure to toxicants of the type present in the Gulf war could affect spermatogenesis, which might be observed as increased levels of infertility."[86]

These "war stories" of male infertility certainly played out in my own study, where forty-three of the men, or more than three-quarters (76 percent), were infertile, most having fled the wars in Lebanon and Iraq. *Il harb*, "the war," was frequently mentioned by my interlocutors as a possible cause of their male infertility problems, with most men mentioning exposure to toxic chemicals. Men in my study knew if they were infertile because all of them had undergone semen testing. Few of them understood the exact cause of their condition, yet most accepted the validity of their diagnosis, especially after multiple semen tests. Outside of the doctor's office, however, few men spoke about their condition, even to family members. In Arab Detroit, male infertility diagnoses were shrouded in secrecy, mostly out of fear of community response. A Lebanese man, who disagreed with this level of secrecy, had this to say: "No one knows about it. I don't know if she told her mother, because she's close to her. Personally, I haven't told anyone, but I wouldn't mind telling. I mean, why not? It's not a big deal. It's not under my control, because it's a physical problem. It won't make me less male or more male. But for some men, it's a matter of pride."

Despite this man's attempt to normalize male infertility as a simple medical condition, feelings of emasculation were prominent for other men, especially at the time of initial diagnosis. One Lebanese man, who had just learned the results of his semen test, told me with great emotion, "I just lost my manhood with that test!" In general, semen test results usually came as a great shock to infertile men, who had always assumed that they could impregnate a woman. Many men described overwhelming sadness, a few of them admitting that they had cried when they learned the bad news.

At IVF Michigan, I spent many hours talking to these devastated infertile men, who poured out their heartache and embodied misery to me. Two brief interview vignettes—one from a short, athletic Iraqi refugee man named Ahmed, and the other from Adnan, whose family had fled from Lebanon to South America before arriving in Arab Detroit—portray the negative outcomes that male infertility may have on a man's sense of masculinity and normality.

Ahmed

When I met Ahmed, the first words out of his mouth were, "I have a problem. I need 'planting' [a colloquial term for IVF and ICSI], but I don't have the money and no insurance." He then went on to tell me about his recent semen analysis. "I was scared maybe something was wrong, so I took my wife to the doctor downstairs, and we found out she's okay," he explained. "Then I did the test for me, and something is wrong. It was watery [the semen], and most of the sperm died, and the [sperm] activity was low. This is my first time back [to the doctor's office]. I'm just by myself today. The doctor will take another test, then I will decide what to do." I then asked Ahmed how he was handling his recent diagnosis:

AHMED: When I found out, I was a little sad. I wasn't feeling good. I'm not like anybody else. I don't feel like other men. I'm different. I feel it just that way. I'm feeling nervous all the time, acting like this, acting like that, and maybe yelling at my wife. But afterward, I talked to my wife to forgive me, because something is wrong with me. She understands, and she's okay. She's sad, but actually she's upset for me.

MARCIA: Do you have any idea about the cause [of the infertility]?

AHMED: Actually, I never thought about it. I know that in the Middle East, there are men just like me, maybe because of the war. But my father and my mother, they have eleven kids, and I see myself, with not even one.

MARCIA: Have you told them about your problem?

AHMED: No, not yet. Not even my brothers, or my friends. And I decided that if I get no kids at all, then I will say it [about the male infertility]. But first, I'm going to try, and *insha'Allah* [God willing], I hope I will get some.

MARCIA: So, you're going to keep it a secret until then?

AHMED: If I tell them, I don't think people will look at me like I'm a person. Especially in our community, if you say, "How are you?," the second question is, "How are your kids?" It's not like American lives, believe me! They embarrass you, too. Some of them won't say it on purpose, but some will. It's about manhood, about being made to feel different. That's why men don't talk about it.

MARCIA: But there are lots of infertile men.

AHMED: I understand that, but I never see them—other infertile men! If I would see them, then I would say, "Cool!"

Adnan

Whereas Ahmed knew no other infertile men, Adnan had an infertile older brother. Both Adnan and his brother suffered from azoospermia, a serious male infertility problem that is probably genetic in nature.[87] Diagnosed years earlier, Adnan had much to say about how azoospermia had changed his reproductive and sexual life, as well as his relationship with his wife:

MARCIA: When you learned about the azoospermia, how did it affect you?

ADNAN: It affected me, oh yeah! In many ways. The sense of being less of a man than you thought you were, a kind of shame, or like something secret came out in your body. It surprises you, and you yourself, you're not expecting it, and it's something shocking! Even though in my family, I was always thinner, shorter, and sick a lot, and I always felt I'm not big enough, I wasn't expecting this when I got married.

MARCIA: So you had no idea?

ADNAN: No, I had no idea, and yeah, I was shocked. My older brother, he told me much later that he's azoospermic. My brother always wanted children, and he never had them. But it helped me a lot, talking with him. It helped me to not feel less of a man, or weak. You also feel that you disappoint your woman. She looks at you like you're less than what she expected. But my wife never *ever* made me feel that way. It's my *own* feeling. You feel like you have to do something *for* your partner—a surgery, or a treatment, or *something*! I have a lot of respect for my wife because she sacrificed her maternity for me.

MARCIA: Has she ever said that to you, that she made this sacrifice for you?

ADNAN: No, I always thought she might be feeling this, but she never said it. But the other thing, maybe it's positive, because my sperm don't come out, maybe that's the reason why I'm so *sexual*, and why I think about sex a lot, *not* to compensate, but in my case, I'm always "hot." My sperm are not being released, and so they have to be absorbed in my body.[88] So I'm very sexual. Friends at my age are beginning to have sexual problems, and I wonder when it will happen to me, but nothing so far. So, that's the good thing; this problem made me a better lover for my wife.

MARCIA: I'm sure she appreciates that!

ADNAN: Well, if I could only get her pregnant, then all of these feelings of mine will disappear!

As seen in both Ahmed's and Adnan's cases, infertile men in my study often had complicated feelings about their reproductive health problems. Yet, even men like Adnan, with little hope of conception, continued to search for a solution to their dire infertility problems.

As I would discover in Arab Detroit, men were often willing to subject their reproductive bodies to a wide variety of diagnostic tests, including repeated semen analysis, genetic testing, and painful testicular biopsies and aspirations. On the therapeutic front, infertile men also put their reproductive bodies on the line. During my study period, for example, a clinical trial was being undertaken to determine whether female hormonal therapies could be used to improve sperm quality. Men were told about the hormones' potential side effects, including gynecomastia, or the swelling of male breast tissue. Yet, several men in my study were willing to enroll in the clinical trial and were especially happy that the expensive hormones, called Profasi and Pergonal, were being given out for free.

Men's treatment seeking was not limited to IVF Michigan. In many cases, men had visited other doctors, especially urologists, who had advised them to undergo a genital surgery called "varicocelectomy." Varicocelectomies involve the removal of "varicoceles," which are abnormal enlargements of the veins in the scrotum. A varicocelectomy strips the scrotum of these varicose veins, purportedly improving male fertility in the process.[89] Because at least 40 percent of infertile men have ultrasound-confirmed varicoceles, varicocelectomies are the most common male infertility surgery. Yet, the efficacy of varicocelectomy as a "cure" for male infertility is hotly debated. Most infertility specialists do not believe that this surgery is effective; thus, the WHO no longer supports it as a treatment for male infertility.[90] Still, the operation continues to be performed around the world, including in the Middle East, where urologists make a handsome profit.

Not surprisingly, eight men in my study had undergone varicocelectomies, including four Yemeni men who had done the surgery back in Yemen. The other four men had undertaken varicocelectomies in the United States, often paying dearly in the process. For example, a Palestinian man, who had left Ramallah when he was seventeen and who described himself as "lower middle class," explained that he was still paying for his $4,000 varicocelectomy, on top of his many other medical bills. The varicocelectomy, he said, was his choice. "Actually, when we went to the doctor, he told us, 'If you go and do the surgery, it's probably not going to solve the problem.' He was up front with us. He was a urologist, and he was honest with us. But it was a process of elimination. We don't know what is causing my problem, so we said, 'Let's do it,' even though it was hard, and I'm paying for it now." In addition to the expense, varicocelectomies can cause complications, as one Lebanese man discovered. After the varicocelectomy, there was no improvement in his low sperm count, but his sperm motility plummeted to zero.

As is clear from these vignettes, infertile Arab men in my study suffered physically, mentally, and financially in the process of diagnosing and solving their infertility problems. Still, they persevered, demonstrating a high degree of what I characterize as *male reproductive agency.* I saw Arab men taking action to improve their reproductive health, a form of agency that is rarely portrayed in anthropological studies of reproduction or in studies of Arab men in general.[91] Yet the infertile Arab men in my study were uniformly willing to take responsibility for their infertility, to make difficult reproductive decisions with and for the wives they loved, to embody the reproductive discomforts of diagnosis and treatment, and to resort to all possible therapies to improve their chances of conception. Their male reproductive agency was replete with love and sacrifice. Many of the men I met said that they were doing this "for her"—for the wives they cherished, but for whom they felt great sympathy, as women who had been deprived of motherhood.

I came to think of these men's physically complicated, emotional struggles to overcome their infertility as men's *war stories of male infertility.* War stories were not just about Arab men's exposures to war. They were about Arab men fighting on many fronts to conquer their infertility. These battles entailed emotional pain, embodied trauma, emasculation, shame, secrecy, and stigma. Being an infertile man was, in effect, being at war with one's own body—using a variety of medical armaments in the difficult battle to become a fertile father.

ICSI—A Masculine Hope Technology?

For those men fighting to overcome their infertility, ICSI was their masculine "hope technology"[92]—their only chance to overcome their childlessness. It is important to begin by explaining why ICSI is the only option for infertile Arab men. Sperm donation—the only other solution for male infertility, one that has been used in the United States for over a century[93]—has been, and continues to be, widely prohibited across the Muslim world, from Morocco to Malaysia.[94] Sperm donation is religiously equated with genealogical confusion, mistaken paternity, and illicit sexuality, and is thus widely refused by Muslim men, who argue that a sperm-donor child "won't be my son."[95] Similarly, legal adoption as it is practiced in the West—where a child takes the adoptive father's surname, can legally inherit from him, and is treated as if he or she is a biological child—is also prohibited for reasons of genealogical confusion and patrilineal impurity.[96] In the absence of sperm donation and child adoption, infertile Muslim men are left with few other avenues to fatherhood other than to try to conceive using their own sperm.

The introduction of ICSI was thus a watershed event in the Muslim world.[97] As a variant of IVF, ICSI solves the problem of male infertility in a way that IVF cannot. With standard IVF, spermatozoa are removed from a man's body through masturbatory ejaculation, and oocytes (eggs) are surgically removed from a woman's ovaries following hormonal stimulation. Once these male and female gametes are retrieved, they are introduced to each other in a petri dish in an IVF laboratory, in the hopes of fertilization taking place. However, "weak" sperm (that is, low numbers, poor movement, misshapen) are poor fertilizers. Through "micromanipulation" of otherwise infertile sperm under a high-powered microscope, they can be injected directly into human oocytes, effectively "forcing" fertilization to occur. As long as one viable spermatozoon can be extracted from an infertile man's body, it can be "ICSI-injected" into an oocyte, leading to the potential creation of a human embryo. With ICSI, then, otherwise "sterile" men can father biogenetic offspring. This includes azoospermic men like Adnan, who produce no sperm in their ejaculate and must therefore have their testicles painfully aspirated or biopsied in the search for sperm. In other words, ICSI gives even the most seriously infertile man a chance of producing a test-tube baby.

Just as IVF was the new hope technology for infertile women when it was introduced in England in 1978,[98] ICSI became the new *masculine hope technology* when it was introduced in Belgium in 1991. Entering the Middle East through Egypt in 1994, ICSI spread rapidly, leading to a virtual "coming out" of male infertility cases across the Arab world.[99] Nearly twenty-five years later, ICSI continues to be used widely in the Middle East, as elsewhere. Today, ICSI has replaced IVF as the world's leading assisted reproductive technology. Whereas IVF leaves fertilization up to chance, ICSI does not. Thus, ICSI provides a more guaranteed way of creating "the elusive embryo."[100]

This dramatic increase in ICSI cycles worldwide has come under recent scrutiny. Following a global survey of assisted reproductive technologies undertaken from 2008 through 2010, Professor Hans Evers, the editor-in-chief of the major European journal *Human Reproduction*, questioned the global overuse of ICSI, calling this trend "disturbing":

> Notwithstanding the fact that it has been shown over and over again that IVF gives better results than ICSI in couples with non-male infertility, we perform

> too much ICSI: on average about twice as many ICSI cycles are initiated as IVF. The incidence of severe male infertility cannot explain this discrepancy. I was puzzled by this finding, however I was dumbfounded by the regional differences. In Asia "only" 1.4 times as much ICSI as IVF is performed, in North America 2.7 as much, in South America 6 times as much, and in the Middle East even 60 (yes, sixty) times as much . . . It's not like the "therapeutic illusion" of old: the patient who will get better without treatment will also do so with treatment. No, this treatment hurts a couple's chances. In the three years under review, ICSI on faulty indications has prevented at least 25,000 couples from getting pregnant.[101]

In other words, in female infertility cases, ICSI fertilization may actually lower a couple's chances of conception. In addition, ICSI entails at least six major challenges for infertile men and their wives. First, the precisely timed collection of semen can produce deep anxiety and even impotence in some men but is imperative for all ICSI procedures. Second, some azoospermic men produce no spermatozoa whatsoever, even within their testicles, eliminating ICSI as an option. Third, ICSI may not succeed, leading to endless rounds of fruitless repetition among those couples who can afford it. Fourth, ICSI involves a grueling surgical procedure, which is highly dependent on the complicated hormonal stimulation and transvaginal extraction of healthy oocytes from women's ovaries. Fifth, whereas the fertility of older men can be salvaged through ICSI, women's fertility is highly age sensitive, with egg quality declining at later stages of the reproductive life cycle. Thus, women in their late thirties and early forties may have "aged out" of ICSI, causing highly gendered, life-course disruptions surrounding women's "biological clocks."[102] Finally, for men, ICSI may succeed after years of other failed treatment options. However, when it does succeed, ICSI may perpetuate genetic defects into future generations, by causing the same sperm defects (and other inherited disorders) carried by infertile men to be passed to their male offspring. The ethics of passing genetic mutations to children—and especially conceiving future generations of infertile male offspring through ICSI—has been a significant cause for concern.[103]

Despite these major challenges, more than 5 million "miracle babies" have now been born around the world via assisted reproductive technologies,[104] and at least a half million of them are ICSI babies. ICSI is men's hope technology, creating the only hope for infertile Muslim men, who are barred from other avenues to fatherhood. In my study, infertile men described ICSI as their "last hope," and their way of "keeping hope" alive for the future. For men with severe infertility problems, ICSI was described as a "last resort" or a "last chance," given that no other treatments were available.

Yet, in Arab Detroit, ICSI hopes conflicted directly with men's abject poverty. ICSI was costly, including at IVF Michigan, where the price list reflected the national averages—namely, $150 for an office visit; $1,600 for bloodwork and ultrasounds; $1,200 for testicular aspiration; $2,500 to $4,000 for hormonal medications; and $8,100 for the ICSI procedure itself, including the surgical egg retrieval, the ICSI fertilization process, and the transfer of the fertilized embryos back into a woman's uterus. When taken together, a cycle of ICSI could cost well over $12,500, and as much as $15,000, a price that very few men in the study could possibly afford. Substantial "discounts" on ICSI were sometimes offered as a form of *zakat*, or Islamic charity, by the sympathetic Lebanese IVF physician. However, in most cases, a "discount" of $2,000 on the ICSI procedure meant that couples still owed more than $10,000 for a single cycle.

Medical insurance did little to cover these ICSI costs. Most Iraqi men in my study had refugee entitlements to some form of health insurance,[105] either Blue Cross Blue Shield through their employers, Aetna insurance provided by the US government for Iraqis who had served as translators during the Iraq War, Medicaid for some unemployed or disabled Iraqi refugees, or, in two cases in my study, Wayne County health insurance for a state employee and a small business owner. However, most of the Lebanese, Yemeni, and Palestinian men in the study were entirely uninsured, some having lost their insurance with unemployment. Yet, even among the insured men, ICSI costs were rarely reimbursed. For example, only four men in the study were able to recover any ICSI costs and then only for their wives' blood work.

In short, with or without health insurance, men in Arab Detroit had to fund their own ICSI cycles. Not surprisingly then, the barriers to ICSI access were overwhelming. Given the hard lives described in Chapter 2, severe economic constraints impinged on these men's abilities to afford ICSI, a problem that they routinely lamented in conversations about the high costs of treatment. Without working wives, most men were responsible for all of their medical bills. Most men did not own credit cards, nor could they defer payments through a layaway plan. Virtually all financial transactions at IVF Michigan were handled in cash, which was exchanged over the counter at the end of clinic visits.

As one Iraqi refugee put it matter-of-factly, "Money is the problem . . . The doctor gave us a discount and said it [ICSI] will cost only $7,000. But I don't have even $100. What can we do?" Similarly, a Lebanese man, who had been unable to accrue the money for ICSI over his five years of marriage, explained, "The problem has been money. I haven't been able to pay. Three years ago, it was $12,000. Right now, it is $15,000, even though he [the doctor] mentioned a study, so the price would be reduced. I was planning to put it on a credit card, but the total cost is still way too much."

As I got to know these men through repeated visits to the clinic, I watched initial hopes for ICSI fade into deep demoralization. Over time, many men came to realize that conceiving a biological child was unlikely without some sort of financial miracle. Among the total group of forty-three infertile men in my study, only twenty-eight ICSI cycles were initiated—but twenty-two of these cycles were undertaken by a small group of six couples with access to greater financial means (usually through small family businesses and family aid). Only six other men, including Saad, had managed to undertake an ICSI cycle. These six men had either taken out a bank loan, borrowed money from friends and family, sold their wives' bridal gold or family land back in the "home country," or put the entire cost of ICSI onto a credit card, going deep into debt in the process. Even after all of this, only two of the twenty-eight ICSI cycles resulted in the birth of children. Both of them were ICSI sons, born to Iraqi refugee fathers.

On Arab and Black Fatherhood

To summarize, then, infertile men in Arab Detroit uniformly desired children in their marriages and were more than willing to undertake ICSI to solve their infertility problems. But the vast majority of them were poor and were prohibited from accessing ICSI due to its high cost. As members of an ethnic minority population living economically and socially marginal lives in the United States, infertile Arab men and their wives faced significant disparities in access to affordable infertility care. Even though they had bypassed cultural barriers by choosing an Arabic-speaking Lebanese American Muslim IVF physician, who respected their religious and cultural beliefs and would not discriminate against them as fellow Arabs, these couples could nonetheless not take full advantage of the clinic's infertility services, by virtue of their absolute poverty.

In this regard, poor infertile couples in Arab Detroit share their structural position with poor infertile blacks in the city. The sole study of infertility among black women in southeastern Michigan showed the degree to which racially based income disparities effectively barred their access to treatment.[106] In Detroit then, both of these minority groups clearly experienced the effects of stratified reproduction, including poverty, lack of access to affordable, high-quality reproductive health care, and ongoing reproductive racism.

As seen in this chapter, reproductive racism extends particularly perniciously to both Arab and black men, who have been vilified as dangerous, untrustworthy "Others" in American society. These controlling images—and the racial profiling that results—are at significant odds with a vision of Arab and black men as loving husbands and fathers. Yet, this is what mattered most to the Arab men in my study. Having found refuge in America, they were now struggling to create new lives—including test-tube baby lives—to achieve their most cherished dreams of fatherhood.

4 What They Feel

Reproductive Exile between Moral Worlds

Reproductive Exile

So far in this book, we have heard the stories of several Iraqi refugees—Fatima and Sadiq, Kamal, Ali, Ibrahim, and Ahmed—as well as the stories of Lebanese men and women—Mahmoud, Mayada, Saad and Hala, and Adnan—who had fled to Arab Detroit to escape the wars in their home countries. Few of the Iraqis were willing or able to return to Iraq, even though many still had family members, including elderly parents, who were caught in the ongoing conflagration. Similarly, many of the Lebanese Shia who had fled from southern Lebanon were afraid to return, even though the Israeli army had ended its occupation in May 2000 and the country had begun to experience a rebirth with the homecomings of its far-flung diaspora. Unfortunately, the Valentine's Day assassination of Prime Minister Rafik Haririi in 2005, followed by the six-week summer war between Israel and Hezbollah in 2006, led to the deaths of thousands of Lebanese civilians and devastated the southern Lebanese countryside to the very edges of Beirut. A woman whose family home was severely damaged in the summer war had this to say:

> I'm from the South, not the extreme South. But last summer the Israeli Army was there [in southern Lebanon], and there were only a couple of places where they did not come. And even our home was damaged. And not just us—our neighbors, everyone! So I'm so scared to go back. Maybe if it was *absolutely*

> necessary to see my parents or to stay with them for a while. But for any other reason, no! Absolutely no!

Similarly, a man who had lived through the Lebanese civil war refused to accompany his wife back to Beirut. When I asked him why, he was adamant:

> No! I have no interest whatsoever! My wife has the interest because she has a sister there in Beirut. So she definitely mentions wanting to go. "You want to go? Me, no thank you!" I'm not comfortable with it. I can probably say that I will *never, ever* travel there. There were a lot of bad stories—too many bad stories—and lots of terrible things happened. Before the first war started, that long war we had from '75 to '90, it was a beautiful country. But now, the instability is too much. And after the summer war [of 2006], that really did it for me!

Even those who wished to return to Lebanon often faced insurmountable challenges. For example, one man whose mother was dying feared that he would never see her again. "To do this, you have to have money," he explained. "It's very expensive. We've been here ten years, and my family is back in Lebanon, and my mom is very sick. She's dying, but I can't go there to see her because of my financial situation. The ticket right now is about $1,000. So you need money to do this."

These fears of return, along with a lack of money and visa restrictions, were prominent among Iraqi refugees as well. As one Iraqi woman put it, "I *wish* I could go back, but now is not the right time. Every time I call, the family says, 'Stay there! Don't come!' It's really, really hard to go back to Iraq, and if something bad happens to you, the medical system there is not working."

Indeed, the destruction of Iraq's medical system was mentioned by many Iraqis in my study as a terrible tragedy. Iraq, they proudly told me, had once been renowned throughout the Middle East for its high-quality medical care, its expert physicians, and its specialized services—all for "free," as health care was subsidized by the state. However, the Iraqi health care system was slowly decimated over time, first by the UN sanctions period, which led to severe shortages of medicine and supplies, and then by the 2003 Iraq War, which led to the targeted killing of medical personnel by militia groups and the subsequent flight of most qualified physicians from the country. The infertile Iraqi refugees in my study were especially dismayed by the loss of the fledgling IVF industry in the country. IVF clinics that had once sprouted in major cities such as Baghdad had been closed or destroyed. The only exception was Iraqi

Kurdistan, where a single clinic was said to be functioning in the northern capital city of Erbil.[1]

Unable to go back home, all of the Iraqis and most of the Lebanese in my study were literally "stuck" in Michigan, where they faced inclement weather, a crumbling auto economy, and an inaccessible IVF system. Each time I drove away from IVF Michigan—passing the gray facade of the Ford Rouge factory with its billowing smokestacks—I felt deep pangs of sympathy for these men and women. Living constrained lives on the polluted margins of Detroit, there was little that they could do to change their situations. They were stranded—impoverished, immobile, and barren.

Over time, I came to think of these stranded men and women as *reproductive exiles.* On the one hand, they were forced to leave their home countries because of war and political violence. But once they arrived in the United States, they found themselves trapped—unable to return home but unable to have access to infertility services due to their poverty and overall structural vulnerability. Exile, thus, had two meanings for this population: first, the forced removal from one's home country, with little hope of return; and second, the feeling of being forced out of the US health care system, where the "hope technologies" of IVF and ICSI were a glimmering but distant mirage.

This sense of reproductive exile—of being unable to gain access to IVF or ICSI in America, yet unable to return to embattled countries with destroyed or diminished health care systems—came closest to my Arab interlocutors' subjectivities, even if this was my term, not theirs. Unable to go "back home" but unable to feel entirely "at home" in America as impoverished, childless refugees, my interlocutors existed in a tragic state of liminality[2]—betwixt and between two countries and cut off from the fertile world of parents and their children. For Iraqi men in particular, who had often suffered through war, torture, imprisonment, refugee camps, and the like, this state of reproductive exile was especially devastating. In a cultural and social world where children were a confirmation of a man's very selfhood and his future immortality, the inability to create new life in the aftermath of all that had been lost represented a genuine existential tragedy.

Between Moral Worlds

The men and women in my study were not only cut off from home countries, but they were literally straddling two "local moral worlds"[3]—the American secular one, where both child adoption and sperm donation are considered "natural" solutions to infertility, and an Islamic moral world where both of these options are morally condemned. Almost without exception,[4] the men and women in my study were observant Muslims. The Iraqis and Lebanese were mostly Shia Muslims, and the Yemenis and Palestinians (who will be introduced later on in this chapter) were all Sunni Muslims. Despite this sectarian divide, both Shias and Sunnis were united in a local moral world where Islamic religious sensibilities mattered deeply. Most of my interlocutors were attempting to understand their infertility and what to do about it from an Islamic moral perspective.

On the one hand, Islam is very clear that the inability to bear a child is a God-given reproductive impairment, one that is explicitly mentioned in the Qur'an. Muslims with intractable cases of infertility are expected to accept their condition of childlessness with patience and grace.[5] On the other hand, a *hadith*, or a saying attributed to the Prophet Muhammad, states that for every disease there is a remedy. Thus, Muslims are enjoined to seek knowledge about their afflictions "from the cradle to grave," and to be active seekers of medical care.[6] Although diseases and infirmities that cannot be cured are generally accepted as "God's will,"[7] medical advancements are seen as being continuously created by human scientists under God's provenance to overcome once-incurable conditions. Scientists and physicians are thus seen as undertaking God's handiwork.[8]

Overall, then, Islam is *technoscientifically agentive*.[9] It encourages the use of science, medicine, and biotechnology as solutions to human suffering. Within the Islamic moral universe, both IVF and ICSI are viewed as "God's gift" to infertile couples. God is seen as having created these assisted reproductive technologies to overcome a particularly difficult reproductive affliction.[10] As both IVF and ICSI have received Islamic clerical approval, the technologies have spread widely across the Muslim world.[11] This inherent appeal of IVF and ICSI in the Muslim world is also linked to Islamic pronatalism—namely, the need to perpetuate an Islamic "multitude," as described clearly in the Islamic scriptures.[12]

Despite the overall moral approval of IVF and ICSI, Islam is not monolithic when it comes to assisted reproduction. In Sunni Islam—which accounts for 80 to 90 percent of the world's Muslim population—religious authorities have permitted IVF and ICSI, but they refuse any form of third-party reproductive assistance, including sperm donation, egg donation, embryo donation, or surrogacy.[13] Sunni religious authorities deem the intervention of a third-party donor into an infertile marriage to be tantamount to adultery. They are also concerned about the potential for half-sibling incest among the offspring of anonymous donors.[14] And, as with adoption, children of anonymous donors will never know their biological relatives, which leads to genealogical confusion and the denial of a child's right to know his or her own lineage. Based on these religious ethical contentions, third-party reproductive assistance has been clinically banned in all Sunni-dominant Muslim countries for more than thirty years.[15]

The situation is quite different in the Shia Muslim world, where most religious authorities have now accepted at least some forms of third-party reproductive assistance, especially egg donation.[16] Since the late 1990s, fatwas, or religious decrees, have emanated from Shia clerics, especially in Iran, where all possible forms of third-party reproductive assistance are currently being practiced.[17] Lebanon, with its Shia-majority population, has followed the Iranian lead, offering egg donation, sperm donation, embryo donation, and surrogacy to patients in some IVF clinics.[18] However, these practices are neither common nor morally accepted by most infertile Muslim patients. Sperm donation in particular is anathema to Muslim men, regardless of whether they are Shia or Sunni.[19] Indeed, only one Shia religious authority—Ayatollah Ali Hussein Khamene'i, the supreme leader of the Islamic Republic of Iran and the hand-picked successor to Iran's Ayatollah Khomeini—has ever issued a fatwa approving of sperm donation as a morally acceptable solution to male infertility.[20] As a result, Iran and, to a much lesser extent, Lebanon are the only two Muslim countries in the world where sperm donation is offered in Shia-serving IVF clinics.

Given this moral landscape, dilemmas may emerge for infertile Muslim men. Specifically, Islam encourages the use of IVF and ICSI as solutions to infertility. But these technologies may be unaffordable, particularly for Muslim couples living in the United States. Sperm donation is much more affordable, costing hundreds of dollars rather than thousands. However, the thought of purchasing donor sperm from a sperm bank and then having these donor sperm inseminated intravaginally into the uterus of one's wife is simply reprehensible to the vast majority of Muslim men, who consider donor insemination to be the moral equivalent of extramarital sex.

These moral objections to sperm donation were prominent in my earlier study in Lebanon, where the vast majority of Muslim men, both Sunni and

Shia, rejected this reproductive option in absolute terms. Among the more than 200 men I interviewed in Lebanon—including many pious Shia Muslim men who followed the moral guidance of Ayatollah Khamene'i in Iran—the overwhelming majority simply could not accept the idea of conceiving or parenting a sperm-donor child. A child created through another man's sperm, they told me, "won't be my son."[21] Not surprisingly, I was able to interview only one Shia Muslim couple who had ever used donor sperm (from a medical student) but only as a "last resort" after nearly two decades of a severe male infertility problem.[22]

At IVF Michigan, I was thus curious to know whether life in America would in any way alter these antidonation moral stances. To that end, I asked infertile men and women in my study, both Sunni and Shia Muslims, whether they would ever consider third-party reproductive assistance, either of egg or sperm donation. Four sets of responses emerged. First, many of these infertile couples, including Shia Muslims, were shocked to learn that third-party reproductive assistance was being offered in Iran and Lebanon. They were entirely unaware that Shia religious authorities had authorized these practices, and they were often surprised, telling me, "This is the first time I've ever heard this!"

Second, many couples, both Shia and Sunni, told me that they had been very concerned about IVF laboratory mistakes that might lead to a kind of "accidental" third-party reproductive assistance, or the "mixing" of sperm and eggs between couples. Accordingly, their "worries," "fears," and "paranoia" about laboratory mix-ups had led them to seek care from an Arab-serving IVF clinic run by a Muslim IVF physician.

Third, attitudes toward sperm donation in particular were uniformly negative, with men often responding, "*Never*!" or "It's *haram*!" (religiously forbidden). Even Shia Muslim men, who were religiously permitted to use donor sperm if they followed the lead of Ayatollah Khamene'i, rejected the idea of sperm donation out of hand. One azoospermic Lebanese Shia man, who was told by his physicians that his only hope might be sperm donation, told me, "Never! No way! Neither here or in Lebanon. If we try, it *must* be sperm from *my* body, and eggs from *my* wife's body. If not, then we don't want kids."

Finally, attitudes toward adoption were similar to those regarding sperm donation. Adopted children, like donor-sperm children, were considered to be "strangers' children," not part of one's own "blood" or "body." Another Lebanese Shia man offered an almost identical rationale to the aforementioned rejection of sperm donation. "Adoption? No, I wouldn't do it!," he said. "I wouldn't!" [Why?] "Because if I need a kid, I need a kid from *my* blood. I wouldn't want a kid from somebody else's blood."

Although some men and women saw the Islamic institution of *kafala,* or the financial guardianship of an orphan, to be a humane act—one that they called a "good deed," done to help "save the life of a child"—the notion of actually raising an orphan in one's home, even as a foster parent, was also rejected by most couples. As with donor children, orphans are viewed as "strangers' children" and are also morally tainted by that fact that they might be "bastards." Thus, even in America, where adoption is widely accepted, few of the men and women at IVF Michigan expressed openness to adoption. The few that did still viewed it as a "last resort."

Marriages on the Brink

The only men and women who seemed to contemplate adoption as a solution to their childlessness were those whose marriages were literally on the brink of dissolution. When infertility could not be overcome, either by virtue of an irremediable medical condition or because repeated IVF and ICSI cycles simply could not be afforded, then sometimes the "final solution" of child adoption was discussed by husbands and wives or at least considered in passing. Several Muslim couples, and a few solo infertile Muslim men, asked me about the practicalities of adoption in the United States and where they might inquire about becoming the parents of an orphaned child. In these cases, I often provided contact information for a southeastern Michigan social service agency, which was known in the area to orchestrate local adoptions.

Ghassan

Ghassan, a Lebanese Shia Muslim, was one of the few men who expressed some interest in adoption. As I was to learn, Ghassan's wife had divorced him over his azoospermia, which was due to the absence of his vas deferens, a sign of genital cystic fibrosis. "We tried to get pregnant," Ghassan explained to me. "Or rather, I tried to get her pregnant, and it didn't work." Ghassan had used all of his savings, plus money from his gas-station-owning parents, to pay for two cycles of ICSI with testicular sperm aspiration. However, neither ICSI cycle produced a pregnancy, and his wife became "impatient," eventually asking Ghassan for a divorce after seven years of marriage.

When I met Ghassan, he was single and going back to college, trying to start over and put his past behind him. Before his divorce, Ghassan had contemplated asking his wife to adopt a child with him. But by that point, Ghassan realized that it was "time to break up." As he told me:

> I was going to ask her about adoption. I thought in our religion we can't do it. Mostly, people say it's not allowable. But I think, "What's wrong with that?" I was thinking that it shouldn't be hard to adopt because it's common here in America. As long as the child's already here, it's a human being. But every person has their own opinion, and you can't change them. I don't know whether she would have seriously considered adoption. But now it doesn't matter because she's remarried and she has two kids, so I don't think so.

Zakaria and Amira

As seen in Ghassan's vignette, even when husbands and wives still loved each other, divorce was sometimes a tragic consequence of male infertility. Within the close-knit Arab community, women were often under great pressure to conceive, with the pressure either from their own families or from constant public scrutiny and questioning. Such was the case with Zakaria and Amira, a young Palestinian couple who had told their families about Zakaria's medical problem. In Zakaria's case, his infertility was due to a congenital condition called Hirschprung disease, in which nerve endings were missing in his lower intestine. Hirschprung disease had led to the related problem of retrograde ejaculation, in which Zakaria's sperm were being released into his bladder, instead of into his ejaculate. Zakaria had sought treatment for his condition, even traveling to St. Louis to consult with a "famous" doctor. (Zakaria found this visit to be remarkable, commenting, "He's a Jew, and I'm Palestinian!"). But, because Zakaria's Hirschprung disease and retrograde ejaculation were difficult problems to solve, even with ICSI, Amira's family began to put pressure on the childless marriage, as the couple told me together:

> ZAKARIA: There *is* some pressure, especially from her side.
>
> AMIRA: My mom just wants us to have kids.
>
> ZAKARIA: She's getting much more pressure than me. Her family has that "back home spirit"!
>
> AMIRA: Actually, there was more pressure before than now.
>
> ZAKARIA: Our people are not educated about technology or infertility. They think, "Oh my God! He's going to have a child with five arms!" They know

that God tests you, and yet they still look at these things as bad. Her family is here in America, but they don't mix with Americans commonly.

AMIRA: His mom and dad are more assimilated.

ZAKARIA: Plus my dad, he went through this [infertility] with my mom.

AMIRA: So our only problem in life is this thing.

ZAKARIA: But her parents have been very nice lately.

AMIRA: They've been behaved!

ZAKARIA: I love her parents. But a lot of it, too, is the community. People always ask, "Do you know who asked me about you guys?" It doesn't help that everyone is gossiping about everyone else.

Hussein

I also encountered some stressed, even devastated husbands, who were in the midst of major marital crises over male infertility. In fact, a number of men in my study admitted that they were currently facing marital duress. I interviewed several of these men alone at IVF Michigan, as most had come by themselves to see the doctor, hoping for some kind of last-ditch medical salvation. One of these men was Hussein, the very first person to volunteer for my study at IVF Michigan. Hussein was a Shia Muslim man from southern Lebanon who was on the verge of a divorce because of his male infertility problem. In his case, he was diagnosed with Klinefelter syndrome (KS), a genetic condition in which a man has an extra X chromosome (XXY) and is sterile. After several painful testicular biopsies where no sperm were found, Hussein was encouraged by his American physicians to turn to sperm donation, as he explained to me:

> Three or four times, they've said the same thing. They kept encouraging me to do this [sperm donation], just in case they found nothing when they put the needle in my testicles. But I will *never* do this! I know that they do it in America. But in Arab men, I don't know who's the father, and so a lot of problems are going to happen in the home. Like I can't say [to the child], "Swear to your father." But if [a donor sperm child] is not my blood, and especially his looks are different, I'll *never* feel that he's my child. Here, you can pick the way you want him to look [based on donor profiles]. What is this—a factory? I can't do that!

Having ruled out sperm donation, Hussein was actually hoping for a divorce. As the youngest son—the "baby of the family"—Hussein had been forced by his "strong-willed" Lebanese mother to marry one of her cousin's daughters. (Cousin marriages are common in the Middle East among both Christians and Muslims but especially among Muslims).[23] However, Hussein had been miserable throughout his three-year marriage, literally pouring out his tale of woe to me:

HUSSEIN: To be honest with you, I think to myself, "If I got remarried, my life would be different." I want to keep hope. Maybe God will give me hope with someone else.

MARCIA: So you want to divorce?

HUSSEIN: Yes. But unfortunately, my mom's family, they think [my wife] is God, and me, I'm the devil! They think I'm trying to "close" the marriage because I'm not happy with my wife. My parents say, "How are we going to tell her parents?" But this is not the only girl who gets divorced. And she's not happy with me either. Honestly, I wanted to get married to someone from my dad's side or to meet different people here [in the United States]. But they say they don't want to give me "out" to the US. If you get a girl from Lebanon, you can have a good life. So I sent my mom over there, and that was a mistake. When I started to get unhappy in my marriage, my grandfather said, "She'll change. She'll get used to you." But instead, they got me a miserable life! It didn't work. It's not like they said it would be. They're killing the emotions of the person.

MARCIA: Have you told them how you feel?

HUSSEIN: They don't want to listen to me. Right now, they want to know if I can have kids or not. If that's it or not. So I'll do an extra test [genetic karyotyping]. And I'm still keeping hope on the side.

MARCIA: So then what will happen?

HUSSEIN: My mom, she came with me to find out what's happening. Nobody knows I'm here. My wife doesn't know I'm seeing doctors. Only my mom and my brother and sister.

MARCIA: So your wife doesn't know?

HUSSEIN: But I told my wife, "I can't get kids right now." Still, her mom is pressuring me. But what can I do? It's too much pressure, mostly from her side. From my side, they say, "If you divorce, who are we going to bring for you [that is, given his infertility]? But everyone has their own eyes. Even the ugliest woman in the world, she could be the most beautiful woman in your eyes. No one can tell you who you should love.

At the time of our first conversation, Hussein had yet to undergo genetic karyotyping. But he actually wanted a genetic test so that he could "claim" his infertility and "release" his wife from their marriage. By the time Hussein learned the devastating news about his KS, his mother had returned to Lebanon, so he was forced to bear the shock of his XXY karyotype alone. Hussein was told by the physician that he could still do ICSI. In fact, ICSI has been used in KS men to successfully deliver non-KS sons (XY males) and daughters (XX females).[24] However, Hussein was in no financial position to pay for a costly ICSI cycle. Instead, he told me, "It's easier to remarry someone who has kids, you know what I mean? That way, I see the child, and I can feel something for the child."[25]

Over time, I was surprised to meet many infertile Arab men coming alone to IVF Michigan. Some, like Hussein, were on their way to a divorce, although others were desperately holding onto their marriages. Five had already been divorced by their wives, as in Ghassan's case discussed earlier. These divorces surprised me, given that I had rarely met infertile men or women in Middle Eastern IVF clinics who had actually gone through a divorce, especially one initiated by a wife. In the Middle East, female-initiated divorce is difficult, stigmatizing, and expensive, which is perhaps why many fertile women stand by their infertile husbands (as most husbands stand by their infertile wives).[26] But, in America, the ease of no-fault divorce seems to have emboldened foreign-born Arab women to free themselves from childless marriages. In my study, a total of five wives—three Iraqi refugees and two Lebanese women—had divorced their infertile husbands, after marriages ranging in length from three to fifteen years (for an average of nine). In three of these divorce cases, the husbands were azoospermic, a condition of infertility that is difficult and sometimes impossible to overcome, even with ICSI.

Laith

Laith was an Iraqi refugee and one of eight men in my study with azoospermia. In many ways, Laith was an American success story. Highly intelligent, he had taught himself English in a Saudi refugee camp, eventually arriving in Houston, Texas, with excellent English skills. Because of this, he was able to enroll in college, eventually completing a master's degree in computer engineering. Together with an Iraqi partner, Laith then opened a successful business. When I met him, he was earning about $60,000 a year—two to four times what most of the men in my study were making. However, Laith's life course had been permanently altered by his intractable azoospermia problem. Although Laith's wife of four years showed no signs of wanting to divorce him, Laith described his feelings of guilt toward her, after having brought her to the United States from a Syrian refugee camp:

> The problem is not for me; it's for my wife. I can't leave her like this without kids. This is what's hurting me. Your mentality, when you feel like it's your responsibility, but it's affecting another person. When I go to bed at night, I think about this. I can't ruin her life. She needs to have kids to have fun with. And if I didn't have this problem, she would have four or even five kids by now. So it's my fault, and I feel bad for her. For me, I can stay like this. But it's my wife—that's what hurts me.

Seeking a Muslim Physician

So what were these morally, maritally, and medically troubled men like Laith to do? Their first line of defense was to seek the help of a Muslim IVF physician—someone who could understand the social plight of infertility, speak the Arabic language fluently, and share the religious sensibilities of their "local moral worlds." *Local moral worlds*, according to Harvard medical anthropologist Arthur Kleinman, who coined this phrase, reflect "what is at stake in everyday experience."[27] As Kleinman explains,

> What precedes, constitutes, expresses, and follows from our actions in interpersonal flows of experience are particular local patterns of recreating *what is most at stake* for us, what we most fear, what we most aspire to, what we are most threatened by, what we most desire to cross over to for safety, and what we jointly take to be the purpose, or the ultimate meaning, of our living and dying.[28]

As Kleinman notes, local moral worlds are most clearly revealed in matters of life and death, when both religion and medicine have much to say about beginnings and endings. In the world of test-tube baby making, the local moral worlds of religion and medicine are often intertwined and complex, given that IVF engenders a complicated "ontological choreography" in the making of new life and new parents.[29]

In the local moral world of IVF in Arab Detroit, seeking the services of a Muslim IVF physician was imperative for many men and women in my study. As they told me, they wanted a physician who could be trusted to understand the Islamic religious nuances of assisted reproduction, as well as the religious prohibitions against sperm donation and adoption. Although Islam does not mandate that patients seek care from a coreligionist, many Muslim patients prefer to be treated by a fellow Muslim physician, based on the assumption of a shared cultural background and religious orientation to medical concerns. For Muslim patients who are especially pious, the desire for a Muslim coreligionist may be a critical moral concern. Furthermore, in the world of IVF, some Muslim patients will want to seek the opinion of a religious authority, either before or during medical treatment. Thus, being able to share these religious opinions with an understanding Muslim physician is important for many Muslim patients as they attempt to "do the right thing" in making an IVF or ICSI baby.

Nabil

For example, an Iraqi man named Nabil had considered undergoing ICSI at a local hospital in the area but described why he ultimately turned to IVF Michigan:

> NABIL: Our religion comes first, and I was scared a little bit because I was worried about what they would do with our embryos [at the hospital].
>
> MARCIA: So what did you do?
>
> NABIL: So I called a *shaykh*, and he said it's okay [to do ICSI], but it's *haram* [prohibited] to give or take [embryos] from anybody else.
>
> MARCIA: But some Shia *shaykh*s say it's okay to donate eggs and sperm.
>
> NABIL: Some are not straight! They allow this. But some, they don't. So that's why we decided to come here. We came here because we were scared about what they would do with our eggs and embryos at that other hospital. For example, do they give them to other people?
>
> MARCIA: So you came here to see the doctor.
>
> NABIL: Because he's a Muslim. And because we saw on TV that some mistakes can be made. Like a white mother did IVF, and she ended up with two black babies. That was a real case someplace in America. So that made us want to do it [ICSI] with a Muslim doctor.

A second major factor compelling men like Nabil to seek a Muslim physician had to do with language. Both infertility and assisted reproduction involve an arcane medical language, with terms like *gamete*, *oocyte*, *epididymis*, *blastocyst*, and *zona pellucida*. Learning this medical language is difficult enough for infertile couples who are native to the country of treatment seeking. However, for infertile Arab couples who speak Arabic as their first and perhaps only language, the thought of going through the medical complexities of infertility diagnosis and treatment in an unfamiliar linguistic register were often incredibly daunting.

To that end, patients in my study desired an Arabic-speaking IVF physician who would use the more familiar Arabic vocabulary surrounding IVF medicine—a discourse that is rich with *seeds*, *planting*, *spermatic animals*, *microscopic injections*, *babies of the tubes*, and the like.[30] The importance of receiving information and instructions in one's native tongue cannot be overestimated. In my study in Arab Detroit, exactly 40 percent of those who participated spoke no English whatsoever, or managed to get by in barely functional "broken English." This was especially true of Yemenis, and particularly Yemeni women, many of whom were illiterate in both Arabic and English. For Iraqi refugees, especially those entering in the aftermath of the 2003 US invasion, many were still struggling with English. Few had yet been able to enroll in English as a second language (ESL) courses, which were being offered at a local community college. Even some Lebanese—the most "acculturated" group in Arab Detroit—were not necessarily proficient in English, especially those who had fled Lebanon in the aftermath of the 2006 summer war.

As many of these monolingual Arabic speakers explained to me, they had come to this particular IVF Michigan clinic in Dearborn because of its Arabic-speaking Muslim IVF physician and its Arabic-speaking, Muslim clinic receptionist. Several couples in the study had actually traveled great distances within the state of Michigan or across state borders to be treated by this particular Arab Muslim IVF physician. For example, a young Lebanese woman who was living on Medicaid and food stamps in Mississippi received enough money from her father to travel to IVF Michigan. Hoping that her Medicaid would somehow cover the cost of the medical visit, she explained why it was important for her to have traveled so far. "I live with my husband in another state," she explained, "but I came here just to see the doctor because I need an Arabic-speaking doctor. It doesn't matter if he's Lebanese or not, but I just need to understand everything in Arabic. I can talk English, and I can understand, but the questions about these medical things are going to be easier for me in Arabic."

Similarly, an Iraqi refugee couple who had been married for twenty-one years and said that they were now "desperate for help" had driven eight hours from Tennessee to Michigan, where they had relatives living in Dearborn. As the wife explained, "We came here from Nashville because the doctor is Arab. When we ask him about our case, he understands us. But the doctors in Nashville don't." The husband added, "We tried too much in Nashville, with three different American doctors. We met a nice American woman doctor who tried to help us. But I'm coming here now because at least we can speak Arabic, and it takes someone who can do that to really understand our problem."

Iraqi refugees, especially those who were newly arrived, could often not speak, read, or write English with any degree of fluency. This was particularly true of refugee women, who, as a group, had often received less education in their home country. Language barriers were thus a huge hindrance to seeking effective medical care. Monolingual Arabic speakers described to me their difficulty in communicating with health care practitioners in the absence of Arabic interpreters or Arabic-language health materials. Describing basic medical information—such as the date of the last menstrual cycle or symptoms involving the uterus and ovaries—was virtually impossible, as was comprehending treatment plans and other health care information delivered in English. In many cases, monolingual Arabic speakers relied on either family members or friends who could speak English to accompany them to medical appointments. Such language barriers—and the concomitant need for Arabic-language medical interpreters and health education aids—were a great frustration for men and women in my study.

Reda

An infertile Palestinian man, Reda, who lived across the border in Windsor, Ontario, told me how he had eventually "given up" on his family physician in Canada and decided to cross the US border to seek an Arabic-speaking Muslim IVF physician in Michigan:

> Even though it's very close—Windsor is only ten minutes beyond the border—there aren't any Arabic-speaking doctors over there. My problem is that the [sperm] count and motility are poor. So I tried to take some medicines given by our family doctor, but these didn't work. He gave me pills, plus Pergonal injections. The amount of the sperm increased, but the motility was still the same. So he said that because I have very little sperm, maybe I should get sperm from somewhere else [a donor]. And this is the *big difference* between Arabs and [North] Americans. When they have a problem like this, American people don't care. They would do [sperm] donation. But by our religion, we can't do

> it. Absolutely, in our religion, we can't do it. So, when that doctor [in Windsor] said that nothing would work because the motility is low, that's when I decided I wanted the *best* doctor who could speak the same language as me. I asked my friends, and this is how I heard about [the doctor] here in Michigan.

In Reda's case, the Canadian physician may not have understood the imperatives of Reda's Muslim moral world. But at least he did try to help Reda within the limits of Canada's national health care system (where both IVF and ICSI are strictly rationed). However, some Arab couples in my study were not so lucky. They described dismissive and patronizing interactions with American health care providers—interactions that were sometimes quite offensive. In particular, women who clearly identified as Muslim by wearing the *hijab* encountered male physicians' negative gender stereotypes—including presumptions of "fundamentalist" religiosity, hyperfertility, and patriarchal oppression by their husbands. Subtle and not-so-subtle forms of cultural insensitivity and frank displays of medical discrimination were often the result.

Nura and Abdullah

Nura and Abdullah were a young Yemeni couple who had lived for ten years in western Michigan. Married in Yemen at the ages of fourteen (Nura) and twenty (Abdullah), they had moved to Michigan to take care of Nura's dying father, who, after thirty-five years of hard labor—first as a California farmworker, then as a Michigan factory worker—had finally succumbed to diabetes and heart disease. Nura was the eldest daughter from her father's first marriage. But when Nura's mother died and her father remarried, she was expected to take care of all the "little children"—seven girls and two boys—in their natal village in Yemen.

Since arriving in Michigan, Nura and Abdullah had faced considerable hardship. Abdullah had been employed in a factory, but three years into his job he was hit by a car when returning home from work. Abdullah suffered from a fractured skull and broken jaw, as well as crushed discs in his neck and lower back.[31] After spending three months in a western Michigan hospital and then two-and-a-half years in rehabilitation, Abdullah remained permanently disabled, with incapacitating headaches and back pain, as well as visible scars across the back of his head and jawline.

When I met Abdullah and Nura, they were surviving on Supplemental Security Income (SSI), the federal program designed to support disabled people. Between the $1,000 monthly SSI payments and Abdullah's Medicaid coverage, they were somehow managing to live. But Abdullah's Medicaid did not cover Nura, which was unfortunate because Nura suffered from PCOS—the condition causing irregular menstrual cycles, anovulation, and diabetes-related insulin resistance. Nura had visited a doctor in Detroit, who told her bluntly to lose weight. Physicians in western Michigan were even more callous. As Nura, who wore the *hijab*, lamented, "If the doctors here were Arab, we could trust them more than Americans." She then went on to describe an interaction with one western Michigan physician:

AMERICAN DOCTOR: Why are you coming?

NURA: We want pregnancy.

AMERICAN DOCTOR: You're young! *You* are babies!

NURA: No, I *want.*

AMERICAN DOCTOR: What *we* think about *you*—we think *you're* babies.

NURA: No, I'm *not* a baby.

In this interaction, Nura quite remarkably defended herself—in English—to an offensive American male physician. In doing so, she claimed her right to be perceived as an adult and as a potential mother of children. The physician's blatant disregard of a young Yemeni couple's justifiable desire to have a child after eleven years of marriage is all the more egregious because of the perceived name-calling—telling an adult couple that they are "babies," too young to be parents. The irony here—and the one that was totally lost on the American physician—is that Nura was *more* than prepared to be a mother, having parented her younger siblings for most of her life. As Nura told me at the end of our meeting, her most ardent desire was to return to Yemen, if only she could raise the money. There, she believed that she could find a "specialist," and she would "not be treated the same as here."

Diasporic Dreams of Reprotravel

At IVF Michigan, I met many infertile Arab men and women like Nura and Abdullah, who were dreaming of returning to home countries—not only to be treated with more respect by Arab physicians but to do IVF or ICSI at a fraction of the cost of these technologies in America. These diasporic dreams of returning home were especially prominent among poor Yemenis like Nura and Abdullah.[32] At the time of my study, Yemenis were still free to travel unimpeded to and from Yemen. But then the Great Recession of 2008 hit, leading to even greater poverty in the local Yemeni community. By 2011, in the wake of the Arab uprisings, Yemen began to divide along sectarian lines. And by 2013 the country had been plunged into a devastating war launched by Saudi Arabia and its Gulf allies. Thus, Yemenis, too, ended up as reproductive exiles, unable to return to their home country because of war and a shattered health care system.

Having said that, before 2008, a few of the Yemenis in my study—two couples and three individual men—had made it back to Yemen for infertility diagnosis and treatment. Many other Yemenis and Lebanese in my study wished that they could travel "back home" for IVF services, if only they had the money. I came to think of these desires as *diasporic dreams of reprotravel.*[33] Reprotravel (short for "reproductive travel"[34]) is a phenomenon that I have encountered ever since I began working with infertile couples in the Middle East more than thirty years ago. When people are desperate to have a child, they will often undertake difficult border crossings—valiant quests for conception that are costly, time consuming, and physically and emotionally arduous.

In my study at IVF Michigan, I met a variety of Arab reprotravelers, some of whom had come to IVF Michigan from other cities or states, as well as four couples who had managed to reprotravel to the Middle East in search of IVF or ICSI. Despite substantial financial and logistical difficulties, one Yemeni couple had traveled to Bahrain, where family members were living and were able to orchestrate a $3,000 ICSI cycle, leading to the birth of the couple's son, now four years old. One Palestinian couple living in Windsor, Ontario, managed to travel to Jordan, where they were able to stay for a month with relatives and complete one ICSI cycle, however unsuccessfully. One Lebanese couple made it back to Lebanon in 2007, even though the husband had vowed never to return after his parents were killed in the tragic 1996 Qana massacre.[35] His decision to reprotravel back to Lebanon was motivated by his inability to afford ICSI in the United States. In Lebanon, he paid only $2,000, although the cycle was unsuccessful. Finally, one Lebanese man in my study, Abbas, whose story will be told in greater detail later, actually moved from his home in Brooklyn, New York, to his mother's home in Beirut to undertake four unsuccessful ICSI cycles in the course of a year. When I met Abbas, he was nearly out of money and extremely demoralized. But he had traveled to IVF Michigan, where I found him and his wife, Huda, "desperate to have a child," as they put it.

I came to think of this particular type of reprotravel back home as a form of *return reproductive tourism*. On the one hand, "reproductive tourism" is not an apt descriptor for couples' painstaking and often traumatic transnational journeys in search of IVF.[36] However, in the case of reprotravel back home, the term *tourism* is appropriate for several reasons. Return reproductive tourism usually entails three distinct features: first, return to a country of origin to undertake assisted reproduction, imagined as a kind of "homecoming" to make a test-tube baby; second, a "holiday" visit to family in the home country, who have often been missed and cherished over the ensuing years; and third, an ardent desire to undertake assisted reproduction in a place of "comfort," where the medical care is viewed as both trustworthy and culturally appropriate and the moral world of assisted reproduction is seen as religiously compatible with one's own value system.

In other words, return reproductive tourism is a special form of reprotravel undertaken by expatriate or diasporic populations—those who are living outside their countries of birth.[37] As we have seen in the case of Arab Detroit, such diasporic communities may confront their own infertility problems, but, instead of relying on host country IVF services, members of these communities dream of making a test-tube baby "back home," and some are able to do so.

At IVF Michigan, I spent untold hours listening to men and women dream about reprotravel—its costs, benefits, and consequences. On a most basic level, the price of an IVF or ICSI cycle in the Middle East was a huge consideration. In countries such as Egypt and Iran (or Syria at that time), a single cycle cost as little as $1,500. Even in the most expensive Arab Gulf countries (such as Kuwait or the UAE), IVF cycles were less than half the cost of the $12,500 US average. However, the costs of reprotravel itself, plus the expectation of gifts for relatives, were a significant disincentive. As one Lebanese man explained to me, "It will be $3,000 just for two round-trip tickets, and that's a lot! And then you need money for over there. It would cost us around $7,000 for the whole trip, and that's without the payment for the IVF. So, it's almost the same as here. Add on all the gifts, you know, and it will be around $10,000!" Other men in the study worried about the unpaid leave from work, as well as the job insecurity that a month's "holiday" to the Middle East might entail.

Still, many of those dreaming of reprotravel back home felt that it would be a net plus if they could somehow manage to do it. I noticed that many Lebanese men and women maintained patriotic attitudes about home-country medical care, a phenomenon that I came to think of as *medical "expatriotism."*[38] At IVF Michigan, Lebanese who were expatriates—not having lived in Lebanon for many years since the war—were still convinced of the superiority of the medical professionals and the "experience" to be found in Lebanese IVF clinics. Even though Lebanon was a relative latecomer to IVF—opening its first centers nearly a decade later than Egypt, Jordan, and Saudi Arabia because of the delays caused by the Lebanese civil war[39]—I was told time and again that prewar Lebanon was the "Switzerland of the Middle East," Beirut was "the Paris of the Arab world," and Lebanese doctors there were "all Western trained." Thus, according to most of the Lebanese in my study, Lebanon's spirit of medical professionalism and resilience could never be thwarted. They trusted the postwar medical system in Lebanon and saw it as much more affordable than health care in the United States.

These issues of trust and affordability extended to IVF services in Lebanon. As one Lebanese man put it, "Don't forget! In Lebanon, they've got experience for this one [IVF] better than here. For this one, Lebanon probably has better experience than the US." Similarly, a Lebanese woman commented, "Medicine in Lebanon is, what do you say? It is like 'progressive,' and I trust them." Another Lebanese man put it even more strongly, "Honestly, Lebanese medicine is number one in the world! We're confident in IVF there 100 percent."[40]

Many husbands in my study were also convinced that taking their wives back to Lebanon for IVF would result in a more optimal IVF experience. In Lebanon, conceptions could happen under the watchful eyes of Muslim physicians, and couples would be surrounded by the tender loving care of their family members, especially the wives' mothers. In the Middle East, mothers and daughters are often extremely close, deeming each other to be "best friends" in life.[41] Thus, if there was a single family member who knew about a couple's IVF seeking, it was generally the wife's mother and often the husband's mother as well. Back in Lebanon, then, IVF clinic waiting areas were often filled with mothers who were there to support their daughters and sons through the trials and tribulations of the "operation" (as IVF and ICSI egg retrievals and embryo transfers were called).[42]

Not only was such maternal support seen as psychologically comforting, but some couples maintained the belief that they would become pregnant if only they could manage to try IVF back in the home country. Return reproductive tourism back home was deemed more "relaxed," more "familiar," and more "comforting"—in short, much less stressful than attempting to get access to and afford IVF in America. This belief in the psychosocial benefits of simply being "at home" while pursuing IVF and ICSI was an important factor and repeating theme among the men and women in my study. Most of those who had reprotraveled were adamant about the comforts of home and the importance of being in the home environment, if at all possible.

A young Lebanese couple, Jaffar and Rima, who had been married for six years, were frustrated by their diagnosis of "unexplained infertility" and were seriously considering a trip to Lebanon to undergo IVF. As Jaffar explained, "Actually, I was thinking of going back to Lebanon because she believes that better doctors are over there and also that she can get pregnant 'by her family.' Her mother is over there. Her father passed away, but her mom is there, and she went to a few doctors to ask about my wife's case. If Rima went back there, it's better for her. Her mom, she also thinks that if Rima goes there, she can get pregnant." Jaffar added, "It's not an issue of money. IVF *is* cheaper there, but it is more about what she believes. She's never been back to Lebanon since she got here in 2003. Psychologically, this could be a good reason to go back."

Medical Horror and Reproductive Damage

A final sad reason why some infertile individuals and couples preferred to return home was because of egregious cases of medical malpractice, which had resulted in ongoing infertility problems. Again, over thirty years of studying infertility, I have heard many of these stories of iatrogenesis, which is usually defined as physician-induced harm.[43] In some of these cases of iatrogeneis, permanent *reproductive damage* is the result.

Abbas and Huda

Such was the case with Abbas, the forty-three-year-old man mentioned earlier, who had traveled to Lebanon to undertake four unsuccessful cycles of ICSI. Abbas and his wife Huda, who was ten years younger, had been married for three years when I met them. However, Abbas's reproductive damage had been sustained years earlier—not in Lebanon but rather in the United States. As we will see, Abbas had been through a veritable medical horror story, which he and Huda narrated together. Their verbatim account is as follows:

ABBAS: From the beginning . . . I'll start from the beginning. We didn't want to wait at all, but the first month, she didn't get pregnant. The second month, she didn't get pregnant. So we started going to doctors.

MARCIA: And did they find something?

ABBAS: Yes, we found a *big* problem. The big problem was about me, not about her. I'll tell you what happened. Before I got married, before I got married, I had hernia surgery, in 2000 exactly, on both sides. What happened is that, when we were trying to get pregnant, the doctors in Lebanon figured out that the problem is through the hernia surgery. During that hernia surgery, they cut the vessels that transfer sperm. And this is the big problem that we've been struggling with ever since.

MARCIA: Oh my gosh! Where was this?

ABBAS: In New York, at [named] hospital in Brooklyn. They basically did a vasectomy.

MARCIA: And you didn't want this?

ABBAS: When it happened, I wasn't even married yet! When I found out, I asked lawyers what to do, but they said, "It's too late, after four to five years, to sue somebody."

MARCIA: What kind of doctor was he? A urologist?

ABBAS: No, he was a general surgeon.

MARCIA: So, do you know if you have any sperm inside [the testicles]?

ABBAS: That's what I was worried about. So that's when I first went to the American University of Beirut. I asked Dr. [named], and he said, "We'll do TESA [testicular epididymal sperm aspiration] for you, to find out if you have sperm." When he gave me the results, it said, "Spermatic normal." So I *do* make sperm. But every time we have to do IVF, it's another TESA. I read something in here [at IVF Michigan] about it. They do something called "aspirate the sperm" with TESA. So every time we have to do IVF, we have to do TESA.[44]

MARCIA: How many times have you done it?

ABBAS: Six times, four in Lebanon, and two here. The first time was with Dr. [named, in Beirut], and we didn't get success. Then we went to Dr. [named, in Beirut], and the second time nothing. Then we did two more times there with [another doctor], and one time with [another doctor]. Here in the United

States, we did one time with Dr. [named] in New York Beth Israel Hospital, and one time here with Dr. [named] on Park Avenue. He's Chinese or something.

MARCIA: Wow! You've been through a lot.

ABBAS: What we've been through, and nothing at all to show for it! No pregnancies. They always said it's not like when you do [IVF] the normal way, where you get millions of sperm. With TESA, there's not that much sperm, but we did get eggs fertilized. We got embryos all the time. Even [the doctor on Park Avenue] froze one and put back only one [embryo]. In most of the other cycles, they put back like five or six.[45] And at least four [embryos] were good quality.

HUDA: They were size twenty to twenty-two.

MARCIA (TO HUDA): You've had to take a lot of medicine.

HUDA: Oh! The injections! Twenty here [pointing to her stomach] and twenty here [pointing to her buttocks].

ABBAS: It's not good, is it?

HUDA: I've taken *a lot* of medicine! *A lot, a lot!*

MARCIA: And the expense—I didn't ask you about your work.

ABBAS: For me, I used to work most of my life. I was working and saving. But I spent them [the savings]. I had something saved before I married. But there is no insurance to cover these kinds of things, these surgeries. We do have government insurance, AmeriChoice. But it only covers little things, like coughs.

HUDA: No medicine, no injections, nothing!

MARCIA: Is that why you did all of those cycles in Lebanon?

ABBAS: We stayed in Lebanon, which is cheaper than here. It was $6,000 in Lebanon for everything, for the doctor and for the medicine. In here, in New York, it is around $15,000, so if you do it two times, it cost $30,000. But $6,000 times four is only $24,000.

MARCIA: So you traveled a lot to Lebanon.

ABBAS: I was there, I got married, and I stayed for one year. I stayed over there to do that and to wait for her results. I stayed in Lebanon for one year to do four times ICSI.

MARCIA: And the total cost?

ABBAS: Maybe $60,000 altogether [in Lebanon and the United States].

MARCIA: Where did you find that kind of money?

ABBAS: Well, I had lived twenty-one years in the US.

MARCIA (TURNING TO HUDA): And you?

HUDA: I, just two years here in the US.

ABBAS: I went back to Lebanon to marry, but I discovered the problem, then stayed. I used to work in a store—a coffee shop owned by my cousins. But we lost the lease in New York. So I decided to go to spend one to two months in Lebanon. It was time to be free! I had been working with my cousins for so many years, and I had saved money. But now I'm almost jobless. I'm a driver now in New York City. I drive a taxi. But there's no insurance for taxi drivers. There's no union for taxi drivers.

MARCIA: So why did you decide to come back [from Lebanon]?

ABBAS: Actually, I decided to complete my life, to go ahead with my life. In Lebanon, I was staying in my mother's house, with no job. I came here to start again.

MARCIA: When did you come back?

ABBAS: Last summer, last June, was when we did the last one [ICSI] in New York. Then, another friend in New York told us, "I went to *a lot* of doctors in New York, and not one of them has helped us." Not until someone said, "Go to Michigan and see [the doctor] at IVF Michigan. We went there, and now we have a baby!" So I called him finally [the doctor at IVF Michigan], and *he himself* picked up the phone! He said, "Don't worry. Just take an appointment with [the receptionist]. Come in, and we'll talk about it." So this is the first day here in the office. We've been here two days. Luckily, I have a sister. She's here only a couple of months in Dearborn, and I only have one sister here with kids and her husband. So we're staying with them, and they drove us here. My nephews brought us to the office.

MARCIA: Did you drive or fly from New York?

ABBAS: We flew in the airplane because it was cheaper than with the cost of gas and the time. From LaGuardia, the Priceline ticket was only $150, so with tax, it was $400 together.

MARCIA: Now that you're here, how are you feeling?

ABBAS: Actually, we are *desperate* about it! Even if we need to call someone to transfer money [for another ICSI cycle].

MARCIA: Do you have someone who can do that?

ABBAS: Yes, I do have family. I have six brothers, but only two of them are okay [financially]—working enough so that they *could* help us. But I've been helping *them* for twenty years, so they can help me now!

MARCIA: Are you the oldest brother?

ABBAS: Actually, I'm their little brother.

MARCIA: And do they know the problem?

ABBAS: We kept it a little bit secret, until they had to know after a while.

MARCIA: Why?

ABBAS: Because I'm the last one to get married, and I was old when I married. My brothers married in their twenties, but I was nearly forty. And my mom is getting old. My mom is still dreaming of us getting a child.

HUDA: And I am, too.

ABBAS: And me, too.

I don't know how Abbas and Huda's diasporic dreams of making a test-tube baby turned out, as I never saw them again in the IVF Michigan clinic. However, I could not help but wonder why a simple hernia repair had turned into an "accidental" vasectomy of a young, unmarried, Lebanese Muslim man. Was this a simple medical error—a case of unintended iatrogenesis? Or was it something much more sinister—an American doctor's attempt to prevent a young Muslim man from ever conceiving a child? Without recourse to a medical malpractice trial, the details of Abbas's reproductive injury would never be revealed in a court of law.

Still, the damage to Abbas's body was permanent. Thus, he had spent his small nest egg—acquired through twenty years of daily labor in a Brooklyn coffee shop—on expensive reprotravel to Lebanon and now Michigan. Ultimately, I never knew whether the caring Muslim physician at IVF Michigan was able to perform a minor miracle for Abbas and Huda by helping them to conceive the dreamed-of ICSI child. But I hope so.

Conclusion: Why America Must Care

The Lives of Arab Refugees

Happy Endings and Refugee Hopes

In a book focusing on Middle Eastern wars, Arab refugees, syndemics of suffering, misdirected resettlement, structural vulnerabilities, concentrated poverty, health disparities, minority infertility, reproductive racism, medical malpractice, marital crisis, and reproductive exile on the margins of Detroit, a city enveloped in a geography of despair, most of the stories have been sad, some even poignant. Nonetheless, a single sustaining thread has quietly woven its way through the pages of this book, beginning with Fatima and Sadiq's "miracle" pregnancy in the Prologue and ending with the diasporic dreams of home in the last chapter. Submerged beneath the sadness has been the lifeline of hope—hope for a happy ending, away from the violence of war, in a peaceful place, where refugees are accepted and supported, able to create new lives and new families. This hope for a happy ending has inspired millions of Arab refugees to flee from places of danger. And it is what sustains them as they search for better lives in safe havens such as Arab Detroit. As anthropologist Henrietta Moore has incisively argued in her work on sub-Saharan Africa, hopes and aspirations are an "animating life force"[1]—reorienting human beings toward what might still be possible and demonstrating that human beings have a capacity for resilience after atrocity.

In Arab Detroit, the men and women I met were still holding onto their hopes and dreams, despite their many hardships and struggles. Arab Detroit was far from a perfect home. But it did offer cultural comfort within an Arab ethnic enclave, a well-established Muslim community, a place of refuge, if not a land of opportunity.

Over five years of listening to refugees' stories in Arab Detroit, I heard about their many hopes and aspirations—among them, learning English, opening a bank account, owning a credit card, finding a well-paid job, securing health insurance, starting a small business, making enough money to send home, and eventually returning home without fear of violence and danger. Furthermore, I was impressed by the small but significant number of Arab men and women who were trying to improve their lives through education. In my study, six men and four women were attending local community colleges, trying to gain entrance to professions including nursing, education, computer engineering and IT, pharmacy, and architecture.

Although there were relatively few clear success stories among my study population—only five that I could count among the nearly 100 men and women I interviewed—Kamal's was one such story. Kamal, as you may recall, was the Iraqi refugee from Chapter 1 who had witnessed "*so many* dead people, *so much* blood" while serving in a tank unit in the Iraqi army. After fleeing as a refugee to Saudi Arabia, Kamal was resettled directly in Arab Detroit, where I met him exactly ten years later.

Kamal

While attending the Friday afternoon infertility clinic, Kamal was downright upbeat. Kamal had accomplished the two things in life that all of the men and women in my study were hoping for: first, the achievement of an economically stable, even prosperous life; and second, the joys of parenthood through the birth of a test-tube baby.

Kamal told me that his initial resettlement in Arab Detroit had been difficult, as he struggled to make ends meet in many different odd jobs, including as a driver, a construction worker, and an auto mechanic. But this allowed him to save enough money to marry his Iraqi sweetheart, Zeinab, whom he had come to know and love during their time in the Saudi refugee camp. Zeinab's family was also resettled in Arab Detroit. And although Kamal "had to do a lot of things to get married to her," his hard work and persistence paid off. Kamal and Zeinab were married in a small ceremony in a Shia mosque in Arab Detroit. Zeinab was only sixteen at the time, but she was happy to become a married woman, and she hoped to become a mother.

Marrying Zeinab was not Kamal's only good fortune. He was bolstered by having his two refugee brothers by his side in Arab Detroit. By the time I met Kamal, he and his brothers had become homeowners, purchasing two small "fixer-uppers," one in Detroit and the other in Dearborn. Kamal's younger brother, who was still not married, lived with Kamal and Zeinab in their Detroit home, while Kamal's older brother, who now had a wife and six children, occupied the nicer residence in Dearborn. Given that home ownership was rare among the Iraqi refugees in my study, Kamal and his two brothers had together achieved a major piece of the American dream.

But Kamal had gone even farther. Through hard work and persistence, he had purchased a small Arab-owned barbershop, teaching himself how to cut men's hair. The business thrived, and by the time I met Kamal, he had purchased his second barbershop, this one serving a "mixed" Arab and American clientele. These barbershops were so profitable that Kamal was taking home about $30,000 a year.

With this money, Kamal had invested in his most important dream—to overcome his male infertility and become a father. Because Kamal was talkative, he had much to say about his treatment quest:

KAMAL: I never felt that this had anything to do with my manhood, because right away, I went to a doctor. After one year of marriage, I took her to a doctor, and they said everything is okay [with her]. So they told me to "Move fast! Don't wait! Because if you delay, it's bad for you. Your success will be less." So then we made *a lot* of [semen] tests. We went to *a lot* of places. And then I made a surgery, too, for a varicocele.

MARCIA: Did it help?

KAMAL: I don't think it helped. [He stood up to show me the incision site in his lower abdomen.]

MARCIA: It usually doesn't.

KAMAL: So then we started doing ICSI. The first one, we got twenty-one eggs and put back five embryos, and the second one, we got eighteen eggs and put back seven [embryos]. But neither was successful.

MARCIA: Did you freeze some of your embryos?

KAMAL: No, for religious reasons, we didn't have any idea if freezing was okay, so we didn't do it at the time. Religiously, I was scared a little bit—worried about what they do with extra embryos. So then we decided to come here, to a Muslim doctor.

MARCIA: So how many times have you done ICSI?

KAMAL: You know, Marcia, three times we did it, and each time we spent *a lot* of money! The first two times, the doctor tried to help me a little bit with the cost. Together, they cost around $15,000, and I put it on a credit card payment. But this last time, it cost more, about $10,000 to $15,000. So it was about $30,000 altogether! If I was working in a factory or gas station, then I couldn't do this. But *alhamdulillah* [praise be to God], I can do it, and this time, we got our son.

Kamal and Zeinab were one of only two couples in my study who had actually conceived and delivered a baby. Pulling a photo from his wallet, Kamal smiled widely when he showed me the picture of little Haydar, his thirteen-month-old ICSI son. As he pointed out proudly, Haydar was an American citizen by birth.

Zeinab then chimed in, telling me that she hoped to have ICSI twins—and at least one girl—with their fourth, upcoming ICSI cycle, to complete their desired family size. However, Kamal surprised me, saying that he would take "anything," including an adopted child. On this point, he and Zeinab disagreed:

KAMAL: We went to see a doctor, a Chaldean [Iraqi Catholic], and she said, "Go to adopt a baby and bring it home." And I said, "Allah is present." If I didn't get a baby, I will think about adoption.

ZEINAB: But I say "No." I told him that. I want to feel the motherhood. She's not my girl, or he's not my son. I want to have a baby *with* him [Kamal].

KAMAL: But I have no problem with adoption. I take the baby, and he's my son.

MARCIA: Do they do this in Iraq?

KAMAL: They *do* do this in Iraq.

ZEINAB: I know families that have done this.

KAMAL: In Iraq, they don't have places to take the babies [orphanages]. So babies are put on the side of the road, in front of the doors of mosques and churches. And people come and take those babies to raise them. So I would do it. If I found one, I would take it and raise it as my own.

Adopting the Orphaned and Hosting the Uprooted

As a Muslim man, Kamal's willingness to adopt an orphaned child was quite unusual. But I also found it highly encouraging, showing that American pro-adoption attitudes might be changing the hearts and minds of potential Muslim adoptive parents. Given the current Middle East wars and refugee crises, parents like these will be needed to take on thousands—and potentially hundreds of thousands—of Muslim war orphans.[2]

As of this writing, the plight of children in the Middle East is dire. On September 6, 2016, UNICEF issued an extremely sobering report, entitled *Uprooted: The Growing Crisis for Refugee and Migrant Children.*[3] According to the report, nearly 50 million children have either migrated across borders or been forcibly displaced, with more than half of these children, or approximately 28 million, fleeing violent conflict and insecurity. Although children make up about one-third of the global population, they account for about one-half of the world's refugees.

In 2015, there were twice as many child refugees as there were in 2005. One-half of the child refugees living under UNHCR's mandate came from just two countries, Syria and Afghanistan. And ten countries, mostly in the Middle East and Africa, accounted for nearly three-quarters of all these child refugees. Another set of ten countries, again mainly in the Middle East and Africa, were "hosting" most of these refugee children and their families. Turkey had taken in the lion's share, with more than 3 million Syrian refugees living inside Turkey's borders. But relative to its population size, Lebanon had taken in more refugees than any other single country—with one in every four people in Lebanon being either a Syrian or Palestinian refugee.[4]

By 2016, the devastating war in Syria had escalated, especially in the northern city of Aleppo. Humanitarian aid efforts, including UN relief convoys, were severely hampered by government blockades of besieged areas, leading to threats of mass starvation and death.[5] By the end of 2016, Syrian government forces had retaken control of Aleppo through escalating military intervention by Russia. But the so-called fall of Aleppo entailed the death and mass exodus of thousands more Syrian civilians.[6] Those refugees who managed to flee from the war-torn city faced dire conditions, including lack of sufficient food and water in overstretched refugee camps. Although international aid organizations and public health officials repeatedly warned that "Syrian refugees desperately need our help,"[7] the global response to the Syrian refugee crisis showed signs of fatigue by the end of 2016, with global attention to the Syrian conflict waning.

As the Syrian crisis entered its sixth year, it was abundantly clear who had—and who had not—assisted the vulnerable Syrian population. On the one hand, the neighboring countries of Turkey, Lebanon, and Jordan had come to the rescue, taking in more than 4 million Syrian refugees. On the other hand, the nearby petro-rich Arab Gulf countries, including Saudi Arabia, Kuwait, Qatar, Bahrain, and Oman, had done little to alleviate the Syrian refugee crisis, justifying their inaction by pointing out that they did not sign onto the 1951 UN Refugee Convention.[8] The United Arab Emirates (UAE), built on the backs of migrant labor,[9] had done slightly better than its regional allies, taking in 200,000 Syrian nationals by 2015,[10] and pledging to bring 15,000 more Syrians to the UAE over a five-year period.[11] However, at the same time, the UAE had become part of the Saudi-led coalition that was launching deadly airstrikes on Yemen—an internecine Middle Eastern war that was leading to another "forgotten" Arab refugee crisis.

In contrast to the frank apathy shown by the rich Arab Gulf nations, a few rich Western European nations did substantially better. By the end of 2015, Europe was hosting 1.8 million refugees, mostly from the three Middle Eastern countries of Syria, Iraq, and Afghanistan. An additional one million asylum-seekers were awaiting the outcome of their asylum applications in Europe. Among those asylum-seeker were thousands of refugee children—70 percent of them coming from Syria, Iraq, and Afghanistan.[12]

However, this massive influx of Middle Eastern refugees caused antirefugee sentiment to begin to grow, including in Germany, the nation that had taken in nearly 300,000 Syrian refugees in the year 2016 alone.[13] Right-wing political parties began winning victories in parts of Germany and other European countries, where calls for a so-called Muslim ban were spurred in part by the deadly ISIS-inspired terrorist attacks on Brussels, Nice, and Berlin. The 2016 UN *Uprooted* report cited "the rise of xenophobia and discrimination toward refugees" as one of the key issues that would need to be confronted for successful refugee resettlement to continue in Europe.[14]

Such calls for a Muslim ban were growing in the United States as well, particularly during the 2016 presidential campaign of Donald Trump. His repeated anti-Muslim pronouncements on the campaign trail—for a ban on incoming Muslim refugees, an "ideological test" for Muslim immigrants and visitors to the United States, a closing of all American mosques, as well as his insults toward a Muslim American Gold Star family who had lost their soldier son in Afghanistan—garnered support across a wide swath of the American public, who, by the end of 2016, had elected him as America's forty-fifth president.[15]

But even before Trump, the US response to the Syrian refugee crisis was tepid. Only 26,000 Syrians had been identified and referred by UN agencies for resettlement in the United States by November 2013, representing a tiny fraction (0.5 percent) of the total number of Syrians who had fled their homeland by that time.[16] A year later, only 132 Syrian refugees had actually been accepted into the United States—a mere 0.2 percent of the 70,000 refugees who arrived legally in the United States that same year and far fewer than the 292,540 refugees offered asylum in the EU.[17] By the end of 2015, the total number of Syrians who had entered the United States was only 2,174, according to the Office of Refugee Resettlement. As noted by the anthropologist of migration, Jeffrey H. Cohen, in his article "Syrian Refugees Next Door?," "That is a number so small as to be almost insignificant. The possibility that a Syrian family might become your neighbor is nearly zero. Syrian refugees represent fewer than 0.0007 percent of the nation's population."[18]

By mid-2016, the total number of Syrian refugees who had entered the United States increased to 8,000, under President Obama's mandate to admit at least 10,000 Syrians during the 2015–2016 fiscal year.[19] According to State Department figures, 78 percent of those Syrians admitted were women and children, with 58 percent being children, almost evenly split between boys and girls.[20] The US government also set up a family reunification program for both Iraqi and Syrian refugees with relatives in the United States. By August 2016, more than 2,000 Syrians were being considered for family reunification, but only twenty individuals had been approved, and none of them had yet arrived in the country by what was then the fifth year of the civil war.[21]

According to an Oxfam International report, the United States had received only 10 percent of its "fair share" of Syrian refugees by the end of 2016, based on the size of its economy and its ability to deploy significantly more personnel to embassies in the affected region.[22] The US admissions cap of 10,000 per fiscal year "pales in comparison to the numbers accepted by other countries."[23] Sweden, for example, with a population equivalent to only 3 percent of the US population, had taken in more than 100,000 Syrians over the first five years of the war. And, over three winter months in 2015 and 2016, Canada managed to resettle 25,000 Syrian refugees, with Canadian Prime Minister Justin Trudeau personally welcoming them into the country.[24]

In fact, Canada had done exactly 248 percent more than its fair share in welcoming vulnerable Syrian refugees into the country.[25] It had done so by deploying almost 500 additional staff members to embassies in countries neighboring Syria to fast-track the resettlement process. The United Kingdom had done slightly better than the United States, but not by much, meeting only 18 percent of its fair share. But according to the Oxfam report, Russia provided the most egregious example of inaction, especially given the death and destruction it had caused in Syria. Despite having signed onto the 1951 refugee convention and having close ties to the Syrian regime over many decades, Russia had resettled only two Syrian refugees by the end of 2016.

Ultimately, Oxfam blamed these "rich countries" for taking in less than 3 percent of the world's 5 million Syrian refugees.[26] Oxfam's lead on the Syrian crisis team, Andy Baker, pointed to a "growing anti-refugee xenophobic backlash" for which vulnerable Syrian refugees were "paying the price."[27] As Baker stated,

> Around 130,000 Syrians spread across the rich countries of the world is a tiny number, particularly when contrasted with Lebanon, where one in five people is a refugee. While resettlement will not solve the crisis, it is a tangible way to provide hope for many refugees and show a concrete act of solidarity with Syria's neighbours which host the vast majority of the men, women and children who have fled the war.[28]

Stopping Wars in the Middle East

As Oxfam's report correctly notes, "resettlement will not solve the crisis."[29] To solve the crisis, the Syrian war itself needs to end. The Syrian war is one of five tragic wars—along with Afghanistan, Iraq, Libya, and Yemen—that continue to haunt the region. As of 2016, the United States was involved in all five of these wars, primarily from the air but also on the ground.

To be specific, in 2016, the United States dropped exactly 26,171 bombs on the world—an alarming 3,027-bomb increase over 2015, according to the Council on Foreign Relations' analysis of Defense Department data.[30] About equal numbers of bombs were dropped on Syria (12,192) and Iraq (12,095), while smaller numbers were dropped on Afghanistan (1,337), Libya (496), and Yemen (34).

By the end of 2016, Afghanistan had become the site of the longest war in modern US history (conducted over sixteen years, with 8,400 US troops still on the ground), followed by the war in Iraq (conducted over fourteen years, with nearly 5,000 US troops still on the ground in the battle to retake the

ISIS-controlled city of Mosul).[31] In many ways, 2016 was a watershed year for US involvement on multiple Middle East fronts. Thus, at the end of President Obama's presidency, these ongoing Middle East wars were a blemish on his presidential record, given his campaign promise to end the wars in Iraq and Afghanistan.

By 2016, Britain had called its own nation to account for its participation in the US-led war in Iraq. On July 6, 2016, a long-awaited report by the UK's Iraq Inquiry Committee was released. It was called the "Chilcot Report," in honor of the retired civil servant, Sir John Chilcot, who led the inquiry. The 2.6-million-word document required twelve volumes and seven years to research and complete.[32]

The main message of the Chilcot report was a blistering critique of the UK government's complicity and military participation in America's Iraq War folly. In particular, the report soundly condemned Prime Minister Tony Blair, who chose "to join the invasion of Iraq before peaceful options for disarmament had been exhausted."[33] Blair's decision, the report opines, was based on flawed intelligence about WMDs that went unchallenged, an unsatisfactory legal rationale, exaggerated public statements, and inadequate military preparedness.[34] Furthermore, the consequences of the invasion were gravely underestimated, with planning and preparations for an Iraq after Saddam Hussein being "wholly inadequate."[35] More than 200 British citizens died as a result of the war, as well as more than 150,000 Iraqis, "probably many more."[36]

In the end, the report deemed Tony Blair at fault for having "overestimated the influence he would have over President George W. Bush."[37] The United Kingdom must never again give its "unconditional support" to the United States in matters of war, the Chilcot report concluded.[38] The major lesson learned by the United Kingdom was that the wrongful decision of the United States to go to war in Iraq ultimately ended up hurting the United Kingdom on the world stage. But, as the report also concluded, it is the Iraqis who ultimately suffered.

In America, the Chilcot report received very little media attention, suggesting that correspondingly few in the United States knew about the report or its findings. Shortly thereafter, Sir Jeremy Greenstock, the former UK Ambassador to the United Nations, who was Britain's special representative to Iraq and one of the country's most highly regarded diplomats, published his critical war memoir, *Iraq: The Cost of War*. In the book, Greenstock spelled out in gripping detail how the United Kingdom was systematically excluded from key pre- and postwar decision making, despite its allegiance to Bush's war effort.[39] As with the Chilcot report, Greenstock's important account of Britain's "doomed diplomacy" also received little US media coverage.[40]

In the current climate in America, there appears to be a deep reluctance to link current events—for example, the rise of ISIS, global terrorism, or the refugee crisis—to US responsibility. To this day, no Iraq War tribunals have been held, nor has former President George W. Bush been held accountable for his premeditated decision to invade Iraq without just cause, on the basis of erroneous evidence. Furthermore, no official apologies, amends, or reparations have been made by the United States to Iraq. Instead, the United States has failed to fix what it has broken.

When I lecture on how America's two wars in Iraq have led to many of the unfortunate consequences described in this book, audiences are often stunned, even on "liberal" college campuses where they are sympathetic to my overall message. Perhaps because the millennial generation in America no longer faces the threat of military conscription, as young people did during the Vietnam War era, millennials and their parents and grandparents have become complacent. This is suggested by the fact that "new millennial" antiwar protest against the US wars in Iraq and Afghanistan has been insignificant when compared to the public protests enacted during the Vietnam War era.

A decade ago, I felt compelled to deliver my Society for Medical Anthropology (SMA) presidential address on "Medical Anthropology against War."[41] I urged my fellow medical anthropologists to take up an antiwar platform, arguing that the war in Iraq was illegitimate and the cause of great human suffering. Similarly, SMA's parent organization, the American Anthropological Association (AAA), issued a statement condemning the Iraq War. The AAA called for a complete end to all US military operations, and full US compliance with the UN Convention against Torture (in the aftermath of the Abu Ghraib scandal and the ongoing imprisonments in Guantanamo). Two resolutions were voted on and adopted by the AAA membership in May 2007. But the resolutions fell on deaf ears in the US government, and little activist protest followed within the anthropological association.

The Middle East wars have been largely ignored within the anthropological community.[42] Although anthropologists are usually deeply critical of journalists for their "shallow" reporting of complex social realities, it is the journalists—not the anthropologists—who have risked their lives in Middle

Eastern war zones.[43] As a profession, anthropologists have been faint of heart and lacking in moral courage in terms of actually entering war-torn countries, much less war zones. In so doing, we have turned away from the brutal realities, the embodied suffering, the psychological devastation, the sexual violence, and the refugee aftermath of Middle Eastern warfare. It is not enough to study so-called structural violence, as important as structural vulnerabilities and everyday forms of violence may be. The legacy of actual *physical violence* in the Middle East wars must be rendered visible by anthropologists. Chapter 1 of this book represents my own scholarly efforts in this regard, and I am pleased to note that a younger generation of medical anthropologists is taking up this charge.[44] Such scholarship begins to lay bare the syndemics of suffering in Middle Eastern war zones and the plight of Arab refugees who have fled to places like Arab Detroit.

Caring for America's Arab Refugees

In his moving article on "Michigan's Iraqi Refugee Crisis," Iraq War veteran and freelance journalist Robert Guttersohn opined,

> For the refugee, Iraq will always be home. But knowing he can never return to his native land, he must instead seek refuge in the country whose very military invasion set off the domino effect leading to his displacement . . . The refugee had the unfortunate luck of living there when the bombs began to fall. Taking in refugees is only half the job. Ensuring they have a fair opportunity to be active participants in the economy is another. An improved refugee program, whether run by the state or the federal government, would be expensive. So is war, though, and a country that starts one should feel the weight of those whose lives are uprooted by it—both its soldiers and the refugees.[45]

What would an improved refugee program look like? Although there are no "perfect" examples, I would like to describe a model program in my own community of New Haven, Connecticut. Like Detroit, New Haven is a poor, black, deindustrialized city, the kind of struggling minority community in which many Iraqi refugees have been resettled.[46] Nonetheless, New Haven has managed to reinvent itself as a "new haven" for fleeing refugees and become an exemplar for successful resettlement. (The city is also a well-known sanctuary city, or "safe haven," for undocumented migrants coming from Latin America).

So, what is New Haven doing right? New Haven clearly benefits from a number of important attributes. The first is Yale, the wealthy private university in the center of the city, which is home to many students and faculty who care about refugee issues. For example, in 2008, five students at Yale Law School founded the Iraqi Refugee Assistance Project (IRAP), to provide direct legal representation to Iraqi refugees overseas, who did not have access to legal counsel. Since then, IRAP (renamed the International Refugee Assistance Project in 2015) has opened twenty-nine chapters at law schools in the United States and Canada, working with over seventy-five international law firms and multinational corporations to provide pro bono legal assistance, including to those refugees arriving in the New Haven area. Similarly, Yale Medical School is home to many physician-activists. For example, Yale–New Haven Hospital runs both pediatric and adult Refugee Clinics, as well as a Yale Center for Asylum Medicine, specifically designed to address the health needs and challenges faced by the local refugee community and victims of torture who are seeking asylum in the United States. Overall, Yale University is the city's major employer; thus, it uses the talents of English-speaking Iraqis who have found living-wage jobs across campus.

Beyond Yale, the key to successful refugee resettlement is New Haven's Integrated Refugee and Immigrant Services (IRIS), the federally funded nonprofit agency that works to resettle refugees in the New Haven community.[47] Founded in the early 1980s by the Episcopal Church in Connecticut, IRIS has helped to resettle about 240 Arab and African refugees annually. Because of its own outreach efforts and its location near a well-to-do university, IRIS receives generous donations—of food, furniture, clothing, and other necessities. Furthermore, many Connecticut religious communities and secular organizations partner with IRIS to help resettle refugees around the state of Connecticut. With more than fifty groups volunteering since the summer of 2015, IRIS was able to ask the US State Department to double its annual quota of refugees to 500.[48]

For IRIS, "resettlement" means many things. It entails meeting and greeting refugees at the airport, bringing them to completely furnished rental apartments with fully stocked refrigerators, insuring that they have a culturally appropriate hot meal, prepared by someone from their home country, on their first night of arrival in the city (this is a federal mandate), and providing them with a phone to let their families know that they have reached New Haven safely. IRIS is also federally mandated to provide each family with a

$1,000 one-time grant for rent and other necessities. In the first week, IRIS staff members take refugees to the Social Security office, help them to navigate public transportation (the New Haven bus system), show them how to get to Yale-New Haven Hospital, and help them enroll their children in school.

Furthermore, IRIS staff members, many of whom are volunteers, offer ongoing refugee support. They provide free English classes for adults every weekday morning, a playgroup for toddlers, academic support for children enrolled in school, and an after-school program to help refugee children with their homework. Older refugee youth are taken on college tours in the area and helped substantially with their applications. Their parents, meanwhile, benefit from IRIS's employment services. Within four months, 70 percent of job-seeking adult refugees find jobs, and 90 percent within six months.[49] However, IRIS cannot promise highly skilled employment opportunities for educated refugees, many of whom end up working in factories or in housekeeping. Thus, processes of recertification for talented refugee professionals remain an ongoing challenge, at IRIS, as elsewhere around the country.[50]

Still, IRIS's mantra is "self-sufficiency," and, over time, many Iraqi refugees coming to the New Haven area achieve this goal. Indeed, I have witnessed this spectacular process with my own eyes. To be exact, I left the University of Michigan in 2008 to join Yale University and to become the Chair of Yale's Council on Middle East Studies (CMES). To my good fortune, I was able to hire a newly arrived Iraqi refugee, the married father of a young son, who had served as a translator with the US forces and was forced to flee from Iraq when his life was being threatened. He and his family were among the first Iraqi refugees to arrive in New Haven. IRIS and the local Unitarian Universalist Church partnered to insure the family's successful resettlement. Among other things, they helped this University of Baghdad-educated man to prepare his English-language resumé, which they circulated among potential Yale employers. When his resumé landed on my desk, I and my CMES Program Manager were eager to give this bilingual translator a chance, hiring him in an administrative position at our center, where his Arabic skills would come in handy.

CMES's young refugee father not only took to his job, but he spread his happiness and optimism throughout our office, where he worked for seven years before receiving a well-deserved promotion within the university. Nearly a decade on, he is living the American dream. He has a stable union job with good benefits, he owns a home, his two children (including a daughter born in the United States) have scholarships to a fine private school, he survived open-heart surgery to correct a congenital heart defect that was detected by Yale physicians, and, over the ensuing years, he has been able to resettle most of his natal Iraqi family in America. My Iraqi colleague's story proves that Arab refugee resettlement—and assimilation—is quite possible.

Furthermore, my refugee colleague brought an infertile Iraqi refugee couple to my attention. I was able to take them to the Yale Fertility Center, where the husband was diagnosed with severe male infertility (only one spermatozoon could be detected in his semen). Although he was a candidate for ICSI and the IVF clinic was willing to discount his treatment, the necessary hormonal medications still cost thousands of dollars, an amount well beyond this new refugee couple's current state of penury. Thus, as in so many other infertile refugee stories, the (fertile) young wife exercised her right to divorce, restarting her American life as a single woman and working in a local hospital on the way to achieving her American dream of becoming a nurse.

Ensuring Health Equity and Reproductive Justice

I hope that this refugee couple's story, and others like it in this book, have spurred ethical reflection about health equity and reproductive justice—or lack thereof—for refugees who must confront the exclusionary tendencies of the US health care system. To that end, my current activist commitment is to the low-cost IVF (LCIVF) movement, one that has gained significant traction globally over the past decade. LCIVF represents a new millennial activist attempt to respond to the Universal Declaration of Human Rights mandate (Article 16:1), which states, "Men and women of full age, without any limitation due to race, nationality or religion, have the right to marry and found a family."[51] LCIVF is thus a reproductive justice movement, driven by the goal of helping the world's infertile, most of whom are located in resource-poor settings,[52] including those in Western nations, such as we have seen in Arab Detroit.

In Europe, a group of prominent IVF scholar-activists, headed by Professor Willem Ombelet in Belgium, have called for a reproductive rights agenda that includes the provision of safe, affordable, and accessible IVF for the world's infertile.[53] As they point out, the vast majority of IVF cycles are delivered in the private medical sector, meaning that the costs may be prohibitive for most ordinary citizens and certainly for the infertile poor. The mission of LCIVF, therefore, is to make safe, affordable, effective IVF services accessible to everyone who needs them, including to disadvantaged minority communities like those in New Haven and Arab Detroit.

Making LCIVF a global reality remains a formidable challenge, but recent efforts and technological innovations to make a simple, transportable IVF laboratory system are certainly a step in the right direction. (And although technologically more difficult, a low-cost ICSI system also needs to be developed, to address the millions of cases of male infertility.) So far, LCIVF has gained support from WHO and the European Society for Human Reproduction and Embryology (ESHRE). In Europe, the LCIVF movement is part of a reproductive justice mission being supported by many prominent IVF clinicians and organizations. For example, the ESHRE Task Force on Ethics and Law has argued explicitly that "low-cost IVF will make treatment more accessible and thus reduce injustice."[54]

In North America, a nonprofit organization called "Friends of Low-Cost IVF" (FLCIVF) was created in 2011 by Professor Alan Trounson, emeritus professor at Monash University in Melbourne, Australia, along with his colleague Karin Hammarberg and a number of North American IVF practitioners (who invited me, as an anthropologist of IVF, to join them).[55] Since 2011, FLCIVF has conducted annual meetings and a postgraduate course through the American Society for Reproductive Medicine (ASRM). FLCIVF raises funds through private donations from individuals and charities interested in the LCIVF cause and works with IVF clinics willing to donate their services pro bono. The two main aims of FLCIVF are to provide simplified clinical IVF services for a minimal cost to reduce the financial burden of IVF services for childless couples who need them and to deliver reproductive health education to minimize the preventable forms of infertility.

My hope is that other global health agencies and philanthropic organizations will eventually take up this charge, including infertility and the LCIVF movement in the global reproductive rights and reproductive justice agendas. As seen in this book, it is aspirations for parenthood—the yearning for children who are wanted, needed, and cherished—that undergird the quest for IVF, even among impoverished communities such as those in Arab Detroit. Parenthood aspirations and child desires are clearly enduring in a world where nearly 95 percent of all adults, both men and women, still express the desire to have children at some point in their reproductive lives.[56]

Thus, on a most basic level, ensuring reproductive justice for the world's infertile people means providing affordable IVF as a basic right and expectation of citizenship. To do so, nation-states, including the United States, must resolve a number of important issues, including, first, whether the infertile have a disease needing treatment or whether having a baby is a "luxury" and thus of little or no concern to the state; second, whether health services are a right or entitlement of citizenship and, if so, whether IVF services should be considered as a part of basic health care; third, whether IVF and all its variants should be fully legalized or whether some aspects are to be constrained by the law; and finally, whether IVF services are an entitlement of citizens only, or whether noncitizens, including immigrants and refugees, can claim the right to IVF.

My personal hopes are two-fold. First, I hope that the US government will come to "mandate" subsidized IVF and ICSI in all fifty states of this country,[57] as do most Western European nations. Second, I hope that a variety of global health agencies and philanthropic organizations, for example, the technologically oriented Bill and Melinda Gates Foundation, will eventually take up the LCIVF challenge, including infertility and IVF as part of the global reproductive rights and reproductive justice agenda.

Given that infertility is a source of profound human suffering, ensuring access to IVF must be viewed as an important humanitarian and reproductive justice issue. Compassion for the infertile, respect for reproductive autonomy, and access to IVF as a basic health care entitlement are important reproductive rights goals for the twenty-first century. If the day comes when *all* infertile people have access to safe, effective, and affordable IVF—and *insha'Allah* (God willing), it will—then the reproductive exile of poor Arab refugees will come to an end. For infertile Arab refugees living on the margins of Detroit, this one small act of compassion would demonstrate beyond a reasonable doubt that America truly cares.

Coda

As I write these final words of *America's Arab Refugees*, it is January 20, 2017, the day of President Donald Trump's inauguration. I cannot help but to reflect on the uncertain future, and the many questions that a Trump presidency will bring. On the domestic level, will Trump actually enact the Muslim ban? Will Arab refugee resettlement in the United States be stopped? Will Iraqi refugees and other Muslims who do not yet have legal citizenship in the United States be deported? Will Islamophobia and hate crimes against Muslims spiral across the country? And what will happen to the Affordable Care Act? Will health care still be available to America's poor, including poor Arab refugees? Will health disparities increase in this country in the future?

On the international front, what will President Trump do about ISIS, given his campaign pledge to stop global terrorism? Will Trump increase the US military presence in the Middle East? Will new Middle East wars be started? Will the nuclear deal with Iran be revoked? What will that mean for Iran's role in an already sectarian-divided and war-torn region? And will Trump ally with Putin in some "grand strategy" for Syria? Or will the war in Syria escalate? Will millions more Syrians have to flee?

On Trump's inauguration day, I cannot begin to answer these questions. But, as a Middle East scholar, I am filled with trepidation. I do not know what a Trump presidency will mean for the world or for the fragile Middle Eastern region. I worry about the plight of Arab refugees, and I am concerned that the United States will lead the way in turning its back on this vulnerable population.

But, always an optimist, I ask readers to imagine a brighter world:

A Middle East that is safe for the people who live there.

An America that proves it still cares about Arab refugees.

Acknowledgments

This book about the lives of poor Arabs who fled from Middle Eastern war zones to Arab Detroit would not have been possible without the help of Dr. Michael Hassan Fakih. During my nearly eight years as a professor at the University of Michigan, Dr. Fakih facilitated all of my Middle Eastern research projects, including this one in Dearborn, Michigan, the so-called capital of Arab America. I owe a scholarly debt of gratitude to Dr. Fakih, whose enthusiasm for my research ideas never flagged and who was an important interlocutor, coauthor, and colleague during my time in Michigan. In addition, this study would not have been possible without the help and support of Dr. Khaled Sakhel, Hanaa Hijazi, and Deanna Darson, all of whom invested themselves in my study and assisted me in various ways. Hanaa in particular provided able research assistance, finding willing participants for my study and occasionally translating when particular Arabic terms or regional dialects proved especially challenging.

My ability to carry out five years of research in the Arab Detroit community was made possible by my location at the University of Michigan (UM) in Ann Arbor, a forty-minute drive to the west of Dearborn. Given the university's commitment to scholarly research of the highest caliber, I was encouraged by my home department to pursue this study, despite my very busy teaching and administrative schedule. To that end, I received excellent administrative support from Beth Talbot and Pauline Kennedy. I also had many wonderful UM colleagues, some of whom served as fine exemplars for how to conduct ethically driven, community participatory research projects in Michigan's many impoverished neighborhoods. These colleagues at the UM School of Public Health included Cleopatra Caldwell, Linda Chatters, Barbara Israel, Sherman James, Mark Padilla, Amy Schulz, Melissa Valerio, and Caroline Wong.

In UM's Center for Middle Eastern and North African Studies, where I served as the director, Marya Ayyash, Gottfried Hagen, Michael Kennedy, Sasha Knysh, Alyssa Surges, Mark Tessler, and Norman Yoffee were my most important friends and interlocutors. At UM, I was also fortunate to have many comrades in the worlds of medical anthropology, reproductive medicine, and science and technology studies, including Rosie Ceballo, Paul Edwards, Gabrielle Hecht, Nancy Hunt, Tim Johnson, Holly Peters-Golden, Elisha Renne, Liz Roberts, Jennifer Robertson, and Abby Stewart. Mary Piontek and Leslie Stainton were also supportive friends and colleagues.

I also mentored more than twenty talented UM graduate students in anthropology, Middle East Studies, public health, and medical history. These included Omowale Adenrele, Kate Allen, Sarah Arvey, Nicole Berry, Isabel Cordova, Sallie Han, Lisa Harris, Laura Heinemann, Lori Ingbar-Barer, Alyson Jones, Loulou Kobeissi, Jessa Leinaweaver, Kate McClellan, Emily McKee, Molly Moran, Mikaela Rogozen-Soltar, Eric Stein, Carla Stokes, Mandy Terc, Cecilia Tomori, and Emily Wentzell. Most of these students are now professors. It has been wonderful to watch their careers unfold.

Of these former UM students, Loulou Kobeissi deserves my biggest debt of gratitude for helping me work through my empirical data from a prior study in Beirut, Lebanon, and for assisting with the research on the health effects of war in Lebanon and Iraq, which appears in Chapter 2. Loulou herself comes from a Lebanese Shia Muslim family who left the country during the civil war, finding a second home in Michigan. I want to thank Loulou for being such an excellent research assistant, coauthor, colleague, and friend. She helped to explain nuanced aspects of Lebanese life in the home country, as well as in the Lebanese diaspora in Michigan, which informed my thinking and writing on this subject.

This study was made possible by generous funding from the National Science Foundation's Cultural Anthropology Program. I received two major NSF grants between 2003 and 2009, which allowed me to carry out my research project in Dearborn. Stuart Plattner and Deborah (Deb) Winslow were extremely helpful NSF program officers. Indeed, I remain extremely grateful to

NSF, as well as to the US government's two Fulbright programs, for funding all of my anthropological research in both the Middle East and the United States since the late 1980s.

As the Middle East continues to implode in political violence, the people whose stories are told in this book—primarily from Iraq, Lebanon, Yemen, and Palestine—remain exiled from countries embroiled in bitter conflict. As the Middle East refugee crisis continues to unfold, it is my Middle East anthropology colleagues to whom I turn for insight and commiseration. Among my many wonderful Middle East colleagues, Soraya Tremayne provides me with daily email camaraderie and scholarly sustenance. Together with our junior, Zeynep Gurtin, we have become a powerful writing trio, able to compare and contrast our disparate Muslim Middle Eastern research locations (Iran, Turkey, and the Arab world). In addition, my dear colleagues Nefissa Naguib, Sallama Shaker, and Lisa Wynn keep my heart connected to Egypt, the place where I started my anthropological journey so many years ago. And today, Daphna Birenbaum-Carmeli and I are in the midst of a binational anthropological research collaboration that is producing exciting results. Indeed, I have developed a wonderful community of colleagues and friends around the world—too many to name here—who make the life of an academic anthropologist a tremendously fascinating and gratifying career.

As an academic book writer, my life as an author has been immeasurably enhanced by working with skillful editors. At Stanford University Press, Kate Wahl cared about this project and provided me with a contract for this book well in advance of its gestation and delivery. Along the way, Michelle Lipinski has been a delightful and supportive anthropology editor, who has cheered me on literally from chapter to chapter. I also greatly benefited from the supportive comments of a number of reviewers, including among them Salmaan Keshavjee and Lucia Volk, who saw the potential of this book to reach multiple audiences. At Stanford University Press, I have also worked with a wonderful set of editorial assistants, including Norah Spiegel and Margaret Pinette, my copyeditor, as well as the design team who helped to create the book's stunning cover. In addition, a number of colleagues were instrumental in helping me to think through the book's title. They include Stan Brunn, Mia Fuller, Avi Shlaim, and Sarah Franklin, to whom I am especially grateful. I have given a number of presentations at their universities, including Cambridge and Oxford, as well as Harvard and Yale, receiving invaluable feedback in the process.

My final and most important thanks go to my cotravelers in life—my husband Kirk, my son Carl, and my daughter Justine. Living with me in the Middle East and accompanying me on many trips to Arab Detroit, they have come to appreciate the Arab world in their own ways and to understand why I have devoted my scholarly life to the region. I want to thank Kirk for being an atypical American man, one who was willing to take many career breaks to travel with me and to carry the heavy loads of both oversized luggage and parenting. Most of all, I want to thank Carl and Justine for enduring our many moves, their entry into new schools full of strangers, and their placement in language courses where they had no preparation whatsoever. I also thank Justine for her photos of Arab Detroit, which help set the scene in the introduction to this book. I have asked more of my family than most wives and mothers in America, yet our family's sacrifices have been nothing when compared to those people whose lives have been described in this book. Through their stories, I hope to have shown why Arab lives matter, and why America must do better—much, much better—in caring for Arab refugees.

Notes

Preface

1. Collins 2000; Crenshaw 1989; and Crenshaw et al. 1996.
2. Mullings 1996 and Schulz and Mullings 2005.

Prologue

1. Walbridge and Aziz (2000) describe the horrific conditions and violence experienced by the Iraqi refugee population before and after they gained entrance to Saudi Arabia.
2. Dewachi 2017.
3. Ali Al-Sistani of Najaf, Iraq, is one of the world's leading Shia Muslim clerics. His fatwas, or written religious rulings, are followed by millions of Shia Muslims.

Introduction

1. Project for the Study of the 21st Century 2015 and Uppsala Universitet Department of Peace and Conflict Research 2017.
2. Barnard 2014 and Heisler, Baker, and McKay 2015.
3. "Exodus," 2015.
4. Cockburn 2016.
5. "An Ill Wind," 2016.
6. Griswold 2016 and Newland 2015.
7. Newland 2015.
8. Friess and Morello 2015.

9. Mowafi 2011.
10. Gelvin 2015.
11. Coll 2004.
12. Hanson 2013 and Katz 2010.
13. Byman 2003.
14. Katz 2010.
15. Li 2005.
16. Byman 2003.
17. Dirik 2014.
18. Basham 2004.
19. Mansfield and Snyder 1995.
20. Li 2005.
21. Daoud 2015.
22. Abukhalil 2004 and al-Rasheed 2007.
23. Daoud 2015.
24. Dorsey 2016a,b.
25. "The Propaganda War," 2015.
26. Fisher 2016.
27. "Sunnis and Shia," 2016.
28. Zakaria 2016.
29. Nasr 2006, pp. 22, 24. Nasr argues that the US invasion of Iraq and American support of an Iraqi Shia-led government allowed Iraq's Shia population to rise up against Sunni political hegemony. As a public intellectual, Nasr has been very influential. He is now dean of the Johns Hopkins School of Advanced International Studies in Washington, D.C., and a senior fellow in foreign policy at the Brookings Institution.
30. Keynoush 2016; Poole 2016; and Ulrichsen 2016.
31. Caro 2015.
32. Bremmer 2015 and Fisk 2016.
33. "Saudi Arabia's Allies Bahrain, Sudan and UAE Act Against Iran," 2016.
34. Zakaria 2016, p. 1.
35. Cockburn 2016 and Gelvin 2012.
36. Cockburn 2016.
37. Guehenno 2015, 2016.
38. Stares 2015.
39. Ibid.
40. Ibid.
41. "ISIS Goes Global," 2016.
42. Arango 2015.
43. Sherlock 2015.
44. Gladstone and Ghannam 2015.
45. United Nations 2015.
46. "Russian Airstrikes in Syria 'Have Killed More Than 1,000 Civilians,'" 2016.
47. United Nations 2016.

48. Ibid.

49. Ibid.

50. United Nations High Commissioner for Refugees 2015a.

51. Mowafi 2011.

52. United Nations High Commissioner for Refugees 2016.

53. For excellent sources on Palestine, see Sa'di and Abu-Lughod 2007 and Taraki 2006. On Lebanon, see Abdelhady 2011; Fisk 2002; and Khalaf 2012.

54. The figures here have been compiled from multiple United Nations and web-based sources. See Inhorn 2011.

55. Peteet 2005.

56. Khater 2001.

57. United Nations Assistance Mission in Afghanistan 2016.

58. Watson Institute of International and Public Affairs 2016.

59. "Sen. McCain Expects a Permanent Presence in Afghanistan," 2015.

60. Hydari 2013.

61. Perkins 2015.

62. U.S. Citizenship and Immigration Services 2013.

63. Svab 2015.

64. United Nations High Commissioner for Refugees 2015b.

65. "Syrian Refugees Inter-Agency Regional Update, January 2016," 2016.

66. Cohen 2016b.

67. Griswold 2016.

68. UNHCR 2017.

69. Eurostat 2016.

70. Guehenno 2015, 2016.

71. Obaid 2016.

72. United Nations Office for the Coordination of Humanitarian Affairs 2017.

73. Yemen Situation Regional Refugee and Migrant Response Plan, January–December 2016.

74. "Refugees at Highest Level Ever, Reaching 65m, UN Says," 2016.

75. Sarroub 2005.

76. Abraham and Shryock 2000 and Schopmeyer 2011.

77. Abraham and Shryock 2000.

78. Baker et al. 2003 and Detroit Arab American Study Team 2009.

79. Warikoo 2016.

80. Sheppard 2011.

81. Notably, many Iraqi Christians have achieved wealth in part through grocery and liquor store ownership in poor black neighborhoods in the city (David 2000).

82. Schulz and Lempert 2004.

83. Abbey-Lambertz 2014.

84. Abraham, Howell, and Shryock 2011.

85. Baker et al. 2003.

86. In their 2011 book, *Arab Detroit 9/11*, editors Abraham, Howell, and Shryock describe "life in the Terror Decade." A number of other books also examine the tragedy of 9/11 for Arabs/Muslims living in America, including the kinds of discrimination, threats of deportation, racial profiling, and imprisonment faced by this now "suspect" religious-ethnic minority community. These include Bakalian and Bozorgmehr's *Backlash 9/11: Middle Eastern and Muslim Americans Respond* (2009); Bayoumi's *How Does it Feel to Be a Problem? Being Young and Arab in America* (2008); Bukhari et al.'s *Muslims' Place in the American Public Square: Hopes, Fears, and Aspirations* (2004); Cainkar's *Homeland Insecurity: The Arab American and Muslim American Experience After 9/11* (2009); Ewing's *Being and Belonging: Muslims in the United States since 9/11* (2008); Grewal's *Islam Is a Foreign Country: American Muslims and the Global Crisis of Authority* (2013); Jamal and Naber's *Race and Arab Americans before and after 9/11: From Invisible Citizens to Visible Subjects* (2008); Peek's *Behind the Backlash: Muslim Americans after 9/11* (2011); Shaheen's *Guilty: Hollywood's Verdict on Arabs after 9/11* (2008); and Shryock's *Islamophobia, Islamophilia: Beyond the Politics of Enemy and Friend* (2010).

87. Bronner 2014.

88. "President Obama's 2016 State of the Union Address," 2016.

89. Abraham and Shryock 2000.

90. Ajrouch and Jamal 2007; Jamal and Naber 2008; and Naber 2000.

91. Ahmed, Kia-Keating, and Tsai 2011.

92. Shah et al. 2008.

93. Ali et al. 2005.

94. Abraham and Shryock 2000.

95. Abraham, Howell, and Shryock 2011.

96. Shryock and Abraham 2000.

97. Inhorn 2003.

98. Bourgois and Hart 2011 and Quesada, Hart, and Bourgois 2011.

99. Braveman 2006.

100. Singer 2009.

101. Ostrach and Singer 2013.

102. Maraniss 2015.

103. Ginsburg and Rapp 1995: 3.

104. Inhorn and Patrizio 2015 and Spar 2006.

105. Inhorn 2011.

Chapter 1

1. Ostrach and Singer 2013.

2. Ibid.

3. Ibid., p. 257.

4. Jamail 2013.

5. Becker 1999.

6. WHO 1978.

7. Ghobarah, Huth, and Russett 2004.

8. Loulou Kobeissi, my former doctoral student at the University of Michigan School of Public Health, helped tremendously in this research on the public health costs of war in Lebanon. We published some of this information in the *Journal of Social Affairs* (Inhorn and Kobeissi 2006). But the journal is published in the United Arab Emirates, and thus the article has never been available to international audiences.

9. Pintak 2003.

10. Tessler 1994.

11. Ibid.

12. Lucia Volk's book, *Memorials and Martyrs in Modern Lebanon* (2010), traces efforts to publicly commemorate Lebanon's modern war history, primarily through the erection of public monuments, including to the assassinated Lebanese Prime Minister Rafik Hariri.

13. Jabbra 2004 and Saxena, Kulczyck, and Jurdi 2004.

14. United Nations Development Programme Lebanon 2002.

15. United Nations Office of Disarmament Affairs 2017.

16. United Nations Mine Action Service 1999.

17. World Health Organization (WHO) Eastern Mediterranean Regional Office 2017a.

18. Baddoura 1990.

19. Yaktin and Labban 1992.

20. World Health Organization (WHO) Eastern Mediterranean Regional Office 2017a.

21. Makdisi 1990.

22. Saab et al. 2003.

23. Karam, Yabroudi, and Melhem 2002 and Karam et al. 2006, 2008.

24. World Health Organization (WHO) Eastern Mediterranean Regional Office 2017a.

25. United Nations Development Programme Lebanon 2002.

26. Joseph 1994, 2004.

27. Inhorn 2012a,b and Inhorn and Kobeissi 2006.

28. Abu-Musa et al. 2008 and Inhorn 2012b.

29. United Nations Development Programme 2002.

30. United Nations Development Programme Lebanon 2002.

31. World Health Organization (WHO) Eastern Mediterranean Regional Office 2004.

32. Joseph 1994, 2004.

33. Makhoul and Harrison 2002; Makhoul, Abi Ghanem, and Ghanem 2003; and Makhoul, Shayboub, and Jamal 2004.

34. Makhoul, Abi Ghanem, and Ghanem 2003: 251.

35. Ibid.

36. The situation of Palestinians in Lebanon is poignantly captured in Julie Peteet's book, *Landscape of Hope and Despair: Palestinian Refugee Camps* (2005). Brazilian anthropologist Gustavo Barbosa (2008, 2013) has also studied the hope and despair of young male Palestinian refugees in Lebanon.

37. World Health Organization (WHO) Eastern Mediterranean Regional Office 2004: 1.

38. Ibid.

39. Hamdan 2002.

40. Ibid.: 181.

41. Ibid.: 182.

42. Ibid.

43. Ibid.: 185.

44. Ibid.: 187.

45. Ghanem 2016.

46. Ibid.

47. Refaat and Mohanna 2013.

48. Ibid.

49. Ibid.: 763.

50. Kurzmann 2013.

51. Ibid.

52. World Health Organization 2003.

53. In a lecture at Yale University on April 27, 2016, entitled "Isis, Syria, and the Future of the Middle East," UCLA historian James Gelvin argued that ISIS's increasing global terrorism is, in fact, a signal of its weakening position in the Middle East itself. Thus, it must inspire spectacular terrorist attacks outside of Iraq and Syria to draw attention to its cause. See Gelvin 2016.

54. Other scholars have written about some of these public health costs of war. They include Dewachi 2011; Dewachi et al. 2014; Harding and Libal 2010; and Hills and Wasfi 2010.

55. Iraq Body Count 2017.

56. Roberts et al. 2004.

57. Burnham et al. 2006.

58. Iraq Family Health Survey Study Group 2008.

59. Hagopian et al. 2013.

60. Iraq Body Count 2017.

61. Iraq Body Count 2017.

62. "Operation Iraqi Freedom," 2017.

63. Alhashawi et al. 2009 and Sadik et al. 2011.

64. Alhashawi et al. 2009.

65. Fleck 2004 and Sadik et al. 2011.

66. al-Saffar 2007.

67. Fleck 2004 and "Iraq Mental Health Deteriorates with Violence," 2006.

68. "Iraq Mental Health Deteriorates with Violence," 2006.

69. A search of Google Scholar reveals numerous studies of the mental health impact of war on US and UK troops deployed in Iraq and Afghanistan. In comparison, only one major study—the Iraq Mental Health Survey (IMHS), conducted in 2007 and 2008—examines the mental health impact of war on Iraqis themselves. The dearth of research on this topic is noted by the members of the IMHS study team (Alhashawi et al. 2009), when compared to the huge literature emerging on US/UK veteran mental health.

70. Alhashawi et al. 2009.

71. Clark 2003.

72. Medical Aid for Iraqi Children (MAIC) 2017. MAIC was registered as a UK-based nonprofit to send medical supplies to Iraqi children after the First Gulf War and during the UN sanctions period. It was operating for the first six years of the Second Gulf War, but it closed on July 31, 2009. Its active website can still be found at www.maic.org.uk/.

73. al-Obaidi, Budosan, and Jeffrey 2010 and Médecins Sans Frontières 2013.

74. World Health Organization Eastern Mediterranean Regional Office 2007.

75. Médecins Sans Frontières 2013.

76. Sadik et al. 2011: 39.

77. Sadik et al. 2011 and Médecins Sans Frontières 2013.

78. Bhutta and Black 2013.

79. World Health Organization 2003.

80. al-Obaidi, Budosan, and Jeffrey 2010.

81. Ghazi et al. 2013.

82. World Health Organization 2003.

83. Bhutta and Black 2013.

84. World Health Organization (WHO) Eastern Mediterranean Regional Office 2007.

85. Alaani et al. 2010, 2011; and Busby, Hamdan, and Ariabi 2010.

86. Taylor et al. 2014.

87. Save the Children 2016.

88. Diamond 2005 and Nasr 2006.

89. Save the Children 2016.

90. Ibid.: 1.

91. Face the Facts, George Washington University 2013.

92. Donaldson et al. 2010.

93. World Health Organization 2003.

94. Sadik et al. 2011.

95. Ibid.

96. Burnham et al. 2012.

97. Heisler, Baker, and McKay 2015.

98. Fahey 1999, 2003, 2004.

99. Fahey 2004: 4.

100. A group of researchers in the United Kingdom conducted follow-up studies of UK veterans of the First Gulf War, including those suffering from so-called Gulf War syndrome (GWS). They did find some evidence of male infertility and increased time to conception among male veterans. But links to other health problems, including cancer and birth defects, could not be discerned, even though those men suffering from GWS complained of a variety of health symptoms. See Doyle et al. 2004, 2006; Maconochie et al. 2003; Maconochie, Doyle, and Carson 2004; Macfarlane et al. 2003, 2005; and Simmons, Maconochie, and Doyle 2004. In her book, *Impotent Warriors: Perspectives on Gulf War Syndrome, Vulnerability and Masculinity*, anthropologist Susie Kilshaw (2008) explores the impact of GWS on UK veterans' lives, claims for disability compensation, and masculinity and sexuality.

101. McDiarmid et al. 2004.

102. Jamail 2013.

103. Fahey 2004.

104. World Health Organization 2003.

105. Ibid.

106. Alaani et al. 2010; 2011 and Busby, Hamdan, and Ariabi 2010.

107. Alaani et al. 2011: 1.

108. Webster 2013.

109. Ibid.

110. Jamail 2013.

111. Fahey 2004: 24.

Chapter 2

1. For information about USRAP, see U.S. Citizenship and Immigration Services (2013, 2017).

2. Ali's story is also told in Inhorn 2012a, Chapter 5.

3. See Seth Holmes's *Fresh Fruit, Broken Bodies: Migrant Farmworkers in the United States* (2013) for an award-winning account of structural vulnerability among Mexican migrant fruit pickers. See also Organista et al. 2013; Quesada, Hart, and Bourgois 2011; Walter, Bourgois, and Loinaz 2004; and Worby et al. 2014.

4. See Philippe Bourgois's *In Search of Respect: Selling Crack in El Barrio* (2003), as well as Sabrina Marie Chase's *Surviving HIV/AIDS in the Inner City: How Resourceful Latinas Beat the Odds* for powerful ethnographic portrayals of structural vulnerability among inner-city Puerto Rican men and women.

5. See Philippe Bourgois and Jeffrey Schonberg's *Righteous Dopefiend* (2009) and Kelly Ray Knight's *addicted.pregnant.poor* (2011) for outstanding and empathic studies of addicted men and women in San Francisco. See also Bourgois, Lettiere, and Quesada 1997; Lopez et al. 2013; Messac et al. 2013; Rhodes et al. 2012; and Rosenblum et al. 2014.

6. Smid, Bourgois, and Auerswald 2010.

7. Hansen, Bourgois, and Drucker 2014.
8. Quesada, Hart, and Bourgois 2011: 340.
9. Bourgois et al. 2017.
10. Ticktin 2011.
11. Quesada, Hart, and Bourgois 2011.
12. Zong and Batalova 2015.
13. U.S. Citizenship and Immigration Services 2015.
14. Human Rights Institute, Georgetown University Law Center 2009.
15. Ibid.
16. Zong and Batalova 2015.
17. Human Rights Institute, Georgetown University Law Center 2009 and Zong and Batalova 2015.
18. Human Rights Institute, Georgetown University Law Center 2009 and Svab 2015. Two recent books focus on the plight of Iraqi interpreters left behind (Johnson 2014), and those that made it to America (Campbell 2016).
19. Data for Table 2.1 come from www.uscis.gov/humanitarian/refugees-asylum/refugees/iraqi-refugee-processing-fact-sheet and Zong and Batalova 2015.
20. Only Burma outstripped Iraq as the top refugee-producing country, at 24 percent of the total.
21. Taylor et al. 2014.
22. Human Rights Institute, Georgetown University Law Center 2009.
23. Ibid.: 19.
24. This section on the systemic flaws in the USRAP program represents a summary of issues outlined in the detailed report on the Iraqi refugee crisis in America, published online by the Human Rights Institute, Georgetown University Law Center, in 2009.
25. UNHCR Iraqi Refugee Data Analysis Report, as reported in Human Rights Institute, Georgetown University Law Center 2009: 30.
26. United Nations High Commissioner for Refugees, Trauma Survey in Syria Highlights Suffering of Iraqi Refugees, as reported in Human Rights Institute, Georgetown University Law Center 2009: 32.
27. Taylor et al. 2014.
28. Human Rights Institute, Georgetown University Law Center 2009: 1.
29. Taylor et al. 2014.
30. Ibid.: 1135.
31. Elsouhag et al. 2015 and Yanni et al. 2013.
32. Elsouhag et al. 2015.
33. US Committee for Refugees and Immigrants, Detroit, 2015.
34. Schopmeyer 2011.
35. Ibid.
36. Instead of moving to Dearborn, new Iraqi refugees are being resettled primarily in the northern Detroit suburbs of Southfield and Sterling Heights.

37. Svab 2015.

38. Data for Table 2.2 come from U.S. Department of State, January 31, 2015, as reported in Svab 2015.

39. Zong and Batalova 2015.

40. Schopmeyer 2011.

41. Sheppard 2011.

42. For more information on the services performed by these organizations, see Arab American and Chaldean Council 2017, and ACCESS 2017.

43. US Committee for Refugees and Immigrants, Detroit, 2015.

44. Guttersohn 2014.

45. Svab 2015.

46. Guttersohn 2014: 3.

47. Ibid.

48. Davey 2014; Davey and Walsh 2013; and Foroohar 2014.

49. Maraniss 2015.

50. Yaccino 2013.

51. MacDonald 2016.

52. Davey 2014.

53. Rose 1978 and Rose and Deskins 1991.

54. Abbey-Lambertz 2014 and United Ways of Michigan 2014.

55. Ibid.

56. Bouffard 2015.

57. Brookings Institution 2016 and Warikoo 2016.

58. Brookings Institution 2016.

59. Warikoo 2016.

60. Ibid.

61. LeDuff 2013 and Maraniss 2015.

62. Aswad 1999.

63. Chetty et al. 2016.

64. As reported in Warikoo 2016.

Chapter 3

1. Crenshaw 1989.

2. Collins 2000: 21.

3. Ibid.: 245.

4. Ibid.: 21.

5. Ibid.: 76.

6. Ibid.; see Chapter 4 for a detailed discussion of controlling images.

7. Ibid.; see Chapter 10 for a detailed discussion of the transnational dimensions of intersectionality.

8. Ibid.: 247.

9. Mullings 1996.

10. Mullings and Wali 2001.

11. Schulz and Mullings 2005.

12. Schulz et al. 2000a, 2000b, 2002, 2006.

13. Inhorn and Fakih 2006; Inhorn and Whittle 2001; and Whittle and Inhorn 2001.

14. David 2000; Haddad 2000; Robinson 2011; and Schopmeyer 2011.

15. Aswad 1999 and Edin and Kefalas 2007.

16. National Urban League 2015.

17. Braveman 2006.

18. Carter-Pokras and Baquet 2002.

19. Institute of Medicine 2002.

20. Edwards 2014.

21. Hassoun 1999, 2005; and Mullings and Wali 2001.

22. Ramos et al. 2010; Taylor et al. 2014; and Yanni et al. 2013.

23. Abdulrahim and Baker 2009 and Taylor et al. 2014.

24. Bridges 2011; Lane 2008; and Mullings and Wali 2001. See also Fujimoto et al. 2010.

25. National Institutes of Health 2006.

26. Nsiah-Jefferson and Hall 1989: 110

27. Ceballo 1999: 9. See also Ceballo, Graham, and Hart 2016.

28. Inhorn 1996, especially Chapter 6 on "Child Desire."

29. Schopmeyer 2011.

30. Ceballo 1999; Mullings and Wali 2001; and Nsiah-Jefferson and Hall 1989.

31. Dodson 1998; Edin and Kefalas 2007; and Mullings and Wali 2001.

32. Edin and Nelson 2013; McAdoo 1993; and Taylor and Johnson 1997.

33. Inhorn 1996, 2003.

34. Inhorn 1994, 2012a.

35. Ceballo 1999.

36. Taylor, Chatters, and Levin 2004.

37. Mackenzie 2013.

38. Caesar and Williams 2002 and Roberts 1998.

39. Kulwicki 1996.

40. Inhorn 2015 and Inhorn and Serour 2011.

41. Krieger et al. 1993 and Roberts 1998.

42. Institute of Medicine 2002.

43. Bridges 2011 and Roberts 1998.

44. Baker 2000 and Thomas 2000.

45. Krieger et al. 1993; Williams 2001; and Williams, Neighbors, and Jackson 2003.

46. Naber 2000.

47. Said 1978.

48. Even some ethnographies by anthropologists and sociologists have portrayed black men in this way. See Mackenzie (2013) for a critique of this portrayal.

49. Caldwell et al. 2004.

50. Altman 2015a, 2015b and Devichand 2016.

51. Abraham, Howell, and Shryock 2011.

52. Sarah Franklin (1997) coined the term *hope technology* to characterize IVF.

53. Roberts 1998.

54. Becker et al. 2006; Feinberg et al. 2007; and Quiroga 2002.

55. Abbey, Andrews, and Halman 1991.

56. Becker 1997, 2000; Greil 1991; Sandelowski 1993; and Thompson 2005.

57. Inhorn, Ceballo, and Nachtigall 2009.

58. Institute of Medicine 2002 and National Institutes of Health 2006.

59. Jain 2006; Jain and Hornstein 2005; Kissil and Davey 2012; Missmer, Seifer, and Jain 2011; and White, McQuillan, and Greil 2006.

60. Bitler and Schmidt 2006 and Stephen and Chandra 2000.

61. Jain and Hornstein 2005.

62. Ginsburg and Rapp 1995: 3. However, Shellee Colen (1995) is the one who coined this term in her chapter on West Indian childcare workers in Ginsburg and Rapp's (1995) seminal edited volume, *Conceiving the New World Order: The Global Politics of Reproduction.*

63. Nsiah-Jefferson and Hall 1989: 18.

64. Edin and Nelson 2013 and Inhorn 2012a.

65. Franklin 2016, personal communication.

66. Becker 2000, Harris 2006; Spar 2006; and Thompson 2005, 2013.

67. The term *take-home baby* is not a CDC term. Rather, it is used widely and colloquially to refer to IVF live births.

68. Sunderam et al. 2015.

69. Boivin et al. 2007.

70. Connolly et al. 2010.

71. Chambers et al. 2009 and Connolly et al. 2010.

72. Boivin et al. 2007.

73. Collins 2002.

74. Chambers et al. 2009.

75. Ibid.

76. The mandate states are Arkansas, California, Connecticut, Hawaii, Illinois, Louisiana, Maryland, Massachusetts, Montana, New Jersey, New York, Ohio, Rhode Island, Texas, and West Virginia.

77. Interview with Barbara Collura, President/CEO of Resolve: The National Infertility Association. November 30, 2015.

78. McCarthy-Keith et al. 2010.

79. Bitler and Schmidt 2006.

80. Buchmueller et al. 2016 and Inhorn and Patrizio 2015.

81. Inhorn 2012a.

82. Ibid.; see Chapter 4.

83. Inhorn 2012b.

84. Abu-Musa et al. 2008 and Kobeissi et al. 2008.

85. Maconochie, Doyle, and Carson 2004.

86. Ibid., p. 196.

87. Some cases of azoospermia are caused by congenital obstructions of the vas deferens, required for sperm transport. Men with this form of azoospermia have a mild genital form of cystic fibrosis, which is an inherited disease.

88. Some men with azoospermia actually produce sperm in their testicles, but obstructions in the sperm-transport vessels prevent the sperm from being released into the ejaculate.

89. Inhorn 2007.

90. Varicocelectomies are associated with surgical complications, such as the development of hydrocele, or the buildup of fluid in the scrotum.

91. Gutmann 2007 and Myntti et al. 2000.

92. Inhorn 2016.

93. Becker 2002.

94. Inhorn and Tremayne 2012.

95. Inhorn 2006, 2012a.

96. Inhorn 1996, 2003, 2012a.

97. Inhorn 2012a.

98. Franklin 1997.

99. Inhorn 2003, 2012a.

100. Becker 2000.

101. Evers 2016.

102. Inhorn 2003.

103. Bittles and Matson 2000 and Spar 2006.

104. Franklin 2012.

105. Taylor et al. 2014.

106. Ceballo, Graham, and Hart 2016.

Chapter 4

1. I have heard that an IVF clinic once operated in the northern Iraqi city of Mosul, which was taken over by ISIS.

2. Liminality is the concept made famous by anthropologists Arnold van Gennep (1906) and Victor Turner (1966), who described the intermediate stage in various rites of passage as the "liminal period." Over the years, liminality has been used more generally to describe the uncertainties and ambiguities of life passages between various states, for example, from illness to health, from home to host countries, from adolescence to adulthood, and so on.

3. Kleinman 1992, 2007.

4. I also interviewed one Lebanese Maronite Catholic man, who had grown up in Venezuela, and one Iraqi Chaldean Catholic man, who had migrated to southeastern Michigan from Iraq.

5. I have written a great deal about understandings and experiences of infertility in the Muslim Middle East. See especially Inhorn 1994, 1996, 2003, 2012a.

6. Ebrahimnejad 2011.

7. Kridli 2002 and Shah et al. 2008.

8. Inhorn 2003.

9. Lotfalian 2004.

10. Inhorn 2003.

11. Abbasi-Shavazi et al. 2008; Clarke 2009; Inhorn and Tremayne 2012; and Serour 1996, 2006, 2008.

12. Inhorn 1996.

13. Inhorn and Tremayne 2012.

14. This is a real concern in societies where anonymous egg and sperm donors have produced multiple offspring. Some sperm donors in countries such as the United States have biologically "fathered" scores of offspring. Thus, informal efforts are being made by some parents of these donor children to locate half-siblings and prevent the possibility of future incestuous relations.

15. Apparently, third-party reproductive assistance is being practiced in the Muslim country of Mali, but without explicit acceptance by Sunni Muslim religious authorities (Hörbst 2016).

16. Egg donation is not viewed as negatively as sperm donation because egg donors are sometimes classified as being similar to co-wives in a polygynous marriage. Furthermore, Muslim societies are patrilineal, and patriliny is not disrupted by egg donation as it is by sperm donation. Finally, women who accept donor eggs are able to develop "milk kinship" with the donor egg child via breast-feeding. These social justifications and mechanisms have made egg donation much more morally acceptable than sperm donation. Many Shia clerics and couples have accepted egg donation as a form of third-party reproductive assistance. Some infertile Sunni Muslim couples have accepted it as well. See Inhorn 2012a, Chapter 8, for a fuller discussion.

17. Abbasi-Shavazi et al. 2008; Clarke 2009; Clarke and Inhorn 2011; and Inhorn and Tremayne 2012.

18. Clarke 2009; Inhorn 2012a; and Inhorn and Tremayne 2012, 2016.

19. See Inhorn 2012a, Chapter 7, for a fuller discussion of sperm donation.

20. Clarke 2007.

21. Inhorn 2006, 2012a.

22. The infertile husband, who was an uneducated, working-class Shia Muslim man, felt the need to "confess" the sperm donation to me, which he did in a private room of the clinic. This confession seemed to provide him with some moral relief, especially when I told him that sperm donation was common in America and other Western countries. See Inhorn 2012a, Chapter 7.

23. In this study, twelve couples were cousins, and of these, four were first cousins (three maternal and one paternal). See Inhorn 2012a, Chapter 4, for a fuller discussion of the cultural causes and genetic consequences of consanguineous (cousin) marriage.

24. Greco et al. 2013.

25. Three men in the study were already stepfathers. Two men had married divorced American women. One was a Syrian man with four American stepchildren, and one was an Iraqi man with three American stepchildren. In the third case, a Lebanese man and woman, who had been "childhood sweethearts" from the same village but who had been prevented from marrying by the woman's father, "found" each other again after many years. She was unhappily married with three children. He had been married only briefly but was divorced without any children. After literally running into each other at an Arab Detroit street fair, they renewed their relationship. She soon divorced her husband and remarried her childhood love, who became the stepfather of her three children. Still, they wanted to have more children together and had become patients at IVF Michigan.

26. Inhorn 1996, 2003, 2012a.

27. Kleinman 1997: 45.

28. Ibid.

29. Thompson 2005.

30. Inhorn 1994, 2003, 2012a.

31. Another Yemeni man tragically lost both hands (and then his lower arms due to infection) in a workplace accident. He, too, was living on SSI disability payments and Medicaid. His wife had to feed and groom him, although he told me that he could still drive a car with the stumps of his arms.

32. Inhorn 2011.

33. Inhorn 2011, 2015.

34. *Reprotravel* is my contraction of the term *reproductive travel* (Inhorn 2015). Similar contractions exist in the literature, for example, *reprogenetics* to signify the intersection of reproductive medicine and genetics.

35. Lebanese civilians who were sheltering in a UN compound in the village of Qana in southern Lebanon were killed by Israeli shelling.

36. I have made this argument elsewhere, including in Inhorn (2015) and Inhorn and Patrizio (2009).

37. Dufoix 2008.

38. Inhorn 2003, 2015.

39. Inhorn 2012a and Inhorn, Patrizio, and Serour 2010.

40. Iraqis shared this sense of pride in their home country's former health care system. However, because of the ongoing conflict, none of them were free to repro-travel to Iraq. Yemenis, on the other hand, were often skeptical of Yemen's health care system. Sometimes they pointed to talented physicians but lamented the lack of a developed medical infrastructure.

41. Inhorn 1996.

42. Indeed, in Lebanon, IVF waiting rooms were often filled with older women dressed in black, to signify their widow status. Such waiting rooms full of mothers would be unusual in an IVF clinic in the United States, where couples often come to their appointments alone.

43. I have written extensively about iatrogenesis and infertility in the Middle East (Inhorn 1994, 2012a, and 2015). But in this case, the iatrogenic infertility was produced by a physician in the United States.

44. TESA is the method used to obtain sperm directly from the testicles in cases of azoospermia. In men who have had vasectomies, TESA can also be used to retrieve sperm in this way.

45. Many Western IVF practitioners will transfer only a single embryo into a woman's uterus, to avoid the risky complication of a high-order multiple pregnancy (HOMP). However, in the Middle East, HOMP pregnancies are common because IVF clinics transfer an excess number of embryos in an attempt to increase the chances of conception (Inhorn 2017).

Conclusion

1. Moore 2011.

2. This will become essential, as it was during and after the Balkan War, when thousands of Bosnian Muslim children lost their parents or were abandoned by mothers who had become pregnant through rape.

3. UNICEF 2016.

4. Gladstone 2016.

5. Elbadawi 2016.

6. Malsin 2016.

7. "Syrian Refugees Seeking Help," 2015 and Toma and Bhabha 2013.

8. Ennaji 2016.

9. Ali 2010; Davidson 2005, 2008; Inhorn 2015; Kanna 2011; and Vora 2013.

10. Enaji 2016.

11. "UAE to Accept 15,000 Syrian Refugees within Five Year," 2016.

12. UNICEF 2016.

13. Luyken 2017.

14. UNICEF 2016: 2.

15. DeYoung 2016.

16. Cohen 2016a.

17. Ibid.

18. Ibid.: 2.

19. Goyette 2016.

20. Turner (2016) asks in an article, "Are Syrian Men Vulnerable Too? Gendering the Syria Refugee Response," which questions why women and children have been

prioritized in humanitarian efforts, sometimes at the expense of husbands and fathers, who are equally as "vulnerable" to death, brutality, and resettlement poverty.

21. Goyette 2016.
22. Oxfam 2016.
23. Goyette 2016: 2.
24. Ibid.
25. Oxfam 2016.
26. Ibid.
27. Ibid.
28. Ibid.
29. Ibid.
30. Zenko 2017.
31. Cooper 2016 and Landler 2016.
32. Erlanger and Castle 2016 and "Chilcot Report: Findings at at Glance," 2016.
33. "Chilcot Report: Findings at at Glance," 2016.
34. Erlanger and Castle 2016 and "Chilcot Report: Findings at at Glance," 2016.
35. "Chilcot Report: Findings at a Glance," 2016.
36. Ibid.
37. Erlanger and Castle 2016: 2.
38. "Chilcot Report: Findings at a Glance," 2016.
39. Greenstock 2016.
40. Malloch-Brown 2016.
41. Inhorn 2008.
42. In 2016, the AAA decided to devote its attention to Israel, debating whether Israeli universities should be officially boycotted by the AAA and its membership. This boycott, divest, and sanction (BDS) resolution was not ultimately approved by the AAA membership during its spring 2016 voting cycle. Some might argue that in the midst of wars in Syria, Iraq, Afghanistan, Libya, and Yemen, boycotting Israeli academic institutions seemed like a misplaced and mistimed AAA measure. Yet, to some degree, it speaks to my point about the AAA membership's lack of antiwar activism and failure to hold the US government, in addition to Israel, responsible for so much of the suffering in the Middle East. Indeed, the United States and many other nations—including Russia, Saudi Arabia, Iran, France, and Turkey, to name only a few—have blood on their hands in escalating rather than defusing the Middle East fighting. Although Israel has certainly caused egregious suffering among the Palestinian population—as well as among the southern Lebanese, whose stories have been told in the pages of this book—the blame for Middle Eastern bloodshed is widespread. Clearly, a great deal of blame must be placed on the United States and its disastrous foreign policy under former US President George W. Bush and his neoconservative regime. The question remains as to whether Bush himself should be tried for war crimes.
43. Before I became an anthropologist, I was a journalist. I have always contended that the two fields overlap considerably, and I believe that I am a better and clearer writer because of my journalistic training. Thus, I am not convinced by the

sanctimonious attitudes of some anthropologists who condemn journalists for their lack of "in-depth" understanding of issues and places. What journalists lack in "depth," they certainly make up for in courage compared to most anthropologists.

44. Lutz, Mazzarino, and Inhorn, forthcoming.

45. Guttersohn 2014: 2.

46. For example, many Iraqi refugees have been resettled in the San Bernadino metropolitan area, known locally as the "Inland Empire." This high-poverty, Latino-majority region in southern California was the site for the infamous San Bernadino terrorist attack on December 2, 2015, in which fourteen people were killed and twenty-two others seriously injured. The San Bernadino shooters were a Pakistani American Muslim couple. They were neither Iraqis nor refugees. To reiterate a crucial point, no refugee has ever committed an act of terrorism on American soil as of this writing.

47. Kalb 2016.

48. Ibid.

49. Ibid.

50. Human Rights Institute, Georgetown University Law Center 2009.

51. United Nations 1948.

52. Bennett 2016 and Hammarburg and Kirkman 2013.

53. Ombelet et al. 2008a, 2008b.

54. ESHRE Task Force 2009: 1009.

55. Friends of Low Cost IVF 2017.

56. Boivin et al. 2007.

57. Interview with Barbara Collura, President/CEO of Resolve: The National Infertility Association. November 30, 2015.

References

Abbasi-Shavazi, Mohammad Jalal, Marcia C. Inhorn, Hajiieh Bibi Razeghi-Nasrabad, and Ghasem Toloo. "'The Iranian ART Revolution': Infertility, Assisted Reproductive Technology, and Third-party Donation in the Islamic Republic of Iran." *Journal of Middle East Women's Studies* 4(2008): 1–28.

Abbey, Antonia, Frank M. Andrews, and L. Jill Halman. "Gender's Role in Responses to Infertility." *Psychology of Women Quarterly* 15 (1991): 295–316.

Abbey-Lambertz, Kate. "Most Detroit Families Can't Afford Their Basic Needs: Report." *The Huffington Post*, September 15, 2014. Available at www.huffingtonpost.com/2014/09/04/detroit-poverty-alice-report_n_5760602.html.

Abdelhady, Dalia. *The Lebanese Diaspora: The Arab Immigrant Experience in Montreal, New York, and Paris*. New York: NYU Press, 2011.

Abdulrahim, Sawsan, and Wayne Baker. "Differences in Self-Rated Health by Immigrant Status and Language Preference among Arab Americans in the Detroit Metropolitan Area." *Social Science & Medicine* 68 (2009): 2097–2103.

Abraham, Nabeel, Sally Howell, and Andrew Shryock, eds. *Arab Detroit 9/11: Life in the Terror Decade*. Detroit, MI: Wayne State University Press, 2011.

Abraham, Nabeel, and Andrew Shryock. eds. *Arab Detroit: From Margin to Mainstream*. Detroit, MI: Wayne State University Press, 2000.

Abukhalil, As'ad. *The Battle for Saudi Arabia: Royalty, Fundamentalism, and Global Power*. New York: Seven Stories Press, 2004.

Abu-Musa, Antoine A., Loulou Kobeissi, Antoine B. Hannoun, and Marcia C. Inhorn. "Effect of War on Fertility: A Review of the Literature." *Reproductive BioMedicine Online* 17(2008): 43–53.

ACCESS. "ACCESS: Assisting, Improving, Empowering Our Community." Retrieved on July 5, 2017, from www.accesscommunity.org/.

Ahmed, S. R., M. Kia-Keating, and K. H. Tsai. "A Structural Model of Racial Discrimination, Acculturative Stress, and Cultural Resources among Arab American Adolescents." *American Journal of Community Psychology* 48 (2011): 181–192.

Ajrouch, Kristine J., and Amaney Jamal. "Assimilating to a White Identity: The Case of Arab Americans." *International Migration Review* 41 (2007): 860–879.

Alaani, Samira, Mozhgan Savabieasfahani, Mohammad Tafash, and Paola Manduca. "Four Polygamous Families with Congenital Birth Defects from Fallujah, Iraq." *International Journal of Environmental Research in Public Health* 8 (2010): 89–96.

Alaani, Samira, Muhammed Tafash, Christopher Busby, Malak Hamdan, and Eleonore Blaurock-Busch. "Uranium and Other Contaminants in Hair from the Parents of Children with Congenital Anomalies in Fallujah, Iraq." *Conflict and Health* 5 (2011): 1–15.

Ali, O. M., G. Milstein, and P. M. Marzuk. "The Imam's Role in Meeting the Counseling Needs of Muslim Communities in the United States." *Psychiatric Services* 56 (2005): 202–205.

Ali, Syed. *Dubai: Gilded Cage*. New Haven, CT: Yale University Press, 2010.

al-Obaidi, AbdulKareem, Boris Budosan, and Linda Jeffrey. "Child and Adolescent Mental Health in Iraq: Current Situation and Scope for Promotion of Child and Adolescent Mental Health Policy." *Intervention* 8 (2010): 40–51.

al-Rasheed, Madawi. *Contesting the Saudi State: Islamic Voices from a New Generation*. Cambridge, UK: Cambridge University Press, 2007.

Alhashawi, Salih, et al., on Behalf of the Iraq Mental Health Survey Study Group. "The Prevalence and Correlates of DSM-IV Disorders in the Iraq Mental Health Survey (IMHS)." *World Psychiatry* 8 (2009): 97–109.

al-Saffar, S. "Integrating Rehabilitation of Torture Victims into the Public Health of Iraq." *Torture* 17 (2007): 156–168.

Altman, Alex. "Black Lives Matter: A New Civil Rights Movement Is Turning a Protest Cry into a Political Force." *Time*, December 21 (2015): 116–125.

———. "Where Black Lives Matter Goes from Here." *Time*, August 31 (2015): 22–24.

Arab American and Chaldean Council. "Arab American and Chaldean Council: MyACC.org." Retrieved on July 5, 2017, from www.google.com/search?q=american+chaldean+council&ie=utf-8&oe=utf-8.

Arango, Tim. "Key Iraqi City Falls to ISIS as Last of Security Forces Flee." *New York Times*, May 17, 2015. Available at www.nytimes.com/2015/05/18/world/middleeast/isis-ramadi-iraq.html.

Aswad, Barbara C. "Attitudes of Arab Immigrants toward Welfare." In *Arabs in America: Building a New Future*, edited by Michael W. Suleiman, 177–191. Philadelphia: Temple University Press, 1999.

Baddoura, C. "Mental Health and War in Lebanon." *Bulletin of the National Academy of Medicine* 174 (1990): 583–590.

Bakalian, Anny, and Mehdi Bozorgmehr. *Backlash 9/11: Middle Eastern and Muslim Americans Respond*. Berkeley: University of California Press 2009.

Baker, M. E. "Cultural Differences in the Use of Advance Directives: A Review of the Literature." *African American Research Perspectives* 6 (2000): 35–40.

Baker, Wayne, Ronald Stockton, Sally Howell, Amaney Jamal, Ann Chih Lin, Andrew Shryock, and Mark Tessler. "Detroit Arab American Study (DAAS), 2003." Retrieved on July 4, 2017, from www.icpsr.umich.edu/icpsrweb/ICPSR/studies/4413.

Barbosa, Gustavo. "Back to the House: Becoming a Man in the First Palestinian Intifada." *Vibrant Virtual Brazilian Anthropology* 5 (2008): 13–44.

———. *Non-Cockfights: On Doing/Undoing Gender in Shatila, Lebanon*. DPhil dissertation. London School of Economics, 2013.

Barnard, Anne. "3 Years of War Put Syria in a Tailspin." *International New York Times*, March 19, 2014, 3.

Basham, Patrick. "No Quick Democracy in Iraq." Cato Institute, May 5, 2004. Available at www.cato.org/publications/commentary/no-quick-democracy-iraq.

Bayoumi, Moustafa. *How Does It Feel to Be a Problem? Being Young and Arab in America*. New York: Penguin, 2008.

Becker, Gay. *Healing the Infertile Family: Strengthening Your Relationship in the Search for Parenthood*. Berkeley: University of California Press, 1997.

———. *Disrupted Lives: How People Create Meaning in a Chaotic World*. Berkeley: University of California Press, 1999.

———. The Elusive Embryo: *How Women and Men Approach New Reproductive Technologies*. Berkeley: University of California Press, 2000.

———. "Deciding Whether to Tell Children about Donor Insemination: An Unresolved Question in the United States." In *Infertility around the Globe: New Thinking on Childlessness, Gender, and Reproductive Technologies*, edited by Marcia C. Inhorn and Frank van Balen, 119–133. Berkeley: University of California Press, 2002.

Becker, Gay, Martha Castrillo, Rebecca Jackson, and Robert D. Nachtigall. "Infertility among Low-Income Latinos." *Fertility and Sterility* 85 (2006): 882–887.

Bennett, Linda Rae. "Infertility and Inequity across the Globe." *Asian Population Studies*, May 2016. Available at www.tandfonline.com/doi/full/10.1080/17441730.2016.1176805.

Bhutta, Zulfiqar A., and Robert E. Black. "Global Maternal, Newborn, and Child Health—So Near and Yet So Far." *New England Journal of Medicine* 369 (2013): 2226–2235.

Bitler, Marianne, and Lucie Schmidt. "Health Disparities and Infertility: Impacts of State-Level Insurance Mandates." *Fertility and Sterility* 85 (2006): 858–865.

Bittles, A. H., and P. L. Matson. "Genetic Influences on Human Infertility." In *Infertility in the Modern World: Present and Future Prospects*, edited by Gillian R. Bentley and C. G. Nicholas Mascie-Taylor, 46–81. Cambridge, UK: Cambridge University Press, 2000.

Boivin, J., I. Bunting, J. A. Collins, and K. G. Nygren. "International Estimates of Infertility Prevalence and Treatment-Seeking: Potential Need and Demand for Infertility Medical Care." *Human Reproduction* 22 (2007): 1506–1512.

Bouffard, Karen. "Census Bureau: Detroit Is Poorest Big City in U.S." *The Detroit News*, September 17, 2015.

Bourgois, Philippe. *In Search of Respect: Selling Crack in El Barrio*, 2nd ed. Cambridge, UK: Cambridge University Press, 2003.

Bourgois, Philippe, and Laurie Kain Hart. "Commentary on Genberg et al. (2011): The Structural Vulnerability Imposed by Hypersegregated US Inner-City Neighborhoods—A Theoretical and Practical Challenge for Substance Abuse Research." *Addiction* 106 (2011): 1975–1977.

Bourgois, Philippe, Mark Lettiere, and James Quesada. "Social Misery and the Sanctions of Substance Abuse: Confronting HIV Risk among Homeless Heroin Addicts in San Francisco." *Social Problems* 44 (1997): 155–173.

Bourgois, Philippe, Seth Holmes, Kim Sue, and James Quesada. "Structural Vulnerability: Operationalizing the Concept to Address Health Disparities in Clinical Care." *Academic Medicine* 92 (2017): 299–307.

Bourgois, Philippe, and Jeffrey Schonberg. *Righteous Dopefiend*. Berkeley: University of California Press, 2009.

Braveman, Paula. "Health Disparities and Health Equity: Concepts and Measurement." *Annual Review of Public Health* 27 (2006): 167–194.

Bremmer, Ian. "Why a More Isolated Saudi Arabia Is Looking Weaker." *Time*, October 26, 2015, 16.

Bridges, Khiara. *Reproducing Race: An Ethnography of Pregnancy as a Site of Racialization*. Berkeley: University of California Press, 2011.

Bronner, Stephen Eric. *The Bigot: Why Prejudice Persists*. New Haven, CT: Yale University Press, 2014.

Brookings Institution. "U.S. Concentrated Poverty in the Wake of the Great Recession." 2016. Available at www.brookings.edu/research/reports2/2016/03/31-concentrated-poverty-recession-kneebone-holmes.

Buchmueller, Thomas C., Zachary M. Levinson, Helen G. Levy, and Barbara L. Wolfe. "Effects of the Affordable Care Act on Racial and Ethnic Disparities in Health Insurance Coverage." *American Journal of Public Health* 106 (2016): 1416–1421.

Bukhari, Zahid H., et al., eds. *Muslims' Place in the American Public Square: Hopes, Fears, and Aspirations*. Walnut Creek, CA: AltaMira, 2004.

Burnham, Gilbert, Riyadh Lafta, Shannon Doocy, and Les Roberts. "Mortality after the 2003 Invasion of Iraq: A Cross-Sectional Cluster Sample Survey." *The Lancet* 368 (2006): 1421–1428.

Burnham, Gilbert, Sana Malik, Ammar S. Dhari Al-Shibli, Ali Rasheed Mahjoub, Alya'a Qays Baqer, Zainab Qays Baqer, Faraj al Qaraghuli, and Shannon Doocy. "Understanding the Impact of Conflict on Health Services in Iraq: Information from 401 Iraqi Refugee Doctors in Jordan." *International Journal of Health Planning and Management* 27 (2012): e51–e64.

Busby, Chris, Malak Hamdan, and Entesar Ariabi. "Cancer, Infant Mortality and Birth Sex-Ratio in Fallujah, Iraq 2005–2009." *International Journal of Environmental Research in Public Health* 7 (2010): 2828–2837.

Byman, Daniel. "Constructing a Democratic Iraq: Challenges and Opportunities." *International Security* 28 (2003): 47–78.

Caesar, Lena G., and David R. Williams. "Socioculture and the Delivery of Health Care: Who Gets What and Why." *The ASHA Leader* 7 (2002): 6–8.

Cainkar, Louise A. *Homeland Insecurity: The Arab American and Muslim American Experience after 9/11*. New York: Russell Sage, 2009.

Caldwell, Cleopatra Howard, Joan C. Wright, Marc A. Zimmerman, Katrina M. Walsemann, Deborah Williams, and Patrick A. C. Isichei. "Enhancing Adolescent Health Behaviors through Strengthening Non-Resident Father–Son Relationships: A Model for Intervention with African-American Families." *Health Education Research* 10 (2004): 1–13.

Campbell, Madeline Otis. *Interpreters of Occupation: Gender and the Politics of Belonging in an Iraqi Refugee Network*. Syracuse, NY: Syracuse University Press, 2016.

Caro, Carlo. "The Syrian Dilemma." *The Huffington Post*, January 9, 2016. Available at www.huffingtonpost.com/carlo-caro/post_10685_b_8714474.html.

Carter-Pokras, Olivia, and Claudia Baquet. "What Is a 'Health Disparity'?" *Public Health Reports* 117 (2002): 426–434.

Ceballo, Rosario. "'The Only Black Woman Walking the Face of the Earth Who Cannot Have a Baby': Two Women's Stories." In *Women's Untold Stories: Breaking Silence, Talking Back, Voicing Complexity*, edited by Mary Romero and Abigail J. Stewart, 3–19. New York: Routledge, 1999.

Ceballo, Rosario, Erin T. Graham, and Jamie Hart. "Silent and Infertile: An Intersectional Analysis of the Experiences of Socioeconomically Diverse African American Women with Infertility." *Psychology of Women Quarterly* 40 (2016): 171–176.

Chambers, Georgina, Elizabeth A. Sullivan, Osamu Ishiharar, Michael G. Chapman, and G. David Adamson. "The Economic Impact of Assisted Reproductive Technology: A Review of Selected Developed Countries." *Fertility and Sterility* 91 (2009): 2281–2294.

Chase, Sabrina Marie. *Surviving HIV/AIDS in the Inner City: How Resourceful Latinas Beat the Odds*. New Brunswick, NJ: Rutgers University Press, 2012.

Chetty, Raj, Michael Stepner, Sarah Abraham, Shelby Lin, Benjamin Scuderi, Nicholas Turner, Augustin Bergeron, and David Cutler. "The Association between Income and Life Expectancy in the United States, 2001–2014." *Journal of the American Medical Association* 315 (2016): 1750–1766.

"Chilcot Report: Findings at a Glance." BBC News, July 6, 2016. Available at www.bbc.com/news/uk-politics-36721645.

Clark, Jocalyn. "Threat of War Is Affecting Mental Health of Iraqi Children, Says Report." *British Medical Journal* 326 (2003): 356.

Clarke, Morgan. "Children of the Revolution: 'Ali Khamenei's 'Liberal' Views on In Vitro Fertilization." *British Journal of Middle Eastern Studies* 34(2007): 287–303.

———. *Islam and New Kinship: Reproductive Technology and the Shariah in Lebanon*. New York: Berghahn, 2009.

Clarke, Morgan, and Marcia C. Inhorn. "Mutuality and Immediacy between *Marja'* and *Muqallid:* Evidence from Male IVF Patients in Shi'i Lebanon." *International Journal of Middle East Studies* 43(2011): 409–427.

Cockburn, Patrick. "The Arab Spring, Five Years On: A Season That Began in Hope, but Ended in Desolation." *Plato's Guns*, January 9, 2016.

Cohen, Jeffrey H. "Syrian Refugees Next Door?" *The Conversation*, April 1, 2016a. Available at http://theconversation.com/syrian-refugees-next-door-56111.

———. "Where Have 4.8 Million Syrian Refugees Gone?" *The Conversation*, April 17, 2016b. Available at https://theconversation.com/where-have-4-8-million-syrian-refugees-gone-57968.

Colen, Shellee. "'Like a Mother to Them': Stratified Reproduction and West Indian Childcare Workers and Employers in New York." In *Conceiving the New World Order: The Global Politics of Reproduction*, edited by Faye E. Ginsburg and Rayna Rapp, 78–102. Berkeley: University of California Press, 1995.

Coll, Steve. *Ghost Wars: The Secret History of the CIA, Afghanistan, and Bin Laden, from the Soviet Invasion to September 10, 2001*. New York: Penguin, 2004.

Collins, John A. "An International Survey of the Health Economics of IVF and ICSI." *Human Reproduction Update* 8 (2002): 265-77.

Collins, Patricia Hill. *Black Feminist Thought: Knowledge, Consciousness, and the Politics of Empowerment*. New York: Routledge, 2000.

Connolly, Mark P., Stijn Hoorens, and Georgina M. Chambers on behalf of the ESHRE Reproduction and Society Task Force. "The Costs and Consequences of Assisted Reproductive Technology: An Economic Perspective." *Human Reproduction* 16(2010): 603–613.

Cooper, Helen. "U.S. to Send 600 More Troops to Iraq to Help Retake Mosul from ISIS." *New York Times*, September 28, 2016. Available at www.nytimes.com/2016/09/29/world/middleeast/obama-troops-iraq.html.

Crenshaw, Kimberlé. "Demarginalizing the Intersection of Race and Sex: A Black Feminist Critique of Antidiscrimination Doctrine, Feminist Theory and Antiracist Politics," *University of Chicago Legal Forum* 1989 (1989): 139–167.

Crenshaw, Kimberlé, Neil Gotanda, Gary Peller, and Kendall Thomas, eds. *Critical Race Theory: The Key Writings That Formed the Movement*. New York: The New Press, 1996.

Daoud, Kamel. "Terror's Lineage." *Time*, November 30–December 7, 2015, 60.

Davey, Monica. "Detroit Is out of Bankruptcy, but Not out of the Woods." *New York Times* December 10, 2014. Available at www.nytimes.com/2014/12/11/us/detroit-bankruptcy-ending.html.

Davey, Monica, and Mary Williams Walsh. "Billions in Debt, Detroit Tumbles into Insolvency." *New York Times* July 18, 2013. Available at www.nytimes.com/2013/07/19/us/detroit-files-for-bankruptcy.html.

David, Gary C. "Behind the Bulletproof Glass: Iraqi Chaldean Store Ownership in Metropolitan Detroit." In *Arab Detroit: From Margin to Mainstream*, edited by

Nabeel Abraham and Andrew Shryock, 151–178. Detroit, MI: Wayne State University Press, 2000.

Davidson, Christopher. *The United Arab Emirates: A Study in Survival.* Boulder, CO: Lynne Rienner, 2005.

———. *Dubai: The Vulnerability of Success.* New York: Columbia University Press, 2008.

Detroit Arab American Study Team. *Citizenship and Crisis: Arab Detroit after 9/11.* New York: Russell Sage, 2009.

Devichand, Mukul. "What Does the Slogan 'Black Lives Matter' Mean Now?" BBC Trending, July 8, 2016. Available at www.bbc.com/news/blogs-trending-36749925.

Dewachi, Omar. "Insecurity, Displacement and Public Health Impacts of the American Invasion of Iraq." Watson Institute Series Paper, Brown University, 2011.

———. *Ungovernable Life: Mandatory Medicine and Statecraft in Iraq.* Stanford, CA: Stanford University Press, 2017.

Dewachi, Omar, Mac Skelton, Vinh-Kim Nguyen, Fouad M. Fouad, Ghassan Abu Sitta, Zeina Maasri, and Rita Giacaman. "Changing Therapeutic Geographies of the Iraqi and Syrian Wars." *The Lancet* 383 (2014): 449–457.

DeYoung, Karen. "Trump Proposes Ideological Test for Muslim Immigrants and Visitors to the U.S." *The Washington Post*, August 15, 2016.

Diamond, Larry. *Squandered Victory: The American Occupation and the Bungled Effort to Bring Democracy to Iraq.* New York: Henry Holt and Company, 2005.

Dirik, Dilar. "The 'Other' Kurds Fighting the Islamic State." Al Jazeera, September 2, 2014. Available at www.aljazeera.com/indepth/opinion/2014/09/other-kurds-fighting-islamic-stat-2014928753566705.html.

Dodson, Lisa. *Don't Call Us Out of Name: The Untold Lives of Women and Girls in Poor America.* Boston: Beacon Press, 1998.

Donaldson, Ross I., Yuen Wai Hung, Patrick Shanovich, Tariq Hasoon, and Gerald Evans. "Injury Burden during an Insurgency: The Untold Trauma of Infrastructure Breakdown in Baghdad, Iraq." *Journal of Trauma—Injury, Infection & Critical Care* 69 (2010): 1379–1385.

Dorsey, James M. "Creating Frankenstein: The Saudi Export of Wahhabism." Lecture at the Institute of South Asian Studies, National University of Singapore, March 2, 2016.

———. "Saudi Arabia's Future: Will al Saud's Partnership with Wahhabism Hold?" *RSIS Commentary*, February 26, 2016.

Doyle, Patricia, Noreen Maconochie, and Margaret Ryan. "Reproductive Health of Gulf War Veterans." *Philosophical Transactions of the Royal Society B*, April 29, 2006. DOI:10.1098/rstb.2006.1817.

Doyle, Pat, Noreen Maconochie, Graham Davies, Ian Maconochie, Margo Pelerin, Susan Prior, and Samantha Lewis. "Miscarriage, Stillbirth and Congenital Malformation in the Offspring of UK Veterans of the First Gulf War." *International Journal of Epidemiology* 33 (2004): 74–86.

Dufoix, Stephane. *Diasporas*. W. Rodarmor, translator. Berkeley: University of California Press, 2008.

Ebrahimnejad, Hormoz. "What Is 'Islamic' in Islamic medicine?" In *Science between Europe and Asia*, edited by F. Gunergun and D. Raina, 259–270. Boston: Springer, 2011.

Edin, Kathryn, and Maria J. Kefalas. *Promises I Can Keep: Why Poor Women Put Motherhood before Marriage*. Berkeley: University of California Press, 2007.

Edin, Kathryn, and Timothy J. Nelson. *Doing the Best I Can: Fatherhood in the Inner City*. Berkeley: University of California Press, 2013.

Edwards, Karethy. "Health Disparities: What Can We Do?" *Journal of Cultural Diversity* 21 (2014): 3.

Elbadawi, Hanan. "No Humanitarian Surge for Syria." *Al Ahram Weekly*, June 30, 2016.

Elsouhag, D., B. Arnetz, H. Jamil, M. A. Lumley, C. L. Broadbridge, and J. Arnetz. "Factors Associated with Healthcare Utilization among Arab Immigrants and Iraqi Refugees." *Journal of Immigrant and Minority Health* 17 (2015): 1305–1312.

Ennaji, Moha. "The Middle East Must Lead on Refugees." *Project Syndicate*, August 21, 2016. Available at www.project-syndicate.org/commentary/middle-east-response-to-refugee-crisis-by-moha-ennaji-2016-08.

Erlanger, Steven, and Stephen Castle. "Chilcot Report on Iraq War Offers Devastating Critique of Tony Blair." *New York Times*, July 6, 2016.

ESHRE Task Force on Ethics and Law, including G. Pennings, G. de Wert, F. Shenfield, J. Cohen, B. Tarlatzis, and P. Devroey. "Providing Infertility Treatment in Resource-Poor Countries." *Human Reproduction* 24 (2009): 1008–1011.

Eurostat. "Record Number of Over 1.2 Million First Time Asylum Seekers Registered in 2015, March 4, 2016. Available at http://ec.europea.eu/eurostat/documents/2995521/7203832/3-04032016-AP-EN.pdf/.

Evers, Hans. "World ART Figures Show Unexplained Differences in ICSI Usage." HR Editor's Highlight, June 27, 2016. Available at journals@eshre.edu.

Ewing, Katherine Pratt, ed. *Being and Belonging: Muslims in the United States since 9/11*. New York: Russell Sage, 2008.

"Exodus: The Epic Migration to Europe & What Lies Ahead," Special Report, *Time*, October 19, 2015.

Face the Facts, George Washington University. "U.S. Spends More Rebuilding Iraq, Afghanistan than Post-WWII Germany," January 18, 2013. Available at www.facethefactsusa.org/facts/us-spends-more-rebuilding-iraq-afghanistan-than-post-wwii-germany.

Fahey, Dan. "Depleted Uranium Weapons: Lessons from the 1991 Gulf War." *INESAP Bulletin*, 1999.

———. "The Use of Depleted Uranium in the 2003 Iraq War: An Initial Assessment of Information and Policies." June 24, 2003. Available at http://wise-uranium.org/pdf/duiq03.pdf.

———. "The Emergence and Decline of the Debate over Depleted Uranium Munitions, 1991–2004." June 20, 2004. Available at http://wise-uranium.org/pdf/duemdec.pdf.

Feinberg, Eve C., Frederick W. Larsen, Robert M. Wah, Ruben J. Alvero, and Alicia Y. Armstrong. "Economics May Not Explain Hispanic Underutilization of Assisted Reproductive Technology Services." *Fertility and Sterility* 88 (2007): 1429–1441.

Fisher, Max. "The Real Roots of Sunni-Shia Conflict: Beyond the Myth of 'Ancient Religious Hatreds." January 5, 2016. Available at www.vox.com/2016/1/5/10718456/sunni-shia.

Fisk, Robert. *Pity the Nation: The Abduction of Lebanon*. New York: Nation Books, 2002.

———. "The Good Old Saudis Have Let Us Down." *Information Clearing House*, January 12, 2016; available at www.informationclearinghouse.info/article43926,htm.

Fleck, Fiona. "Mental Health a Major Priority in Reconstruction of Iraq's Health System." *Bulletin of the World Health Organization* 82 (2004): 555.

Foroohar, Rana. "Detroit's Turnup: An Unlikely Deal Lifts Motown out of Bankruptcy." *Time* (November 24, 2014): 25–28.

Franklin, Sarah. *Embodied Progress: A Cultural Account of Assisted Conception*. New York: Routledge, 1997.

Franklin, Sarah. "Five Million Miracle Babies Later: The Biocultural Legacies of IVF." In *Reproductive Technologies as Global Form: Ethnographies of Knowledge, Practices, and Transnational Encounters*, edited by Michi Knecht, Stefan Beck, and Maren Klotz, 27–60. Chicago: University of Chicago Press, 2012.

Friends of Low Cost IVF. "Remedying Infertility and Empowering Women Globally." Retrieved on July 5, 2017, from www.friendsoflcivf.org.

Friess, Steve, and Carol Morello. "For Syrians in Michigan, Call to Block Refugees Is a Gut Punch." *The Washington Post*, November 16, 2015.

Fujimoto, Victor Y., Tarun Jain, Ruben Alvero, Lawrence M. Nelson, William H. Catherino, Moshood Olatinwo, Erica E. Marsh, Diana Broomfield, Herman Taylor, and Alicia Y. Armstrong. "Proceedings from the Conference on Reproductive Problems in Women of Color." *Fertility and Sterility* 94 (2010): 7–10.

Gelvin, James. *The Arab Uprisings: What Everyone Needs to Know*. Oxford, UK: Oxford University Press, 2012.

———. *The Modern Middle East: A History*, 4th ed. Oxford, UK: Oxford University Press, 2015.

———. "ISIS, Syria, and the Future of the Middle East," Council on Middle East Studies Colloquium, Yale University, April 27, 2016.

Ghanem, Esperance. "Will Short-Term Solution Help Lebanon Solve Trash Crisis?" *AlMonitor*, March 21, 2016. Retrieved on June 29, 2016, from www.al-monitor.com/pulse/originals/2016/03/lebanon-trash-crisis-government-plan-landfills.html.

Ghazi, H. F., J. Mustafa, S. Aljunid, Z. Isa, and M. A. Abdalqader. "Malnutrition among 3 to 5 Years Old Children in Baghdad City, Iraq: A Cross-Sectional Study." *Journal of Health and Population Nutrition* 31 (2013): 350–355.

Ghobarah, Hazem, Paul Huth, and Bruce Russett. "The Post-War Public Health Effects of Civil Conflict." *Social Science & Medicine* 59 (2004): 869–884.

Ginsburg, Faye D., and Rayna Rapp. "Introduction: Conceiving the New World Order." In *Conceiving the New World Order: The Global Politics of Reproduction*, edited by Faye E. Ginsburg and Rayna Rapp, 1–17. Berkeley: University of California Press, 1995.

Gladstone, Rick. "Nearly 50 Million Children Are Refugees, UNICEF Report Finds." *New York Times*, September 6, 2016.

Gladstone, Rick, and Mohammad Ghannam. "Syria Deaths Hit New High in 2014, Observer Group Says." *New York Times*, January 25, 2015.

Goyette, Jared. "Most Syrian Refugees Coming to U.S. Are Women, Children." *GlobalPost*, August 9, 2016.

Greco, E., F. Scarselli, M. G. Minasi, V. Casciani, D. Zavaglia, D. Dente, J. Tesarik, and G. Franco. "Birth of 16 Healthy Children after ICSI in Cases of Nonmosaic Klinefelter Syndrome." *Human Reproduction* 28(2013): 1155–1160.

Greenstock, Jeremy. *Iraq: The Costs of War*. London: William Heinemann, 2016.

Greil, Arthur L. *Not Yet Pregnant: Infertile Couples in Contemporary America*. New Brunswick, NJ: Rutgers University Press, 1991.

Grewal, Zareena. *Islam Is a Foreign Country: American Muslims and the Global Crisis of Authority*. New York: NYU Press, 2013.

Griswold, Eliza. "Why Is It So Difficult for Syrian Refugees to Get into the U.S.?" *New York Times*, January 20, 2016.

Guehenno, Jean-Marie. "10 Wars to Watch in 2015." *Foreign Policy*, January 2, 2015; available at http://foreignpolicy.com/2015/01/02/10-wars-to-watch-in-2015/.

———. "10 Conflicts to Watch in 2016." *Foreign Policy*, January 3, 2016; available at www.crisisgroup.org/en/regions/op-eds/2016/guehenno-10-conflicts-to-watch-in-2016.aspx.

Gutmann, Matthew. *Fixing Men: Sex, Birth Control, and AIDS in Mexico*. Berkeley: University of California Press, 2007.

Guttersohn, Robert. "Michigan's Iraqi Refugee Crisis." *Detroit Metro Times*, July 15, 2014. Available at www.metrotimes.com/detroit/michigans-iraqi-refugee-crisis/Content?oid=2202760.

Haddad, Sharkey. "The American Journey of a Chaldean from Iraq." In *Arab Detroit: From Margin to Mainstream*, edited by Nabeel Abraham and Andrew Shryock, 205–217. Detroit, MI: Wayne State University Press, 2000.

Hagopian, Amy, Abraham D. Flaxman, Tim K. Takaro, Sahar A. Esa Al Shatari, Julie Rajaratnam, Stan Becker, Alison Levin-Rector, Lindsay Galway, Berq J. Hadi al-Yasseri, William M. Weiss, Christopher J. Murray, and Gilbert Burnham. "Mortality in Iraq Associated with the 2003–2011 War and Occupation: Findings from a National Cluster Sample Survey by the University Collaborative Iraq Mortality Study." *PLOS Medicine* October 15, 2013. Available at http://dx.doi.org/10.1371/journal.pmed.1001533.

Hamdan, Fouad. "The Ecological Crisis in Lebanon." In *Lebanon's Second Republic: Prospects for the Twenty-first Century*, edited by Kail C. Ellis, 175–187. Gainesville: University Press of Florida, 2002.

Hammarberg, Karin, and Maggie Kirkman. "Infertility in Resource-Constrained Settings: Moving towards Amelioration." *Reproductive BioMedicine Online* 26 (2013): 189–195.

Hansen, Helena, Philippe Bourgois, and Ernest Drucker. "Pathologizing Poverty: New Forms of Diagnosis, Disability, and Structural Stigma under Welfare Reform." *Social Science & Medicine* 103 (2014): 76–83.

Hanson, Victor Davis. "Why Did We Invade Iraq?" *National Online Review*, March 26, 2013. Available at www.nationalreview.com/article/343870/why-did-we-invade-iraq-victor-davis-hanson.

Harding, Scott, and Kathryn Libal. "War and the Public Health Disaster in Iraq." In *The War Machine and Global Health: A Critical Medical Anthropological Examination of the Human Costs of Armed Conflict and the International Violence Industry*, edited by Merrill Singer and G. Derrick Hodge, 59–88. Lanham, MD: Altamira Press, 2010.

Harris, Lisa. "Challenging Conception: A Clinical and Cultural History of In Vitro Fertilization in the United States." PhD dissertation, University of Michigan, 2006.

Hassoun, Rosina J. "Arab-American Health and the Process of Coming to America: Lessons from the Metropolitan Detroit Area." In *Arabs in America: Building a New Future*, edited by Michael Suleiman, 157–176. Philadelphia: Temple University Press, 1999.

Hassoun, Rosina J. *Arab Americans in Michigan*. Lansing: Michigan State University Press, 2005.

Heisler, Michele, Elise Baker, and Donna McKay. "Attacks on Health Care in Syria: Normalizing Violations of Medical Neutrality?" *New England Journal of Medicine* 373 (2015): 2489–2491.

Hills, Elaine A., and Dahlia S. Wasfi. "The Causes and Human Costs of Targeting Iraq." In *The War Machine and Global Health: A Critical Medical Anthropological Examination of the Human Costs of Armed Conflict and the International Violence Industry*, edited by Merrill Singer and G. Derrick Hodge, 119–156. Lanham, MD: Altamira Press, 2010.

Holmes, Seth. *Fresh Fruit, Broken Bodies: Migrant Farmworkers in the United States*. Berkeley: University of California Press, 2013.

Hörbst, Viola. "You Cannot Do IVF in Africa as in Europe: The Making of IVF in Mali and Uganda." *Reproductive BioMedicine and Society* 2 (2016): 108–115.

Human Rights Institute, Georgetown University Law Center. "Refugee Crisis in America: Iraqis and Their Resettlement Experience." 2009. Available at http://scholarship.law.georgetown.edu/cgi/viewcontent.cgi?article=1001&context=hri

_papershttp://scholarship.law.georgetown.edu/cgi/viewcontent.cgi?article=1001&context=hri_papers.

Hydari, Zaid. "Afghanistan's Forgotten Refugees." *Foreign Policy in Focus*, January 14, 2013. Available at http://fpif.org/afghanistans_forgotten_refugees/.

"An Ill Wind: In Europe and at Home, Angela Merkel's Refugee Policy Is Being Blown Away." *The Economist*, January 23, 2016. Available at www.economist.com/news/europe/21688896-europe-and-home-angela-merkels-refugee-policy-being-blown-away-ill-wind.

Inhorn, Marcia. C. *Quest for Conception: Gender, Infertility, and Egyptian Medical Traditions*. Philadelphia: University of Pennsylvania Press, 1994.

———. *Infertility and Patriarchy: The Cultural Politics of Gender and Family Life in Egypt*. Philadelphia: University of Pennsylvania Press, 1996.

———. *Local Babies, Global Science: Gender, Religion, and in Vitro Fertilization in Egypt*. New York: Routledge, 2003.

———. "'He Won't Be My Son': Middle Eastern Muslim Men's Discourses of Adoption and Gamete Donation." *Medical Anthropology Quarterly* 20 (2006): 94–120.

———. "Masculinity, Reproduction, and Male Infertility Surgeries in Egypt and Lebanon." *Journal of Middle East Women's Studies* 3 (2007): 1–20.

———. "Medical Anthropology against War." *Medical Anthropology Quarterly* 22 (2008): 416–424.

———. "Diasporic Dreaming: Return Reproductive Tourism to the Middle East." *Reproductive BioMedicine Online* 23 (2011): 582–591.

———. *The New Arab Man: Emergent Masculinities, Technologies, and Islam in the Middle East*. Princeton, NJ: Princeton University Press, 2012a.

———. "Why Me? Male Infertility and Responsibility in the Middle East." *Men and Masculinities* 16(2012b): 49–70.

———. *Cosmopolitan Conceptions: IVF Sojourns in Global Dubai*. Durham, NC: Duke University Press, 2015.

———. "Medical Cosmopolitanism in Global Dubai: A Twenty-First-Century Transnational Intracytoplasmic Sperm Injection (ICSI) Depot." *Medical Anthropology Quarterly* 2016, doi:10.111/maq.12275.

———. "Wanted Babies, Excess Fetuses: The Middle East's In Vitro Fertilization, High-Order Multiple Pregnancy, Fetal Reduction Nexus." In *Abortion Pills, Test Tube Babies, and Sex Toys: Emerging Reproductive Health Technologies in the Middle East and North Africa*, edited by Lisa L. Wynn and Angel Foster. Nashville, TN: Vanderbilt University Press, in press.

Inhorn, Marcia C., Rosario Ceballo, and Robert Nachtigall. "Marginalized, Invisible, and Unwanted: American Minority Struggles with Infertility and Assisted Conception." In *Marginalized Reproduction: Ethnicity, Infertility, and Reproductive Technologies*, edited by Lorraine Culley, Nicky Hudson, and Floor van Rooij, 181–97. London: Earthscan, 2009.

Inhorn, Marcia C., and Michael Hassan Fakih. "Arab Americans, African Americans, and Infertility: Barriers to Reproduction and Medical Care." *Fertility and Sterility* 85 (2006): 844–852.

Inhorn, Marcia C., and Loulou Kobeissi. "The Public Health Costs of War in Iraq: Lessons from Post-War Lebanon." *Journal of Social Affairs* 23 (2006): 13–47.

Inhorn, Marcia C., and Pasquale Patrizio. "Rethinking Reproductive 'Tourism' as Reproductive 'Exile.'" *Fertility and Sterility* 92 (2009): 904–906.

———. "Infertility around the Globe: New Thinking on Gender, Reproductive Technologies, and Global Movements in the 21st Century." *Human Reproduction Update* 21 (2015): 411–426.

Inhorn, Marcia C., Pasquale Patrizio, and Gamal I. Serour. "Third-Party Reproductive Assistance around the Mediterranean: Comparing Sunni Egypt, Catholic Italy, and Multisectarian Lebanon." *Reproductive BioMedicine Online* 21 (2010): 848–853.

Inhorn, Marcia C., and Gamal I. Serour. "Islam, Medicine, and Arab Muslim Refugee Health in Post-9/11 America." *The Lancet* 378 (2011): 935–943.

Inhorn, Marcia. C., and Soraya Tremayne. *Islam and Assisted Reproductive Technologies: Sunni and Shia Perspectives.* New York: Berghahn, 2012.

Inhorn, Marcia C., and Soraya Tremayne. "Islam, Assisted Reproduction, and the Bioethical Aftermath." *Journal of Religion and Health* 55 (2016): 422–430.

Inhorn, Marcia C., and K. Lisa Whittle. "Feminism Meets the 'New' Epidemiologies: Toward an Appraisal of Antifeminist Biases in Epidemiological Research on Women's Health." *Social Science & Medicine* 53 (2001): 553–567.

Institute of Medicine. *Unequal Treatment: Confronting Racial and Ethnic Disparities in Health Care.* Washington, DC: National Academies Press, 2002.

Iraq Body Count. Retrieved on July 4, 2017, from www.iraqbodycount.org/.

Iraq Family Health Survey Study Group. "Violence-Related Mortality in Iraq from 2002 to 2006." *New England Journal of Medicine* 358(2008): 484–493.

"Iraq Mental Health Deteriorates with Violence," NPR Morning Edition, May 3, 2006. Available at www.npr.org/templates/story/story.php?storyId=5378517.

"ISIS Goes Global: Over 70 Attacks in 20 Countries." Gant News, CNN Affiliate, February 2, 2016. Available at gantdaily.com/2016/02/17/isis-goes-global-over-70-attacks-in-20-countries/.

Jabbra, Nancy W. "Family Change in Lebanon's Biqa Valley: What Are the Results of the Civil War?" *Journal of Comparative Family Studies* 35 (2004): 25–270.

Jain, Tarun. "Socioeconomic and Racial Disparities among Infertility Patients Seeking Care." *Fertility and Sterility* 85 (2006): 876–881.

Jain, Tarun, and Mark D. Hornstein. "Disparities in Access to Infertility Services in a State with Mandated Insurance Coverage." *Fertility and Sterility* 84 (2005): 221–223.

Jamail, Dahr. "Iraq War's Legacy of Cancer." *Al Jazeera English*, March 15, 2013. Available at www.aljazeera.com/indepth/features/2013/03/201331517195183 8638.html.

Jamal, Amaney, and Nadine Naber, eds. *Race and Arab Americans before and after 9/11: From Invisible Citizens to Visible Subjects.* Syracuse, NY: Syracuse University Press, 2008.

Johnson, Kirk W. *To Be a Friend Is Fatal: The Fight to Save the Iraqis America Left Behind.* New York: Scribner, 2014.

Joseph, Suad. "Problematizing Gender and Relational Rights: Experiences from Lebanon." *Social Politics* 1 (1994): 270–285.

———. "Conceiving Family Relationships in Post-War Lebanon." *Journal of Comparative Family Studies* 35 (2004): 271–293.

Kalb, Peggy Edersheim. "Putting out the Welcome Mat for Refugees." *Yale Alumni Magazine* March/April 2016: 26.

Kanna, Ahmed. *Dubai: The City as Corporation.* Minneapolis: University of Minnesota Press, 2011.

Karam, Elie G., Zeina Mneimneh, Hani Dimassi, Aimee N. Karam, John A. Fayyad, Soumana C. Nasser, Somnath Chatterji, and Ronald C. Kessler. "Lifetime Prevalence of Mental Disorders in Lebanon: First Onset, Treatment, and Exposure to War." *PLOS Medicine* (2008). Available at http://dx.doi.org/10.1371/journal.pmed.0050061.

Karam, Elie G., Zeina Mneimneh, Aimee N. Karam, John A. Fayyad, Soumana C. Nasser, Somnath Chatterji, and Ronald C. Kessler. "Prevalence and Treatment of Mental Disorders in Lebanon: A National Epidemiological Survey." *The Lancet* 367 (2006): 1000–1006.

Karam, Elie C., Philippe F. Yabroudi, and Nadine M. Melhem. "Comorbidity of Substance Abuse and Other Psychiatric Disorders in Acute General Psychiatric Admissions: A Study from Lebanon." *Comprehensive Psychiatry* 43 (2002): 463–468.

Katz, Mark N. "The U.S. and Democratization in Iraq: War on Terror in Perspective." *Middle East Policy Council*, October 14, 2010; available at www.mepc.org/articles-commentary/commentary/us-and-democratizatioin-iraq.

Keynoush, Banafsheh. *Saudi Arabia and Iran: Friends or Foes?* London: Palgrave Macmillan, 2016.

Khalaf, Samir. *Lebanon Adrift: From Battleground to Playground.* London: Saqi Books, 2012.

Khater, Akram F. *Inventing Home: Emigration, Gender, and the Middle Class in Lebanon, 1870-1920.* Berkeley, CA: University of California Press, 2001.

Kilshaw, Susie. *Impotent Warriors: Perspectives on Gulf War Syndrome, Vulnerability and Masculinity.* Oxford, UK, and New York: Berghahn Books, 2008.

Kissil, Karni, and Maureen Davey. "Health Disparities in Procreation: Unequal Access to Assisted Reproductive Technologies." *Journal of Feminist Family Therapy* 24 (2012): 197–212.

Kleinman, Arthur. "Local Worlds of Suffering: An Interpersonal Focus for Ethnographies of Illness Experience." *Qualitative Health Research* 2 (1992): 127–134.

———. *Writing at the Margins: Discourse between Anthropology and Medicine.* Berkeley: University of California Press, 1997.

———. *What Really Matters: Living a Moral Life amidst Uncertainty and Danger.* Oxford, UK: Oxford University Press, 2007.

Knight, Kelly Ray. *addicted.pregnant.poor.* Durham, NC: Duke University Press, 2011.

Kobeissi, Loulou, Marcia C. Inhorn, Antoine B. Hannoun, Najwa Hammoud, Johnny Awwad, and Antoine A. Abu-Musa. "Civil War and Male Infertility in Lebanon." *Fertility and Sterility* 90 (2008): 340–345.

Kridli, Suha Al-Oballi. "Health Beliefs and Practices among Arab Women." *American Journal of Maternal/Child Nursing* 27 (2002): 178–182.

Krieger, Nancy, Diane L. Rowley, Allen A. Herman, Byllye Avery, and M. T. Phillips. "Racism, Sexism, and Social Class: Implications for Studies of Health, Disease, and Well-Being." In *Racial Differences in Preterm Delivery: Developing a New Research Paradigm*, edited by Diane Rowley and Heather Tosteson, 82–122. Oxford, UK: Oxford University Press, 1993.

Kulwicki, Anahid. "Health Issues among Arab Muslim Families." In *Family and Gender among American Muslims: Issues Facing Middle Eastern Immigrants and Their Descendants*, edited by Barbara Aswad and Barbara Bilge, 187–207. Philadelphia: Temple University Press, 1996.

Kurzmann, Charles. "Death Tolls of the Iran–Iraq War." October 13, 2013. Available at http://kurzman.unc.edu/death-tolls-of-the-iran-iraq-war/.

Landler, Mark. "Obama Says He Will Keep More Troops in Afghanistan Than Planned." *New York Times*, July 6, 2016.

Lane, Sandra D. *Why Are Our Babies Dying? Pregnancy, Birth, and Death in America.* New York: Routledge, 2008.

LeDuff, Charlie. *Detroit: An American Autopsy.* New York: Penguin Books, 2013.

Li, Quan. "Does Democracy Promote or Reduce Transnational Terrorist Incidents?" *Conflict Resolution* 49 (2005): 278–297.

Lopez, Andrea M., Philippe Bourgois, Lynn D. Wenger, Jennifer Lorvich, Alexis N. Martinez, and Alex H. Kral. "Interdisciplinary Mixed Methods Research with Structurally Vulnerable Populations: Case Studies of Injection Drug Users in San Francisco." *International Journal of Drug Policy* 24 (2013): 101–109.

Lotfalian, Mazyar. *Islam, Technoscientific Identities, and the Culture of Curiosity.* Washington, DC: University Press of America, 2004.

Lutz, Catherine, Andrea Mazzarinno, and Marcia C. Inhorn. "Introduction: The Health Costs of War." In *War and Health: The Case of Serial War in Iraq and Afghanistan*, edited by Catherine Lutz and Andrea Mazzarinno. Unpublished manuscript.

Luyken, Jörg. "Germany Took in 160 Times More Syrian Refugees in 2016 Than UK," April 27, 2017. Available at www.thelocal.de/20170427/germany-took-in-three-quarters-of-all-syrian-refugees-in-eu-last-year.

MacDonald, Christine. "Detroit Population Rank Is Lowest since 1850." *The Detroit News* May 20, 2016. Available at www.detroitnews.com/story/news/local/detroit-city/2016/05/19/detroit-population-rank-lowest-since/84574198/.

Macfarlane, Gary J., Anne-Marie Biggs, Noreen Maconochie, Matthew Hotopf, Patricia Doyle, and Mark Lunt. "Incidence of Cancer among UK Gulf War Veterans: Cohort Study." *The British Medical Journal* 327 (2003): 1373.

Macfarlane, Gary J., Matthew Hotopf, Noreen Maconochie, Nick Blatchley, Alison Richards, and Mark Lunt. "Long-term Mortality Amongst Gulf War Veterans: Is There a Relationship with Experiences During Deployment and Subsequent Morbidity?" *International Journal of Epidemiology* 34 (2005):1403-1408.

Mackenzie, Sonja. *Structural Intimacies: Sexual Stories in the Black AIDS Epidemic.* New Brunswick, NJ: Rutgers University Press, 2013.

Maconochie, Noreen, Pat Doyle, and Claire Carson. "Infertility among Male UK Veterans of the 1990–91 Gulf War: Reproductive Cohort Study." *British Medical Journal* 329 (2004): 196–201.

Maconochie, Noreen, Pat Doyle, Graham Davies, Samantha Lewis, Margo Pelerin, Susan Prior, and Patrick Sampson. "The Study of Reproductive Outcome and the Health of Offspring of UK Veterans of the Gulf War: Methods and Description of the Study Population." *BMC Public Health* 3 (2003): 1–11.

Makdisi, Jean Said. *Beirut Fragments: A War Memoir.* New York: Persea Books, 1990.

Makhoul, Jihad, Dana Abi Ghanem, and Mary Ghanem. "An Ethnographic Study of the Consequences of Social and Structural Forces on Children: The Case of Two Low-Income Beirut Suburbs." *Environment & Urbanization* 15 (2003): 249–259.

Makhoul, Jihad, and Lindsey Harrison. "Development Perspectives: Views from Rural Lebanon." *Development in Practice* 12 (2002): 613–624.

Makhoul, Jihad, Rawan Shayboub, and Jinan Jamal. "Violence: The Silent Determinant of Child Labor." *Journal of Children & Poverty* 10 (2004): 131–147.

Malloch-Brown, Mark. "Doomed Diplomacy: Jeremy Greenstock's Memoir of Iraq." *The Financial Times*, November 8, 2016. Available at www.ft.com/content/b0471a8c-a4f2-11e6-8898-79a99e2a4de6?mhq5j=e3.

Malsin, Jared. "With Aleppo's Fall, Syria's Civil War Reaches a Grim Turning Point," *Time*, December 18, 2016. Available at http://time.com/4606073/with-aleppos-fall-syrias-civil-war-reaches-a-grim-turning-point/.

Mansfield, Edward D., and Jack Snyder. "Democratization and the Danger of War." *International Security* 20 (1995): 6–20.

Maraniss, David. *Once in a Great City: A Detroit Story.* New York: Simon & Schuster, 2015.

McAdoo, John L. "The Roles of African American Fathers: An Ecological Perspective." *Families in Society* 74 (1993): 35–38.

McCarthy-Keith, Desiree M., Enrique F. Schisterman, Randal D. Robinson, Kathleen O'Leary, Richard S. Lucidi, and Alicia Y. Armstrong. "Will Decreasing Assisted Reproduction Technology Costs Improve Utilization and Outcomes among Minority Women?" *Fertility and Sterility* 94 (2010): 2587–2589.

McDiarmid, Melissa A., Susan Engelhardt, Marc Oliver, Patricia Gucer, P. David Wilson, Robert Kane, Michael Kabat, Bruce Kaup, Larry Anderson, Dennis Hoover,

Lawrence Brown, Barry Handwerger, Richard J. Albertini, David Jacobson-Kram, Craig D. Thorne, and Katherine S. Squibb. "Health Effects of Depleted Uranium on Exposed Gulf War Veterans: A 10-Year Follow-Up." *Journal of Toxicology and Environmental Health* 67 (2004): 277–296.

Médecins Sans Frontières. "Healing Iraqis: The Challenges of Providing Mental Health Care in Iraq," 2013. Retrieved on July 4, 2017, from www.msf-me.org/en/resource/resources-and-publications/special-reports-1/healing-iraqis-the-challenges-of-providing-mental-health-care-in-iraq.html.

Medical Aid for Iraqi Children. Retrieved on July 3, 2017, from www.maic.org.uk/.

Messac, Luke, Dan Ciccarone, Jeffrey Draine, and Philippe Bourgois. "The Good-Enough Science-and-Politics of Anthropological Collaboration with Evidence-Based Clinical Research: Four Ethnographic Case Studies." *Social Science & Medicine* 99 (2013): 176–186.

Missmer, Stacey A., David B. Seifer, and Tarun Jain. "Cultural Factors Contributing to Health Care Disparities among Patients with Infertility in Midwestern United States." *Fertility and Sterility* 95 (2011): 1943–1949.

Moore, Henrietta L. *Still Life: Hopes, Desires and Satisfactions*. Cambridge, UK: Polity, 2011.

Mowafi, Hany. "Conflict, Displacement and Health in the Middle East." *Global Public Health* 6 (2011): 472–487.

Mullings, Leith. *On Our Own Terms: Race, Class, and Gender in the Lives of African-American Women*. New York: Routledge, 1996.

Mullings, Leith, and Alaka Wali. *Stress and Resilience: The Social Context of Reproduction in Central Harlem*. New York: Springer, 2001.

Myntti, Cynthia, Abir Ballan, Omar Dewachi, Faysal El-Kak, and Mary E. Deeb. "Challenging the Stereotypes: Men, Withdrawal, and Reproductive Health in Lebanon." *Contraception* 65 (2000): 165–170.

Naber, Nadine. "Ambiguous Insiders: An Investigation of Arab American Invisibility." *Ethnic and Racial Studies* 23 (2000): 37–61.

Nasr, Vali. *The Shia Revival: How Conflicts within Islam Will Shape the Future*. New York: W. W. Norton, 2006.

National Institutes of Health. "Disparities in Infertility Treatment," Special Issue of *Fertility and Sterility* 85 (4), April 2006.

National Urban League. "2015 State of Black America: Executive Summary and Key Findings," 2015. Available at http://soba.iamempowered.com/sites/soba.iamempowered.com/files/SOBA2015%20Executive%20Summary.pdf.

Newland, Kathleen. "The U.S. Record Shows Refugees Are Not a Threat." Migration Policy Institute, October 2015. Available at www.migrationpolicy.org/news/us-record-shows-refugees-are-not-threat.

Nsiah-Jefferson, Laurie, and Elaine J. Hall. "Reproductive Technology: Perspectives and Implications for Low-income Women and Women of Color." In *Healing Technology: Feminist Perspectives*, edited by Kathryn Strother Ratcliff, 93–117. Ann Arbor: University of Michigan Press, 1989.

Obaid, Nawaf. “The Salman Doctrine: The Saudi Reply to Obama’s Weakness,” The National Interest, March 30, 2016. Available at http://nationalinterest.org/feature/the-salman-doctrine-the-saudi-reply-obamas-weakness-15623.

Ombelet, Willem, Ian Cooke, Silke Dyer, Gamal I. Serour, and Peter Devroey. “Infertility and the Provision of Infertility Medical Services in Developing Countries.” *Human Reproduction Update* 14 (2008a): 605–621.

Ombelet, Willem, Peter Devroey, L. Gianaroli, and E. te Velde, eds. “Developing Countries and Infertility.” Special Issue of *Human Reproduction* 2008b.

“Operation Iraqi Freedom,” icasualties.org. Retrieved on July 4, 2017, from http://icasualties.org/Iraq/USCasualtiesByState.aspx.

Organista, Kurt C., Paula A. Worby, James Quesada, Sonya G. Arreola, Alex H. Kral, and Sahar Khoury. “Sexual Health of Latino Migrant Day Labourers under Conditions of Structural Vulnerability.” *Culture, Health & Sexuality* 15 (2013): 58–72.

Ostrach, Bayla, and Merrill Singer. “Syndemics of War: Malnutrition–Infectious Disease Interactions and the Unintended Health Consequences of Intentional War Policies.” *Annals of Anthropological Practice* 36 (2013): 257–273.

Oxfam. “Less than 3% of 5 Million Syrian Refugees Resettled in Rich Countries,” December 16, 2016. Available at www.oxfam.org/en/pressroom/pressreleases/2016-12-16/less-3-five-million-syrian-refugees-resettled-rich-countries.

Peek, Lori. *Behind the Backlash: Muslim Americans after 9/11*. Philadelphia, PA: Temple University Press, 2011.

Perkins, Derrick. “Marine Vet Seeks Benefits for Afghan Interpreters.” USA Today, February 2, 2015. Available at http://www.usatoday.com/story/news/nation/2015/02/02/marine-vet-seeks-government-benefits-interpreters/22733231/.

Peteet, Julie. *Landscape of Hope and Despair: Palestinian Refugee Camps*. Philadelphia: University of Pennsylvania Press, 2005.

Pintak, Lawrence. *Seeds of Hate: How America’s Flawed Middle East Policy Ignited the Jihad*. London: Pluto Press, 2003.

Poole, Thom. “Iran and Saudi Arabia’s Great Rivalry Explained.” BBC News, January 4, 2016, Available at www.bbc.com/news/world-middle-east-35221569.

“President Obama’s 2016 State of the Union Address,” January 12, 2016. Available at https://medium.com/@ObamaWhiteHouse/president-obama-s-2016-state-of-the-union-address-7c06300f9726.

Project for the Study of the 21st Century. “Death Toll in 2014’s Bloodiest Wars Sharply Up on Previous Year,” March 17, 2015. Available at www.pcr.uu.se/research/ucdp/charts_and_graphs/#tocjump_9344588684030047_0.

“The Propaganda War,” *The Economist*, August 15, 2015, 41–42.

Quesada, James, Laurie Kain Hart, and Philippe Bourgois. “Structural Vulnerability and Health: Latino Migrant Laborers in the United States.” *Medical Anthropology* 30 (2011): 339–362.

Quiroga, Seline Szkupinski. “Disrupted Bodies: The Effect of Infertility on Racialized Identities.” PhD Dissertation, University of California, San Francisco, 2002.

Ramos, M., P. Orozovich, K. Moser, C. R. Phares, W. Stauffer, and T. Mitchell. "Health of Resettled Iraqi Refugees—San Diego County, California, October 2007–September 2009. *Morbidity and Mortality Weekly Report* 69 (2010): 1614–1618.

Refaat, Marwan M., and Kamel Mohanna. "Syrian Refugees in Lebanon: Facts and Solutions." *The Lancet* 382 (2013): 763–764.

"Refugees at Highest Level Ever, Reaching 65m, UN Says," BBC News, June 20, 2016. Available at www.bbc.com/news/world-36573082.

Rhodes, Tim, Karla Wagner, Steffanie A. Strathdee, Kate Shannon, Peter Davidson, and Philippe Bourgois. "Structural Violence and Structural Vulnerability within the Risk Environment: Theoretical and Methodological Perspectives for a Social Epidemiology of HIV Risk among Injection Drug Users and Sex Workers." *Rethinking Social Epidemiology*, edited by P. O'Campo and J. R. Dunn, 205–30. New York: Springer 2012.

Roberts, Dorothy. *Killing the Black Body: Race, Reproduction, and the Meaning of Liberty.* New York: Vintage Books, 1998.

Roberts, Les, Riyadh Lafta, Richard Garfield, Jamal Khudhairi, and Gilbert Burnham. "Mortality before and after the 2003 Invasion of Iraq: Cluster Sample Survey." *The Lancet.* October 29, 2004:1–8.

Robinson, Eugene. *Disintegration: The Splintering of Black America.* New York: Anchor, 2011.

Rose, Harold M. "The Geography of Despair." *Annals of the Association of American Geographers* 68 (1978): 453–464.

Rose, Harold M., and Donald R. Deskins Jr. "The Link between Black Teen Pregnancy and Economic Restructuring in Detroit: A Neighborhood Scale Analysis." *Urban Geography* 12 (1991): 508–525.

Rosenblum, Daniel, Fernando Montero Castrillo, Philippe Bourgois, Sarah Mars, George Karandinos, George Jay Unick, and Daniel Ciccarone. "Urban Segregation and the US Heroin Market: A Quantitative Model of Anthropological Hypotheses from an Inner-City Drug Market." *International Journal of Drug Policy* 25 (2014): 543–555.

"Russian Airstrikes in Syria 'Have Killed More Than 1,000 Civilians.'" *The Guardian*, January 20, 2016. Available at www.theguardian.com/world/2016/jan/20/russian-airstrikes-in-syria-have-killed-more-than-1000-civilians.

Saab, B. R., M. Chaaya, M. Doumit, and L. Farhoud. "Predictors of Psychological Distress in Lebanese Hostages of War." *Social Science & Medicine* 57 (2003): 1249–1257.

Sa'di, Ahmad H., and Lila Abu-Lughod, eds. *Nabhka: Palestine, 1948, and the Claims of Memory.* New York: Columbia University Press, 2007.

Sadik, Sabah, Saad Abdulrahman, Marie Bradley, and Rachel Jenkins. "Integrating Mental Health into Primary Health Care in Iraq." *Mental Health in Family Medicine* 8 (2011): 39–49.

Said, Edward. *Orientalism.* New York: Vintage Books, 1978.

Sandelowski, Margarete. *With Child in Mind: Studies of the Personal Encounter with Infertility.* Philadelphia: University of Pennsylvania Press, 1993.

Sarroub, Loukia K. *All American Yemeni Girls: Being Muslim in a Public School.* Philadelphia: University of Pennsylvania Press, 2005.

"Saudi Arabia's Allies Bahrain, Sudan and UAE Act Against Iran." BBC News, January 4, 2016. Available at www.bbc.com/news/world-middle-east-35222365.

Save the Children. "Uncertain Futures: The Impact of Displacement on Syrian Refugee and Iraqi Internally Displaced Youth in Iraq," April 26, 2016. Available at www.google.com/search?q=Save+the+Children+Uncertain+Futures&ie=utf-8&oe=utf-8.

Saxena, Prem C., Andrzej Kulczyck, and Rozzet Jurdi. "Nuptiality Transition and Marriage Squeeze in Lebanon: Consequences of Sixteen Years of Civil War." *Journal of Comparative Family Studies* 35 (2004): 241–258.

Schopmeyer, Kim. "Arab Detroit after 9/11: A Changing Demographic Portrait." In *Arab Detroit 9/11: Life in the Terror Decade*, edited by Nabeel Abraham, Sally Howell, and Andrew Shryock, 29–63. Detroit, MI: Wayne State University Press, 2011.

Schulz, Amy J., Clarence C. Gravlee, David R. Williams, Barbara A. Israel, Graciela Mentz, Zachary Rowe, et al. "Discrimination, Symptoms of Depression, and Self-Rated Health among African American Women in Detroit: Results from a Longitudinal Analysis." *American Journal of Public Health* 96 (2006): 1265–1270.

Schulz, Amy, Barbara Israel, David Williams, Edith Parker, Adam Becker, and Sherman James. "Social Inequalities, Stressors and Self Reported Health Status among African American and White Women in the Detroit Metropolitan Area." *Social Science & Medicine* 51 (2000a): 1639–1653.

Schulz, Amy J., and L. B. Lempert. "Being Part of the World: Detroit Women's Perceptions of Health and the Social Environment." *Journal of Contemporary Ethnography* 33 (2004): 437–465.

Schulz, Amy J., and Leith Mullings, eds. *Gender, Race, Class and Health: Intersectional Approaches.* New York: Jossey-Bass, 2005.

Schulz, Amy, David Williams, Barbara Israel, Adam Becker, Edith Parker, Sherman A. James, and James Jackson. "Unfair Treatment, Neighborhood Effects, and Mental Health in the Detroit Metropolitan Area." *Journal of Health and Social Behavior* 41 (2000b): 314–332.

Schulz, Amy J., David R. Williams, Barbara A. Israel, and Lora Bex Lempert. "Racial and Spatial Relations as Fundamental Determinants of Health in Detroit." *Milbank Quarterly* 80 (2002): 677–707.

"Sen. McCain Expects a Permanent U.S. Presence in Afghanistan." NPR Morning Edition, October 7, 2015. Available at www.npr.org/2015/10/07/446499466/sen-mccain-expects-a-permanent-u-s-presence-in-afghanistan.

Serour, Gamal I. "Bioethics in Reproductive Health: A Muslim's Perspective." *Middle East Fertility Society Journal* 1(1996): 30–35.

———. "Religious Perspectives of Ethical Issues in ART: Contemporary Ethical Dilemmas." In *Assisted Reproduction*, edited by Francoise Shenfield and Claude Sureau, 99–113. London: Informa Health Care, 2006.

———. "Islamic Perspectives in Human Reproduction." *Reproductive BioMedicine Online* 17 (Suppl. 2) (2008): 34–38.

Shah, S. M., C. Ayash, N. A. Pharaon, and F. M. Gany. "Arab American Immigrants in New York: Health Care and Cancer Knowledge, Attitudes, and Beliefs." *Journal of Immigrant Minority Health* 10 (2008): 429–436.

Shaheen, Jack. *Guilty: Hollywood's Verdict on Arabs after 9/11*. New York: Olive Branch Press, 2008.

Sheppard, C. "Hard Time for Iraqi Refugees in Weak U.S. Job Market." Reuters, March 3, 2011. Available at www.reuters.com.

Sherlock, Ruth. "In Syria's Civil War, Alawites Pay Heavy Price for Loyalty to Bashar al-Assad." *The Telegraph*, April 7, 2015. Available at www.telegraph.co.uk/news/worldnews/middleeast/syria/11518232/In-Syrias-war-Alawites-pay-heavy-price-for-loyalty-to-Bashar-al-Assad.html.

Shryock, Andrew, ed. *Islamophobia/Islamophilia: Beyond the Politics of Enemy and Friend*. Bloomington: Indiana University Press, 2010.

Shryock, Andrew, and Nabeel Abraham. "On Margins and Mainstreams." In *Arab Detroit: From Margin to Mainstream*, edited by Nabeel Abraham and Andrew Shryock, 15–35. Detroit, MI: Wayne State University Press, 2000.

Simmons, Rebecca, Noreen Maconochie, and Pat Doyle. "Self-Reported Ill Health in Male UK Gulf War Veterans: A Retrospective Cohort Study." *BMC Public Health* 4 (2004): 27.

Singer, Merrill. *Introduction to Syndemics: A Critical Systems Approach to Public and Community Health*. New York: Jossey-Bass, 2009.

Smid, Marcela, Philippe Bourgois, and Colette L. Auerswald. "The Challenge of Pregnancy among Homeless Youth: Reclaiming a Lost Opportunity." *Journal of Health Care for the Poor and Underserved* 21 Supplement (2010): 140–156.

Spar, Debora L. *The Baby Business: How Money, Science, and Politics Drive the Commerce of Conception*. Boston: Harvard Business School Press, 2006.

Stares, Paul B. *Preventive Priorities Survey 2015*. New York: Council on Foreign Relations, Center for Preventive Action, 2015.

Stephen, Elizabeth Hervey, and Anjani Chandra. "Use of Infertility Services in the United States: 1995." *Family Planning Perspectives* 32 (2000): 132–137.

Sunderam, Saswati, Dmitry M. Kissin, Sara B. Crawford, Suzanne G. Folger, Denise J. Jamieson, Lee Warner, and Wanda D. Barfield. "Assisted Reproductive Technology Surveillance—United States, 2013." *Morbidity and Mortality Weekly Report* 64 (SS11) (2015): 1–25.

"Sunnis and Shia: Islam's Ancient Schism." BBC News, January 4, 2016. Available at www.bbc.com/news/world-middle-east-16047709.

Svab, Petr. "110,000 Iraqi Refugees in US, Where Are They?" *The Epoch Times*, January 31, 2015.

"Syrian Refugees Inter-Agency Regional Update, January 2016." Reliefweb, January 31, 2016. Available at http://reliefweb.int/report/syrian-arab-republic/syrian-refugees-inter-agency-regional-update-january-2016.

"Syrian Refugees Seeking Help." *The Lancet* 385 (2015): 202.

Taraki, Lisa. *Living Palestine: Family Survival, Resistance, and Mobility under Occupation*. Syracuse, NY: Syracuse University Press, 2006.

Taylor, Eboni M., Emad A. Yanni, Clelia Pezzi, Michael Guterbock, Erin Rothney, Elizabeth Harton, Jessica Montour, Collin Elias, and Heather Burke. "Physical and Mental Health Status of Iraqi Refugees Resettled in the United States." *Journal of Immigrant and Minority Health* 16 (2014): 1130–1137.

Taylor, Robert Joseph, Linda M. Chatters, and Jeff Levin. *Religion in the Lives of African Americans: Social, Psychological, and Health Perspectives*. Thousand Oaks, CA: Sage, 2004.

Taylor, Robert J., and Waldo E. Johnson Jr. "Family Roles and Family Satisfaction among Black Men." In *Family Life in Black America*, edited by Robert Joseph Taylor, James S. Jackson, and Linda M. Chatters, 248–261. Thousand Oaks, CA: Sage, 1997.

Tessler, Mark. *A History of the Israeli–Palestinian Conflict*. Bloomington: Indiana University Press, 1994.

Thomas, S. B. "The Black Organ and Tissue Donor Shortage: A Review of the Literature." *African American Research Perspectives* 6 (2000): 11–23.

Thompson, Charis. *Making Parents: Reproductive Technologies in a Biomedical Age*. Cambridge, MA: MIT Press, 2005.

———. *Good Science: The Ethical Choreography of Stem Cell Research*. Cambridge, MA: MIT Press, 2013.

Ticktin, Miriam. *Casualties of Care: Immigration and the Politics of Humanitarianism in France*. Berkeley: University of California Press, 2011.

Toma, Warda, and Jacqueline Bhabha. "Syrian Refugees Desperately Need Our Help." *Canadian Medical Journal* 5 (2013): 1464.

Turner, Lewis. "Are Syrian Men Vulnerable Too? Gendering the Syria Refugee Response." Middle East Institute, November 29, 2016. Available at www.mei.edu/content/map/are-syrian-men-vulnerable-too-gendering-syria-refugee-response.

Turner, Victor. *The Ritual Process: Structure and Anti-Structure*. Ithaca, NY: Cornell University Press, 1966.

"UAE to Accept 15,000 Syrian Refugees within Five Years," Al Arabiya English, September 23, 2016. Available at http://english.alarabiya.net/en/News/middle-east/2016/09/23/UAE-to-accept-15-000-Syrian-refugees-within-five-years-.html.

Ulrichsen, Kristian Coates. "Iran–Saudi Crisis 'Most Dangerous for Decades.'" BBC News, January 4, 2016. Available at www.bbc.com/news/world-middle-east-35219693.

United Nations. "The Universal Declaration of Human Rights." 1948. Retrieved on September 18, 2016, from www.un.org/en/universal-declaration-human-rights/.

United Nations. "Alarmed by Continuing Syria Crisis, Security Council Affirms Its Support for Special Envoy's Approach in Moving Political Solution Forward," August 17, 2015. Available at www.un.org/press/en/2015/sc12008.doc.htm.

United Nations. "Staggering Civilian Death Toll in Iraq." United Nations Report, January 19, 2016. Available at www.un.org/apps/news/story.asp?NewsID=53037.

United Nations Assistance Mission in Afghanistan. "Afghanistan, Midyear Report 2016: Protection of Civilians in Armed Conflict," July 2016. Available at https://unama.unmissions.org/sites/default/files/protection_of_civilians_in_armed_conflict_midyear_report_2016_final.pdf.

United Nations Development Programme. "National Human Development Report—Lebanon 2001–2002: Globalization Towards a Lebanese Agenda." Beirut, 2002.

United Nations Development Programme Lebanon. "Lebanon's Report to the World Summit on Sustainable Development," Johannesburg 2002.

UNICEF. *Uprooted: The Growing Crisis for Refugee and Migrant Children*. 2016. Retrieved on September 18, 2016, from www.unicef.org/emergencies/childrenonthemove/uprooted/.

United Nations High Commissioner for Refugees. "Iraq: Global Appeal 2015 Update," January 2015a. Available at www.unhcr.org/en-us/publications/fundraising/5461e60613/unhcr-global-appeal-2015-update-iraq.html.

———. "More Than Four Million Syrians Have Now Fled War and Persecution." July 9, 2015b. Available at www.unhcr.org/en-us/news/latest/2015/7/559d648a9/four-million-syrians-fled-war-persecution.html.

———. "Global Forced Displacement Hits Record High," June 20, 2016. Available at www.unhcr.org/en-us/news/latest/2016/6/5763b65a4/global-forced-displacement-hits-record-high.html.

———. "Syria Regional Refugee Response," July 3, 2017. Available at http://data.unhcr.org/syrianrefugees/regional.php.

United Nations Mine Action Service. "Joint Assessment Mission Report: Lebanon." Beirut, 1999.

United Nations Office for the Coordination of Humanitarian Affairs. "Yemen: Crisis Overview." Retrieved on July 4, 2017, from http://www.unocha.org/yemen/crisis-overview.

United Nations Office of Disarmament Affairs. "Landmines." Retrieved on July 5, 2017, from www.un.org/disarmament/convarms/Landmines/.

United Ways of Michigan. "ALICE: Asset Limited, Income Constrained, Employed." September 2014. Available at /www.scribd.com/document/254495166/United-Way-Michigan-ALICE-Report.

Uppsala Universitet Department of Peace and Conflict Research. "The Uppsala Conflict Data Program." Retrieved on July 4, 2017, from www.pcr.uu.se/research/ucdp/charts_and_graphs/#tocjump_9344588684030047_0.

U.S. Citizenship and Immigration Services. "Iraqi Refugee Processing Fact Sheet," June 6, 2013. Available at www.uscis.gov/humanitarian/refugees-asylum/refugees/iraqi-refugee-processing-fact-sheet.

———. "Refugees & Asylum," November 12, 2015. Available at www.uscis.gov/humanitarian/refugees-asylum.

———. “The United States Refugee Admissions Program (USRAP) Consultation and Worldwide Processing Priorities.” Retrieved on July 5, 2017, from www.uscis.gov/humanitarian/refugees-asylum/refugees/united-states-refugee-admissions-program-usrap-consultation-worldwide-processing-priorities.

U.S. Committee for Refugees and Immigrants, Detroit. “Dearborn: Home away from Home for Iraqi Refugees.” Retrieved on December 15, 2015, from http://refugees.org/field-office/detroit/.

van Gennep, Arnold. “Rites de Passage.” *L'Annee Sociologique* 11 (1906): 200–2002.

Volk, Lucia. *Memorials and Martyrs in Modern Lebanon*. Bloomington: Indiana University Press, 2010.

Vora, Neha. *Impossible Citizens: Dubai's Indian Diaspora*. Durham, NC: Duke University Press, 2013.

Walbridge, Linda S., and T. M. Aziz. “After Karbala: Iraqi Refugees in Detroit.” In *Arab Detroit: From Margin to Mainstream*, edited by Nabeel Abraham and Andrew Shryock, 321–342. Detroit, MI: Wayne State University Press, 2000.

Walter, Nicholas, Philippe Bourgois, and H. Margarita Loinaz. “Masculinity and Undocumented Labor Migration: Injured Latino Day Laborers in San Francisco.” *Social Science & Medicine* 59 (2004): 1159–1168.

Warikoo, Niraj. “Muslims Look to Make a Difference in Hamtramck.” *The Detroit Free Press*, January 24, 2016a. Available at www.freep.com/story/news/local/michigan/wayne/2016/01/24/muslim-majority-council-reflects-hamtramck-diversity/78438858/.

———. “Detroit Has Highest Concentrated Poverty Rate among Top 25 Metro Areas.” *The Detroit Free Press*, April 26, 2016b. Available at www.freep.com/story/news/local/michigan/2016/04/26/detroit-has-highest-concentrated-poverty-rate/833955.

Watson Institute of International and Public Affairs, Brown University. “Costs of War: Afghan Civilians.” August 2016. Available at http://watson.brown.edu/costsofwar/costs/human/civilians/afghan.

Webster, Paul C. “Questions Raised over Iraq Congenital Birth Defects Study.” *The Lancet* 382 (2013): 1165–1166.

White, Lynn, Julia McQuillan, and Arthur L. Greil. “Explaining Disparities in Treatment Seeking: The Case of Infertility.” *Fertility and Sterility* 85 (2006): 853–857.

Whittle, K. Lisa, and Marcia C. Inhorn. “Rethinking Difference: A Feminist Reframing of Gender/Race/Class for the Improvement of Women's Health Research.” *International Journal of Health Services* 31 (2001): 147–165.

Williams, David R. “Ethnicity, Race, and Health.” In *International Encyclopedia of the Social and Behavioral Sciences*, edited by N. K J. Smelser and P. B. Baltes, 4831–4838. Oxford, UK: Elsevier Science, 2001.

Williams, David R., Harold W. Neighbors, and James S. Jackson. “Racial/Ethnic Discrimination and Health: Findings from Community Studies.” *American Journal of Public Health* 93 (2003): 200–208.

Worby, Paula A., Kurt C. Organista, Alex H. Kral, James Quesada, Sonya Arreola, and Sahar Khoury. “Structural Vulnerability and Problem Drinking among Latino

Migrant Day Laborers in the San Francisco Bay Area." *Journal of Health Care for the Poor and Underserved* 25 (2014): 1291–1307.

World Health Organization (WHO). "The Declaration of Alma-Ata." 1978. Retrieved on June 29, 2016, from www.who.int/publications/almaata_declaration_en.pdf?ua=1.

———. "Potential Impact of Conflict on Health in Iraq." 2003. Retrieved on June 29, 2016, from www.who.int/features/2003/iraq/briefings/iraq_briefing_note/en/.

World Health Organization (WHO) Eastern Mediterranean Regional Office. "Health System Profile: Lebanon, 2004" Retrieved on July 4, 2017, from http://apps.who.int/medicinedocs/documents/s17301e/s17301e.pdf.

———. "Lebanon: Mental Health." Retrieved on July4, 2017, from http://www.emro.who.int/lbn/programmes/mental-health.html.

———. "Health Systems Profile: Iraq." Cairo: WHO Eastern Mediterranean Regional Office, 2007. Retrieved on June 29, 2016, from www.who.int/maternal_child_adolescent/epidemiology/profiles/maternal/irq.pdf.

Yaccino, Steven. "Kwame M. Kilpatrick, Former Detroit Mayor, Sentenced to 28 Years in Corruption Case." *New York Times* October 10, 2013. Available at www.nytimes.com/2013/10/11/us/former-detroit-mayor-kwame-kilpatrick-sentencing.html.

Yaktin, U. S., and S. Labban. "Traumatic War: Stress and Schizophrenia." *Journal of Psychosocial Nursing and Mental Health Services* 30 (1992): 29–33.

Yanni, Emad A., Marwan Naoum, Nedal Odeh, Pauline Han, Margaret Coleman, and Heather Burke. "The Health Profile and Chronic Diseases Comorbidities of US-Bound Iraqi Refugees Screened by the International Organization for Migration in Jordan: 2007–2009." *Journal of Immigrant and Minority Health* 15 (2013): 1–9.

"Yemen Situation Regional Refugee and Migrant Response Plan, January–December 2016," Reliefweb, December 15, 2015. Available at http://reliefweb.int/report/yemen/yemen-situation-regional-refugee-and-migrant-response-plan-january-december-2016.

Zakaria, Fareed. "America Can't Stop the Sectarian Tidal Wave." *The Washington Post*, January 8, 2016. Available at https://search.yahoo.com/yhs/search?p=fareed+zakaria+america+can%27t+stop+the+sectarian+tidal+wave&ei=UTF-8&hspart=mozilla&hsimp=yhs-001.

Zenko, Micah. "How Many Bombs Did the United States Drop in 2016?" Council on Foreign Relations. January 5, 2017. Available at http://blogs.cfr.org/zenko/2017/01/05/bombs-dropped-in-2016/.

Zong, Jie., and Jeanne Batalova. "Refugees and Asylees in the United States." Migration Policy Institute Report. *Migration Information Source*, October 28, 2015. Available at www.migrationpolicy.org/article/refugees-and-asylees-united-states.

Index